Information TECHNOLOGY

for CSEC Examinations

Dr. O'Neil Duncan

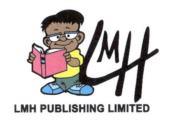

LMH PUBLISHING LIMITED

All LMH titles, imprints and distributed lines are available at special quantity discounts for bulk purchases for sales promotion, premiums, fund-raising, educational or institutional use.

Written by: Dr. O'Neil Duncan
Cover design: Roshane Mullings
Typeset & book layout: Roshane Mullings

Published by: LMH Publishing Limited
Suite 10-11
Sagicor Industrial Park
7 Norman Road
Kingston C.S.O., Jamaica
Tel.: 876-938-0005; Fax: 876-759-8752
Email: lmhbookpublishing@cwjamaica.com
Website: www.lmhpublishing.com

Printed in the U.S.A.   ISBN:978-976-8245-58-8

CATALOGUING-IN-PUBLICATION DATA AVAILABLE AT THE NATIONAL LIBRARY OF JAMAICA

Table of Contents

SECTION 1
COMPUTER FUNDAMENTALS AND INFORMATION PROCESSING

A Concise History of the Computer

The **Abacus** was probably the first counting machine. The French philosopher Blaise Pascal (1452-1519) then invented and built the first adding machine called the **PASCULINE**. In 1890, Dr. Herman Hollerith proposed a solution to the U.S Census Bureau that the data should be fed to the computer on **punched cards**. Eventually, in 1946, John Mauchly and J. Presper Eckert invented the **first electronic computer** at the University of Pennsylvania. The device used electronic switches and radio vacuum tubes and it was known as the **Electronic Numerical Integration and Calculation (ENIAC)**. This device signaled the beginning of the first generation of computers.

The First Generation Computer (1940s - 1955). It was characterized by the use of vacuum tubes. The CPU consisted of two parts: a data processing unit and a program control unit.

The Second Generation Computer (1955-1964). This was mainly characterized by the change from vacuum tubes to *transistor technology*. A *transistor* is a small electronic device containing a semi-conductor and having at least three electrical contacts, used in a circuit as an amplifier, a detector, or a switch. Memories were made up of magnetic ferrite cores. Input-Output processors were used to supervise I/O operations thus allowing the CPU to handle the more important operations. Computer manufacturers began to provide system software such as compilers, subroutine libraries, and batch monitors. The Operating system was introduced.

The Third Generation Computer (1964-1971). Transistors were replaced by Integrated Circuits (IC). Results were a substantial reduction in physical size and cost. Semiconductor memories replaced the magnetic ferrite cores in main memory of which the main types were RAM and ROM. Widespread use of operating systems and mass production of small low cost computers called MINICOMPUTERS was made.

The Fourth Generation Computer (1971-present). This involved the use of thousands of integrated circuits called Very Large Scale Integration (VSLI). The VSLI technology made it possible to fabricate an entire CPU, main memory or similar device within a single IC that could be mass-produced at a very low cost. This has resulted in new classes of machines such as inexpensive personal computers, and high performance parallel processors that contain thousands of CPUs.

The Fifth Generation Computer (Present - Future). Today we have ultralight notebooks and tablets, as well as smart phones which are really just small computers. However, the fifth generation continues. Computing devices, based on artificial intelligence are still in development, though there are some applications, such as voice recognition, that are being used today. The use of parallel processing and superconductors is helping to make artificial intelligence a reality. Quantum computation and molecular and nanotechnology will radically change the face of computers in years to come. The goal of fifth-generation computing going forward is to develop devices that respond to natural language input and are capable of learning and being self-organized.

Systems

A computer system consists of all the parts that work together to carry out the work required by the user.

A **computer** is defined as ***an electronic device that accepts and processes data under the direction of instructions and presents the result of processing as information or stores it for later use.*** A computer therefore carries out the following functions :

- Accepts or allows data to be input to it - Input
- Processes or manipulates the data accepted - Process
- Outputs or gives the result of processing - Output
- Stores or saves the output for later use - Store

A computer goes through a basic Input, Process, Output, Process (IPOS) cycle as shown below.

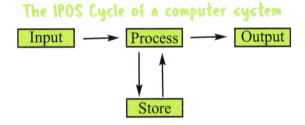

The IPOS Cycle of a computer system

Basic components of a computer system

To perform its functions, the computer must have the appropriate hardware and software component. **Hardware** is the physical part of the computer that you are able to touch. It includes those parts attached around the system unit which houses the **Motherboard – the main circuit board**, those parts on the motherboard and the cables and connectors.

The non-physical parts or aspects of the computer system include its intelligence, the bits, instructions and programs that make the computer function. These are called the **software** of the system.

Hardware may be simply categorized into :

1. Input Devices   2. Processing Device   3. Output Devices   4. Storage Devices

These will be explored further as we progress in learning.

TYPES OF COMPUTER SYSTEMS

The **Types of Computers** are supercomputers, mainframes, minicomputers, microcomputers.

Supercomputers

Supercomputers are superior to other computers in terms of processing speed, memory size, physical size and cost. Since they are number crunchers, they can process trillions of floating point operations per second. Its main memory is measured in millions of bytes. Tremendous heat is generated by the circuitry; therefore special cooling devices and separate computer rooms are required. Cost ranges from several million to US$ 27 million. Among the first supercomputer was the *Cray CDC 6600* which was installed around 1976 and named after US Electrical Engineer Seymour Cray.

Mainframes

Mainframes are smaller, less powerful and less expensive than supercomputers. They process data at a rate of millions of instructions per second. The memory size is measured in millions of bytes and designed primarily to support enterprise-wide information systems. They also process a number of applications concurrently - multiprocessing. In 2010, IBM introduced the zEnterprise system, an extraordinary mainframe computer.

Minicomputers

Minicomputers: - These were developed to do specialized tasks. They are smaller, less powerful and less expensive than mainframes. Prices range from a few thousand pounds to several thousand pounds.

Microcomputers

Microcomputers: - The microcomputer is the most popular type of computer used. Different varieties of microcomputers are: desktop systems, laptops, notepads, subnote pads, pocket PCs, electronic organizers, palmtop computers, pen computers and Personal Digital Assistants.

THE COMPUTER MACHINE CYCLE AND THE CENTRAL PROCESSING UNIT

The four basic functions of a computer mentioned earlier is more complex than one can imagine as the computer constantly works with the data it receives.

The stages in the cycle as the computer executes instructions to transform the data are as follows: **fetching, decoding, executing and storage**.

Data is accepted or input to the computer via Input devices and is briefly stored in registers under the direction of the *CU*. The *CU* then gets the data and decodes or interprets it. If there are calculations to be done or logical operations, the *CU* sends the data to the *ALU* to work on the data after which it is sent to stay a while in another register for storage and then to main memory, or a secondary storage device or to an output device.

The next instruction is fetched and this cycle is repeated continuously by the Central Processing Unit (CPU) beginning when you boot (turn on) the computer until you shut it off.

* Control Unit (CU)
* Arithmetic Logic Unit (ALU)

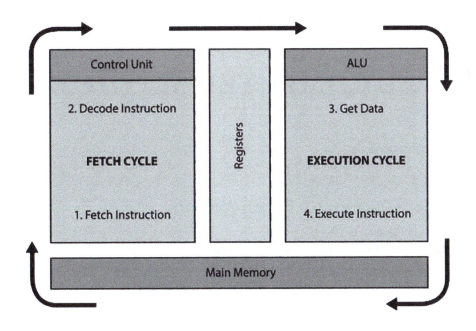

COMPONENTS OF THE CENTRAL PROCESSING UNIT(CPU)

The **CPU/Processor** is a chip that is termed the "brain" of the computer system.

The Control Unit (CU)

The **CU** is the part that sequences, decodes and synchronizes the execution of program instructions i.e. it generates the proper timing and controls signals necessary to complete the execution of an instruction. It directs the flow of data in and out of the computer system.

Arithmetic Logic Unit - The ALU

This is the part that is responsible for processing **arithmetic (mathematical) and logical operations**. This is the reasoning part of the computer system.

Registers

A **register** is a very small area reserved to hold data and instructions which the CPU is using immediately. It is a very tiny section of Random Access Memory (RAM) reserved for quick access to data. There are different types of registers which carry out different functions.

A LITTLE COMPUTER MATHEMATICS

Converting decimal numbers to binary numbers

1. Divide the decimal digit by 2 and record the remainder.
2. Keep dividing the decimal digit by 2 and record the remainder each time.
3. Write down the remainders from bottom up starting from the bottom of what you have then move upward until you are where you started.

Examples:

Convert the decimal number 32 to binary:

1. First we divide the number 32 by 2. This gives us a result 16 with a remainder 0.
2. Divide 16 by 2. We get 8 with remainder 0.
3. Divide 8 by 2. We get 4 with remainder 0.
4. Divide 4 by 2. We get 2 with remainder 0.
5. Divide 2 by 2, we get 1 with remainder 0.
6. Now list the remainders from bottom to top, starting with the final result 1.

> List remainders from bottom to top

Therefore 32 in binary system is 100000 written as 100000_2 where the 2 tells that it is base 2 or binary.

Convert the number 75 into the binary system:

1. Divide 75 by 2. We get 37 with remainder 1.
2. Divide 37 by 2. We get 18 with remainder 1.
3. Divide 18 by 2. We get 9 with remainder 0.
4. Divide 9 by 2. We get 4 with remainder 1.
5. Divide 4 by 2. We get 2 with remainder 0.
6. Divide 2 by 2. We get 1 with remainder 0.
7. Now list the remainders from bottom to top , starting with final result 1.

> List remainders from bottom to top

Therefore 75 in binary system is 1001011_2.

Convert the number 119 into the binary system:

1. Divide 119 by 2. We get 59 with remainder 1.
2. Divide 59 by 2. We get 29 with remainder 1.
3. Divide 29 by 2. We get 14 with remainder 1.
4. Divide 14 by 2. We get 7 with remainder 0.
5. Divide 7 by 2. We get 3 with remainder 1.
6. Divide 3 by 2. We get 1 with remainder 1.
7. Now list remainders from bottom to top, starting with the final result 1.

Therefore 119 in binary is 1110111_2.

Converting binary numbers to decimal numbers

Write the positional value over each of the binary digits. **See the table shown for assistance.**

The positional value of binary digits					
...2^5	2^4	2^3	2^2	2^1	2^0
32	16	8	4	2	1

Multiply each place value by its corresponding binary digit and add them together.

Examples:

Convert 110001 to decimal:

$$110001 = 1 * 2^5 + 1 * 2^4 + 0 * 2^3 + 0 * 2^2 + 0 * 2^1 + 1 * 2^0$$
$$= 1 * 32 + 1 * 16 + 0 * 8 + 0 * 4 + 0 * 2 + 1 * 1$$
$$= 32 + 16 + 0 + 0 + 0 + 1$$
$$= 49$$

Therefore 110001_2 in decimal is 49.

Convert 10101010 to decimal:

$$10101010 = 1 * 2^7 + 0 * 2^6 + 1 * 2^5 + 0 * 2^4 + 1 * 2^3 + 0 * 2^2 + 1 * 2^1 + 0 * 2^0$$
$$= 1 * 128 + 0 * 64 + 1 * 32 + 0 * 16 + 1 * 8 + 0 * 4 + 1 * 2 + 0 * 1$$
$$= 128 + 0 + 32 + 0 + 8 + 0 + 2 + 0$$
$$= 170$$

Therefore 10101010_2 in decimal is 170.

Convert 101011 to decimal:

$$101011 = 1 * 25 + 0 * 24 + 1 * 23 + 0 * 22 + 1 * 21 + 1 * 20$$
$$= 1 * 32 + 0 * 16 + 1 * 8 + 0 * 4 + 1 * 2 + 1 * 1$$
$$= 32 + 0 + 8 + 0 + 2 + 1$$
$$= 43$$

Therefore 101011_2 in decimal is 43.

Representation of integers

There are different systems for handling binary numbers:
- One's complement
- Two's complement

Each system has its own method of representing negative and positive integers. The representation of positive integers looks the same in all three systems but the first bit or Most Significant Bit (MSB) – sign bit, is derived differently in each system. Negative numbers are obtained by negating the positive number.

In order to subtract a number, the CPU adds the negative of the number. For example, $15 - 9$ is treated as $15 + (-9)$ by the processor, i.e. we add 15 to negative 9. It is very important therefore to be able to find the negative of a number. The procedures for finding the representation for negative numbers are shown below.

One's complement representation	The one's complement of a binary number is obtained by flipping the bits i.e. change the 0's to 1's and 1's to 0's. **Example 1: Find the one's complement of 01101.** Solution: The one's complement of 01101 is 10010. **Example 2: What is the one's complement representation of 37 using 8 bits.** Solution: 1. Find the binary equivalent of 37: That is, $37 \equiv 00100101$ (using 8 bits – add 2 0s to the left to get 8 bits) 2. Flip the bits of the binary equivalent: 11011010 3. Write the representation: The one's complement representation of -37 is 11011010_2
Two's complement representation	Find the one's complement of the number using the specified number of bits then add 1 to the result. **Example 1: Find the two's complement of 1001 using six bits.** Solution: 1. Write the number using the specified number of bits: 001001 (add 2 zeroes to the left) 2. Find the one's complement: 110110 3. Add 1: $110110 + 1 = 110111$ 4. Therefore, the two's complement representation of 1001 using six bits is: 110111_2.

Two's complement representation	**Example 2: Find the two's complement of -25 using six bits.** **Solution:** **1.** Write down the binary equivalent of 25 using 6 bits: 011001 **2.** Flip the bits of the binary equivalent: 100110 **3.** Add 1 to the result: $100110 + 1 = 100111$ 4. Therefore the two's complement representation of -25 is: 100111_2
Binary coded decimal (BCD) representation	Another method used to represent integers is the binary coded decimal (BCD) representation. In the BCD system, each digit and the sign of the denary number is represented by a **four bit** binary pattern. **Example: Represent 548_{10} using BCD.** **Solution:** Write the 4-bit binary equivalent for each digit $5 \equiv 0101$; $4 \equiv 0100$; $8 \equiv 1000$ Therefore: 548_{10} is 010101001000BCD **Example: Represent 947_{10} using BCD.** **Solution:** Write the 4-bit binary equivalent for each digit: $9 \equiv 1001$; $4 \equiv 0100$; $7 \equiv 0111$ Therefore 947_{10} is to 100101000111BCD **Example: Represent 623_{10} using BCD** **Solution:** Write the 4-bit binary equivalent for each digit: $6 \equiv 0110$; $2 \equiv 0010$; $3 \equiv 0011$ Therefore 623_{10} is to 011000100011BCD
Binary Subtraction using 2's complement	Consider the following operation: $30 - 7 = 23$ The processor considers this operation in the following format: $30 + (-7) = 23$ To perform binary subtraction, you have to first represent the number to be subtracted in its 2's complement form then add the numbers. Let us consider $30 - 7$. **1.** Find the two's complement of 7. • The binary equivalent of 7 is 111. • We are using six bits so we add three 0's to the left. So $7 = 000111$. • The 1's complement representation of 7 is 111000 • Now add 1 to the 1's complement representation. • The 2's complement representation of 7 is 111001.

Binary Subtraction using 2's complement	2. Now find the binary representation of 30.
	
	• 30 in binary representation is 11110
	• We are using six bits so we add one zero to the left = 011110.
	3. Now add this number to the 2's complement representation of
	
	    011110
	+ 111001
	   (1)010111
	
	4. The result is 010111.
	   Note that the final carry is ignored.

STORAGE DEVICES AND MEDIA

Types of Storage

You will need to save your documents for use at a later date. Saving may be done on the computer or off the computer. There are various devices and media available for saving or storing data depending on the type of files and their content, the sizes of files and how often the files will be needed for processing.

Storage may be categorized into **two types**: **Primary Storage** and **Secondary Storage**.

Primary Storage

Primary Storage (semiconductor memories) can be thought of as a collection of systematically arranged boxes in which computer *words* are stored. The boxes are arranged so that each word has its own unique location, which is specified by a number. This number is referred to as the memory location's address. When the microprocessor wishes to access a particular box to store or retrieve data, it does so by generating the address of that particular storage space, along with special signals required to perform the operation.

Generally speaking, Primary storage:

- is that part of the computer where instructions and data to be used by the computer, are stored.

- is directly accessible by the CPU

- consists of high-speed semiconductor devices that are compatible with the microprocessor's speed so as not to significantly slow its operation.

Two main **types** of Primary Memory

- **Read-Only Memory (ROM)** - used to hold data in a permanent form.

- **Random Access Memory (RAM)** - used for temporary storage of data and programs.

ROM Memory

- ROM generally holds data that was programmed into it at the factory and is not intended to be changed.

- There are several types of ROM, some of which can be erased and reprogrammed but not during the normal operation of the computer:

  - Programmable ROM (PROM) - can be custom-programmed by the user (once) using special circuitry.

  - Erasable-Programmable ROM (EPROM) - can also be programmed and erased by the user using ultraviolet light and special circuitry external to the computer.

  - Electrically Erasable PROM (EEPROM) - can be erased and reprogrammed by special circuitry within the computer. i.e. the computer system can be changed through the use of software rather than replacing the ROM.

- All forms of ROM are all non-volatile. This means that the data contained in the memory is not lost when the computer is turned off or when electrical power is lost. This enables the computer to begin reading instructions and data from this type of memory as soon as the power is turned on.

ROM Applications

- Firmware storage - the computer's operating system programs and language interpreters are stored in ROM devices so that the computer can begin operation as soon as it is turned on (booting).
  The term – firmware means that software is stored in hardware on a permanent basis.

- Lookup tables – storage of trigonometric functions and code conversion tables, which do not change. e.g. instead of performing a calculation each time a function such as sine, cosine, etc. is needed, the microprocessor simply looks up the value associated with the function in a ROM table.

RAM

- RAM holds programs and data currently being used by the microprocessor.

- Random Access means that any address location in the memory can be accessed as quickly as another location.

- RAM is fast enough to work directly with the microprocessor without slowing it down significantly.

- During the execution of a program, RAM address locations store the intermediate or final results of processing.

- RAM has the disadvantage of being volatile. This means that any data stored in RAM is lost if power to the computer is disrupted for any reason.

Bistable Devices and Units of Storage

Data and instructions are easily understood by users when presented in a written or typed format. Computers, on the other hand, cannot immediately use information presented in this format. Instead, all data and instructions input into the computer are translated into codes which the computer can store and process (use). To accomplish this in a relatively simple way, **bi-stable devices** are used for storing and coding in the computer.

These devices are so called because they are able to represent data using *only two states*. An example of a bi-stable device you can appreciate is a light switch, for which two states are "ON" and "OFF". The two states used in the computer system are the digits 0 and 1. As you may recall from mathematics, the number system which only uses these two digits is called the **Binary system**. (Human Beings use a more complex way of representing their information, namely a mixture of the letters of the alphabet, all digits 0 – 9 and other special characters). In the computer system, all information used occupies storage space.

The smallest unit for measuring storage space is a **Bit** and each of the digits used in the computer, i.e. the 0 and 1, occupies one bit of space.

A **Byte** is generally described as a collection of 8 bits of space, and is the space required to hold the binary code which represents any character (a-z, 0-9, special characters).

A **Word** is also described as a collection of bits but normally it is thought of as being bigger than a byte. The number of bits in a word is called the **word size**. Typical word sizes are 16, 24, 32 and 64.

Word sizes may be different for different computers. On a given computer, **word** is normally the storage space required to store one instruction. Each **word** of storage has a unique number permanently associated with it, called the *address* of the word. The word also has an *address content* which is the actual data or instruction stored in it.

The word length is so important to a computer that it is often used to describe the computer, because all its internal hardware devices are constructed to accommodate a given word length.

In general, computers that use larger word sizes are more powerful than those with smaller word sizes since more information can be transferred at one time. A larger range of numeric values, and a greater number of characters and symbols that can be represented with a large word size.

The size of the storage devices for a computer is commonly quoted in terms in some denomination of the byte, i.e. the kilobyte, the megabyte, the megabyte or the gigabyte, which are defined below:

1 kilobyte (KB) = 2^{10} bytes (approximately 1000 bytes)
1 megabyte (MB) = 2^{20} bytes (approximately 1,000,000 bytes)
1 gigabyte (GB) = 2^{30} bytes (approximately 1,000,000,000 bytes)

The storage capacity of primary storage devices, e.g. RAM, is normally quoted in MB while that for

Secondary Storage is quoted in higher units, e.g. hundreds of MB, GB and TB.

Task 1

1. Examine each of the following statements carefully. State whether you agree or disagree with the statement and give reasons for your answer.

   a. When I have written a letter, I store it in RAM so I can edit it later. RAM is a part of main memory.

   b. I use the hard disk to store programs and data. When I run a program it first has to be copied onto ROM. ROM is a part of main memory.

2. What is a bi-stable device? State two examples.

3. A computer has main memory containing RAM and ROM. What is RAM used for?

   a. What is ROM used for?

   b. State and explain the main differences between RAM and ROM.

3. Define the term 'media'.

5. Distinguish between the following terms:

   a. Word and word size

   b. Byte and kilobyte

   c. Firmware and software

Secondary Storage Media and Devices

The main purpose of Secondary storage devices is to store large amounts of data on a permanent, or semi-permanent basis, as cheaply as possible. Secondary storage devices are used for long-term storage of programs and data, or to hold masses of programs and data too large to be held in the Primary memory and are used to make back-up copies of data in case of system failure or data corruption.

Secondary storage is too slow to be used directly with the computer's microprocessor. The secondary memory unit holds the information and transfers it in batches to the computer's faster internal memory when requested. A **buffer** may be used in these situations to compensate for varying speeds.

A **buffer** is a temporary storage area, which is used to hold data being transmitted between components of a computer system, often to compensate for different working speeds or for grouping data. This technique is most frequently used when transmitting data to or from peripheral devices.

The materials (tape, disk, paper, cards, etc) used to store information on secondary storage devices are collectively called **Media**.

Characteristics of common Storage Media:

For our purposes, when we describe the characteristics of a storage medium the following areas should be considered:

- Physical description of the medium.

- How is data stored on the medium?

- Which device writes to/reads from the medium?

- Storage capacity (in bytes) of the medium.

- Type of access method - Serial or random access?

- Advantages/disadvantages associated with the use of the medium.

- How does it compare with other media?

SECONDARY STORAGE DEVICES AND THEIR CHARACTERISTICS

Term	Definition/Characteristics
Magnetic Media	
Magnetic tape	• A storage medium consisting of a flexible plastic strip covered with magnetic material on one side, used to store data. • Sequential/serial access medium • Capable of storing large amounts of data and information at a low cost • A tape drive reads from and writes data and information on a tape • A tape cartridge is a small, rectangular, plastic housing for tape used in today's tape drives • Used by business and home users to backup personal computer hard disks • Both external and internal tape units are used for personal computers. Larger computers use tape cartridges mounted on a separate cabinet called a tape library • Portable - can be carried around
Magnetic Disks:	
Floppy disk	• A flexible magnetic coated disk, commonly used with microcomputers on which data can be stored magnetically. • Random access method is used to access data. • Storage capacity - 80KB - 1.44MB • Uses a Floppy Disk Drive (FDD) which contains a read/write head which accesses (reads) data from and places (writes) data on a magnetic disk repeatedly.

Micro-floppy disk	Refers to 3.5" floppy disks. A storage medium, which consists of a thin, circular, flexible plastic material with a magnetic coating and enclosed in a square-shaped plastic shell. **Characteristics:** • A portable, inexpensive storage medium. • Standard disk size is 3.5 in diameter. • Housed in rigid plastic casting having a sliding shutter covering an opening to the recording surface which automatically closes when the disk is removed from the disk drive. • Has a small opening called a write protect notch with a cover that you slide up or down protects floppy disks from accidentally being erased. • A typical floppy disk stores data on both sides of the disk • Random access medium. • Most floppy disks today are high density (HD) with a capacity of 1.44 MB arrived at as follows: 80 tracks per side x 18 sectors per track x 2 sides per disk x 512 bytes per sector = 1,474,560 bytes = 1.44MB
ZIP disk, Jaz disk, SparQ disk • Disks that can store	100MB, 1GB and 1GB respectively. • Random access media.
Hard disk 	A rigid metallic disk used for storing data magnetically. **Charateristics:** • Its rigid construction allows for higher storage densities. • Access times for a hard disk are much faster than for floppy disks. • A hard disk spins constantly, while a floppy disk starts spinning only when it receives a read or write command. • Random access medium. • Typically stores 1 to 40 GB. • Contains more than one platter. Tracks are arranged in cylinders.

Optical disks	Storage Medium in which laser technology is used to etch the surface of the disk, forming minute patterns which represent data. CD-ROM, compact disk, and DVD-ROM, digital video disk are examples. **Characteristics:** • Random access medium • A flat, round, portable, metal storage medium that is usually 4.75 inches in diameter and less than one-twentieth of an inch thick. • A compact disc typically stores items on a single track; It spirals from the center of the disc to the edge of the disc • The track is divided into evenly sized sectors in which items are stored • Has massive storage capacity • High quality sound and pictures are possible with this device
CD-ROMs	A silver-colored compact disc that uses the same laser technology as audio CDs for recording music • Can contain text, graphics, audio, and video. **Characteristics:** • The manufacturer writes, or records, the contents of standard CD-ROMs • A CD-ROM drive or CD-ROM player is used to read items on a CD-ROM • A typical CD-ROM holds about 650 MB of data, instructions, and information • Manufactures use CD-ROMs to store and distribute today's multimedia software and other complex software **Types available:** • CD-R (compact disc-recordable) A multi-session compact disc onto which you can record your own items such as text, graphics, and audio. You write on the CD-R using a CD recorder or a CD-R drive and special software. • CD-RW - (compact disc-rewritable) An erasable disc you can write on multiple times
DVD-ROM (digital video disc- ROM)	• An extremely high capacity compact disc capable of storing from 4.7 GB to 17 GB. • Looks just like a CD-ROM but data, instructions, and information is stored in a slightly different manner to achieve a higher storage capacity. • You must have a DVD-ROM drive or DVD player to read a DVD-ROM

Magneto Optical Disk	• A hybrid between magnetic disks and optical disks. i.e. A type of disk drive that combines magnetic disk technologies with CD-ROM technologies. • Data are written to a disk using a laser beam and a magnetic read\write-head • A portable high storage capacity - more than 200 megabytes that can be read from and written to.
Microfilm and Microfiche	• Store microscopic images of documents on roll or sheet film. • Images recorded onto film using a computer output microfilm (COM) recorder • Images can only be read with a microfilm or microfiche reader. • Microfilm and microfiche are inexpensive and have the longest life of any storage medium
USB Storage	• This storage medium eliminates the use of the floppy drive and facilitates faster transfer at high speeds with large capacities with note book or any desktop computer with a functional USB port. • Capacities range from 8MB - more than 1TB storage capacity in GB are more popular today.
SCSI	**SCSI (Small Computer Systems Interface) Bus** This bus system is a standard for connecting peripheral devices to a computer system. Most manufacturers and computer systems support it. The SCSI standard has been superceded by SCSI-2, which adds new features, and is itself split into two parts, wide and wide and fast. The main features are • support for a wide range of media types, CD-ROM, tape, optical, scanners • each host adapter can support seven devices • the connecting cable can be 6 meters long (single ended) • devices can be externally mounted • each device has a ROM which contains the device's parameters • each device has its own address and device driver • data transfer rates up to 4 Mb per second Up to SEVEN devices are supported by the SCSI bus. One of these devices is the controller card. An ID number identifies each device; usually, ID 7 is the controller card. The 50 wire flat ribbon (or 25pair twisted) cable is strung along from device to device, and TWO special terminators are placed at EACH end of the cable. The idea behind SCSI is the ability of the host system to accept a wide variety of devices without special drivers or interfaces. Each device accepts a common core set of commands, which helps make writing software drivers simple.

IDE	**IE (Integrated Drive Electronics) or ATA Bus**
	Western Digital and Compaq Corporation developed this in 1989. It is also known as the ATA interface. The major features are • developed from the ST-506 disk interface • uses the BIOS INT 13h routines to interact with the drive • supports two drives (master and slave) • the drives must be magnetic (no support for CD-ROM or optical) • no special drivers required (supported by the BIOS) • there is a limit of 528MB for IDE disk drives supported via the BIOS and the IDE configuration data • controller electronics is on the drive • low cost and inexpensive to implement • data transfer rates up to 4.1MB per second
Flash Memory	Flash Memory is capable of retaining digital information under certain conditions • This retained material might be operational code or data files or a combination of the two. • The ideal memory subsystem optimizes density • Preserves critical material in a nonvolatile condition, is easy to program and re-program • Can be read fast • Is cost-effective for the application.

TERMS ASSOCIATED WITH STORAGE & RETRIEVAL OF DATA FROM SECONDARY STORAGE MEDIA

Term	Description
Read/write head (R/W)	Read/write head is the set of electromagnets and necessary circuitry used to magnetise the magnetic material used for storage
Fixed head	R/W head does not move. e.g. Tape units have fixed heads and the tape moves past them.
Moving head	Most disk units have heads on an arm which moves the heads from track to track.
Sector	The smallest addressable portion of a track and the smallest unit of data that is written to or read from a disk. (see Figure1)
Tracks	The path on a tape, disk or drum along which data is stored. (see Figure1) On a disk these paths are concentric circles; on a tape there are several tracks parallel to the edge of the tape; on a drum there are bands of equal size along the circumference of the drum.
Cylinders	In a disk pack, a set of tracks one above the other, for example the tenth track on each disk, is called a cylinder. (see Figure1) Figure 1
Access time	The time a program or device takes to locate a single piece of information and make it available to the computer for processing. e.g. *disk access time* - The time taken to get data from a disk = the time taken to move the head to the right track + the time taken for the disk to rotate to the correct part of the track.

Sequential access	When there is sequential acess the items are read, one at a time, from the start of the file, in key value order. Therefore the records need to be sorted in the order in which they are to be processed. A magnetic tape uses sequential access.
Direct/random	This is when any item can be retrieved immediately, provided its position in the file is known. (Example of media with random access: floppy disk, CD, hard disk.)
Read	Process of transferring data, instructions, and information from a storage medium into main memory. **Read,** gets input from a computer.
Write	Transfer of data from main memory to secondary storage media
Storage capacity	The number of bytes (characters) a storage medium can hold. Manufacturers use many terms to define the capacity of storage
Storage Density	The number of bits per unit area on a storage medium.

Comparison between Primary and Secondary Storage

Secondary Storage is also called auxiliary storage, permanent storage, or mass storage. It is non-volatile Storage - Permanent storage of data, programs, instructions, and information for future use. It is used for backing up data.

Primary Storage on the other hand is referred to as main memory and is a temporary holding place for data and instructions. It is volatile memory.

CLOUD STORAGE AND LOCAL STORAGE

We may store our files nearby using Secondary Storage devices and Media including the hard disk or we may choose to store our files further away.

Storage on or nearby our computer on a physical device where we are in charge of what is stored is considered **local storage** while storage in space or the cloud or the internet, which is remote from us and is controlled by a third party is considered **Cloud storage**.

Local Storage is beneficial as it:

- Is relatively cheap compared to Cloud storage as it does not cost us any additional money once we have our storage devices.
- Allows the user to be in charge and responsible for the data stored
- Access is limited to authorised users via passwords or encryption
- Allows data to be transferred easily from one device to another

Local Storage carries some challenges as :

- It is limited to access as you have to possess the storage device or be in the location of the device in order to access your data
- Devices can become physically damaged thus leading to loss of data

Cloud Storage is beneficial as it:

- Offers ready access from almost anywhere as it is via the internet
- Allows access via portable devices including your smart phone.
- Offers remote backup for its users
- Requires less space than local Storage

Cloud Storage carries a few concerns:

- The main concern is security as it is often a target for Hackers.
- If you do not have access to the internet then you are denied access to your data.
  It is managed by "outsiders" which can become risky should a problem develop and you are denied access to your data.
- The cost will vary depending on who is providing you with the service and should you require additional space it would come with additional cost.

Task 2

Examine each of the following statements carefully. State what is wrong with the statement.

a. "I prefer to store my files on tape and not on disk. The tape has sequential access, which means I can retrieve the data much faster than from a disk using direct or random access."

b. "On a floppy drive I can store about 1.44MB."

c. "A sector is the smallest, addressable portion of a tape. It is the smallest unit of data that is read from or written to a tape."

d. "Paper and film are both media."

e. "A CD-ROM or compact disk, uses laser technology to read and write from the disk. The CD-ROM drives in room 23 can write to compact disks, but not read from them. Drives that can both write and read to a compact disk cost between 500 and 1,000 dollars."

f. Both tape and disk drives use fixed heads to read from and write to the media."

g. Since the CPU is much faster than the peripheral units, special storage is used to hold data being transmitted between them. This storage area is called 'buffer'."

h. "Disk access time is the time taken to move the head to the right track plus the time taken for the disk to rotate to the correct frame."

i. "A Jaz disk can store more than 650 floppy disks."

j. "The most common media used with computers are magnetic tape, magnetic disk and optical disk. A hard disk is a magnetic disk while a compact disk is an optical disk."

k. "The set of electromagnets and circuitry used to magnetise disks and tapes is called a read/write hand."

l. "If you type 100 words a minute and each word average eight characters, you have to type non-stop for more than twenty years to fill a hard disk of 10GB."

m. Tapes use a sequential access method to obtain data while disks use a random access method. Explain the difference between sequential access and random access.

Task 3

1.   How is data written to an optical disk?

2.   Make a simple drawing of a disk and shade one track and one sector.

3.   What is a 'buffer'?.

4.   What is media?

5.   Name the device used to write to and read from a floppy disk.

6.   Name three media the computer can use to store data.

7.   What is a read/write head?

8.   Name one media that used moving read/write head.

9.   Explain the difference between
     a) direct and sequential access methods.
     b) serial and sequential access methods.

10. Why is secondary storage needed when we already have main memory?

INPUT DEVICES AND MEDIA

Input devices are devices that accept input from outside the computer, that is, any hardware component that allows you to enter data, programs, commands, and user responses into a computer. The input device may be used to enter programs and data into the memory device before execution, or it may be used to enter data directly to the microprocessor during execution. It may also be in a human readable format or a machine readable format or both.

Human readable data is data that can be read by a human, like text and drawings, but not magnetic patters.

Machine readable data is data that can be input into a computer using a suitable input device without the need for any preparation from humans.

A Closer look at Input Devices

Keyboard

This device has keys like a typewriter whose primary function is textual data entry. There are keys for letters, digits, arithmetic operations, punctuation marks, special symbols like &, navigation keys (arrows and Home, PageUp etc.), special keys like Ctrl, function keys (F1-F12), different lock keys, Enter, Delete, Backspace, Spacebar and more. It typically has 104 keys.

Key-to disk is keyboard entry of data directly to magnetic disk without previous preparation on another medium.

Scanner

This device captures the data by scanning it into the computer. The input may later be edited graphically or in a word processor if OCR software is used.

Optical Mark Reader (OMR)

This reads marks made in predetermined positions on special forms (or cards) by a light-sensing method. It is used to mark multiple-choice papers.

Optical Character Reader (OCR)

This machine recognition of printed characters by light-sensing methods. It is used to read typed post codes when mail is automatically sorted.

Magnetic Ink Character Reader (MICR)

This machine recognition of stylised characters printed in magnetic ink. Used to read the cheque number, the branch number and the account number on bank cheques. These characters are both machine and human readable.

Mouse

This an input device that controls the movement of the cursor. The cursor moves in response to the movement of the mouse on a flat surface. The mouse can select objects, drag objects and make menu choices.

Joystick

This device uses a lever to control cursor movement or graphic images and is often used in gaming.

Graphics pad/Graphic tablet

This device is used to input line drawings into a computer. The user draws with a stylus onto a flat pad or tablet, either copying a drawing or working freehand.

Light pen

This is a light-sensitive input device which when it touches the screen detects the presence or absence of light. It is used to select an entry or indicate a position.

Touch terminal

Also called a touch screen. A device that allows data to be input by touching a screen with the finger or other object. The surface of the screen consists of a number of programmed touch points each of which may trigger a different action when selected by the user.

Barcode Reader/
Point of sale (POS) Scanner

This device can scan bar codes and get the cost and item description from a database connected to the network that all the POS are on.

Bar code

This is a pattern of parallel black-and-white lines used to represent a code number, which can then be read automatically.

Voice data entry (VDE) Speech Recognition

This a process of analysing a spoken word and comparing it with those known to the computer system. It is used to give limited set of commands to a computer operated wheel-chair and is also used to "read-in" complete documents into a word processor.

Biometric systems

Biometrics is the automated recognition of individuals based on their behavioral and biological characteristics. By measuring an individual's suitable behavioral and biological characteristics in a recognition inquiry and comparing these data with the biometric reference data which had been stored during a learning procedure, the identity of a specific user is determined.

Biometric Characteristics includes fingerprint, signature, facial geometry, iris, retina, hand geometry, voice and DNA.

Sensor

A sensor is a device that measures a physical attribute or a physical event. It outputs a functional reading of that measurement as an electrical, optical or digital signal. That signal is data that can be transformed by other devices into information. The information can be used by either intelligent devices or monitoring individuals to make intelligent decisions and maintain or change a course of action. A smart sensor is simply one that handles its own acquisition and conversion of data into a calibrated result in the units of the physical attribute being measured. For example,

a traditional thermocouple simply provided an analog voltage output. The voltmeter was responsible for taking this voltage and transforming it into a meaningful temperature measurement through a set of fairly complex algorithms as well as an analog to digital acquisition.

A smart sensor would do all that internally and simply provide a temperature number as data. Smart sensors do not make judgments on the data collected unless that data goes out of range for the sensor.

Remote control

This refers to a program's or device's ability to control a computer system from a remote location. Remote-control programs for PCs enable you to access data stored on your home system even when you are traveling.

Remote control is different from remote access. In remote control, only keystrokes and screen updates are transmitted between the two machines as all processing originates in the remote-control device. In a remote access setup, the user is logged onto the network, using the phone line as an extension to the network. Thus, all traffic has to flow over a low-speed telephone line.

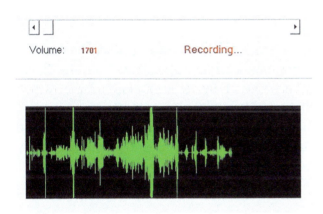

Sound Capture

Capture is the process or means of obtaining and storing external data, particularly images or sounds, for use at a later time. There are various ways in which this can be done; the best method depends on the application. In biometric security systems, capture is the acquisition of, or the process of acquiring, an identifying characteristic such as a finger image, palm image, facial image, iris print, or voice print. (All but the last of these examples involves video data; the last involves audio data.) In order to capture the data, a transducer is employed that converts the actual image or sound into a digital file. The file is then stored. At a later time, it can be analyzed by a computer, or compared with other files in a database to verify identity or to provide authorization to enter a secured system. Most serious computer users are familiar with the term screen capture. The intent of a screen capture is to store the image on a monitor or display exactly as it appears at a specific time.

Braille Keyboards

Braille keyboards are electronic devices which use the Braille technology. The Braille technology has been instrumental in allowing thousands of people to engage in a virtual world that cannot be perceived by their eyes. This technology is commonly used by blind or visually impaired people as it allows them to perform common tasks such as writing, browsing the Internet, typing and printing, etc. Braille keyboards were commonly used with Braille typewriters. These keyboards are extremely rare nowadays.

Output Devices

As input devices are used to read data from external sources into a computer system, **output devices** do exactly the opposite. There are so many output devices which we see in real life like printers, monitors, etc. We see that their primary use is to display the results of the processing done by the computer system on the input which we fed. We will be dealing with output devices in the following section.

Visual Display Units

Visual Display Units are abbreviated as VDUs. They are also known as screens or monitors. This is the standard output device for every computer system. A Visual Display Unit comprises of the display device, internal circuitry and an enclosure. There are many types of display devices.

Cathode Ray Tube (CRT) Monitors

Older systems used the CRT (Cathode Ray Tube) monitors. These monitors are shaped like a television and operate on the CRT technology. The first CRTs were monochrome. The images used to flicker and were of poor quality. However, in the 1980s, IBM introduced the color graphics adapter which enabled the CRTs to display four colors with a resolution of 320 by 200 pixels. As time passed, IBM introduced the enhanced adapter which was capable of producing 16 colors with a resolution of 640 by 350 pixels. CRT technology has remained dominant for the most part of the previous century because it is quiet cheap to manufacture. The **CRT technology** is shown in the following figure:

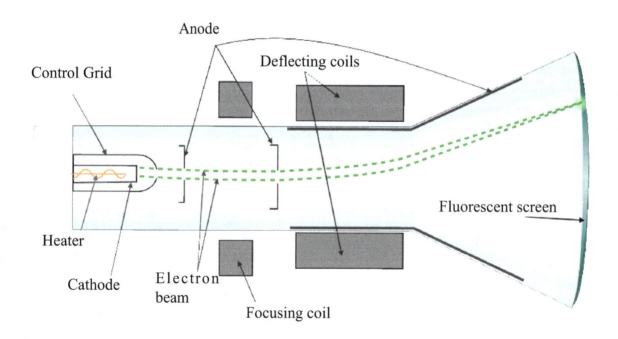

The technology is simple. The heated cathode results in an electron beam which passes through the anodes. The focusing coil helps in projecting the beam on the screen. The deflecting coils help in positioning the beam towards the required pixel position. The screen is fluorescent and has a phosphorous lining. A typical CRT unit is shown.

The Liquid Crystal Display

These are primarily used in laptops; however, they have been replacing the CRTs in desktop based systems as well. The LCDs are placed at a price higher than the CRTs but they have lighter weight, lower power consumption, and smaller physical size. There is another variation of LCD called as TFT-LCD. This variation is mostly used in desktop systems.

Printers

A printer is an output device which produces text and graphics on paper media. Printers can be divided into two major categories. They are:

1. Impact Printers
2. Non-Impact Printers

Impact Printers

Impact Printers are those printers which produce text and images when the print head actually comes in contact with the inserted paper.

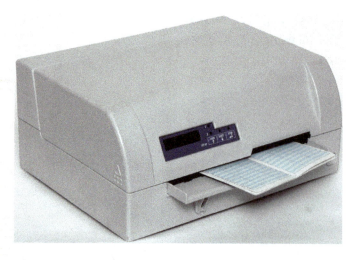

Dot Matrix Printers

This is the only impact printer on the market now. The printing is done when the tiny wire pins on its print head strikes the paper which is inserted into it. The print head runs back and forth like a typewriter. When the ink ribbon presses on the paper as it passes through the print head, it creates dots. *These dots make up the text and the images.* To get more quality, a dot matrix printer should be able to print more dots per character. To do this, a dot matrix printer should have higher number of wire pins. These printers were popular in the 1970s and the 80s. However, these were soon replaced by the inkjet printers. This does not mean they are extinct today. They are still used but only in point of sale terminals.

There are **advantages** to using a dot matrix printer. Some of which are:
1. It can print on carbon copies.
2. It has a low printing cost per page.
3. It can be used on continuous form paper. Hence it is useful for data logging.
4. It is reliable and durable.

However, there are some **disadvantages**:
1. It is very noisy.
2. It has got limited printing quality.
3. It has low printing speed.
4. It has limited color printing abilities.

Non-Impact Printers

Non-impact printers are the complete opposite of impact printers. They do not strike the surface of the paper at all while carrying out their operations. Most printers these days, are non-impact printers. Let us examine a few.

Inkjet Printers

They are the most common type of printers used in homes and business organizations. These print text and images on paper by spraying tiny drops of liquid ink on it. Currently, they either use thermal inkjet technology or piezoelectric inkjet technology.

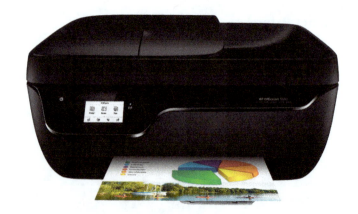

Thermal Inkjet Technology

Uses heating element to heat the liquid ink. A vapor bubble is formed which forces the ink droplets onto the paper through the nozzlc. It uses aqueous ink.Most manufacturers use this technology.

Piezoelectric Inkjet Technology

Used on all Epson and industrial printers. Instead of the heating element, this technology uses a piezoelectric crystal in each of the printer's nozzle. This crystal changes shape and size depending upon the electric current received. This change forces the ink droplets onto the paper from the nozzle.

It uses a wide variety of inks like UV ink, solvent inks, dye-sublimation inks, etc.

The printer head of the inkjet printer can be classified into two categories:
1. Fixed head
2. Disposable head

Fixed head is built into the printer and should last for the whole life of the printer. It produces better output than the disposable head. These heads are also quite cheap. However, if the head is damaged, the entire printer has to be replaced.

Disposable head is included in the replacement ink cartridge. It is replaced each time the cartridge runs out of ink. Costs are higher and the quality is also compromised.

Advantages of an Inkjet Printer:

1. Low cost.
2. Capable of producing fine and smooth details.
3. Capable of printing in vivid color. Good for printing pictures.
4. It is easy to use.
5. It is reasonably fast.
6. It does not make any noise.
7. No warm up time is required.

Disadvantages of Inkjet Printer:

1. The print head is less durable. It is prone to clogging and damage.
2. The ink cartridges are expensive.
3. It is not good for high volume printing.
4. Printing speed not as fast as laser printers.
5. Ink bleeding occurs occasionally.
6. Cannot use highlight markers on inkjet printouts.
7. Aqueous ink is sensitive to water.

Laser Printers

These printers can print text and images in high speed and high resolution ranging from 600 to 1200 dpi. They use toner inks instead of liquid inks. It consists of the following components:

1. *Drum Cartridge:* It rotates as the paper is fed through.

2. *Rotating Mirror:* It deflects laser beam across the drum surface.

3. Toner Cartridge: The laser beam creates a charge which causes the toner to stick to the drum. As the drum rotates and presses on the paper, the toner ink is released from the cartridge from the drum to the paper, creating the output.

4. Rollers: The rollers use heat and pressure to fuse toner to paper. Normally three passes are required.

Advantages of a Laser Printer:

1. It works with high resolutions.
2. It has a high print speed.
3. There is no smearing of the print.
4. It has a low cost per when compared to the inkjet printer.
5. Printout is not sensitive to water.
6. Is excellent for high volume printing.

Disadvantages of a Laser Printer:

1. It is quite expensive.
2. Is less capable of printing pictures.
3. Requires time to warm up before starting
4. They are quite bulky in nature.
5. The cost of replacement is high.

Plotters

A plotter is like a printer but for the purpose of displaying vector graphics on paper. They are widely used in computer-aided design (CAD) for printing blueprints and other drawings. However, plotters are now being replaced by conventional printers.

Audio Output Devices

Many of us play music/videos on our computers or smart phones. The audio or sound is possible through speakers, headsets and headphones - the audio/sound comes out of the device to the user output devices come in the form of speakers, headsets and headphones.

Speakers

These external devices having a low power internal amplifier. The standard audio connections used are 3.5 mm jacks which are often green in colour. There are a few, however, which use RCA connectors. With the advent of the USB technology, there have been widespread use of USB speakers. The first speakers came from Altec Lansing in 1990. Laptops and some desktops come with in-built speakers although external speakers may be connected to amplify the sound.

Headphones and Headsets

Headphones are a pair of small loudspeakers which are designed in such a way that they fit right within the human ears. They are also known to us as earphones, earspeakers, or occasionally, cans. Headsets, however, are like headphones but they are held in a place close to the human ears. Headsets and headphones have wires which are connected to an audio source. With the advent of wireless technology, Bluetooth headsets have made their in-roads into the technology market.

Consider **ONE** of the following business environments:
Airline reservation – Travel agency, Supermarket, Restaurant, Library.
For the selected business environment, identify

a) The input:
   i)   Inputs to the system
   ii) The method used to capture data.
   iii) Devices used to capture input data into the system and classify these devices into direct and indirect methods of data entry.

b) The Processing:
   i)   What kind of processing is carried out on the data.

c) Outputs from the system
   i)   Identify the outputs from the system (include any outputs that are stored)
   ii) Identify devices used to output data

2. "An input device should be fast, accurate and easy to use." Do you agree with this statement? Give reason (s) for your answer.

3. Name an input device that can be used to:
   a) mark multiple-choice SAT papers
   b) read post codes on envelopes
   c) read a barcode on a library lending card
   d) read magnetic codes on a cheque

4. Text can be input in many ways, some understandable by humans and some by machines. Complete the table below:

| ways of storing text method of data capture | human readable? | | machine readable | | Name of Machine readable input device(s) |
	Yes	No	Yes	No	
printed text on paper					
hand written text					
sound waves					
magnetic patterns on a credit card					
magnetic patterns on a disk					
bar code patterns					
magnetic ink characters					

5. I see an article in a newspaper or magazine. How can I get it into MS Word so that it can be edited?

6. Describe three different uses of a mouse.

7. In the old days, you would use the keyboard to play games. The z-key would move you left, the x-key right, and so on. Describe how game playing is better with a joystick or similar game device used with Nintendo, Sega or a computer.

8. It is difficult to draw accurately with a mouse. Which other device exist to draw on a computer?

9. Why does the barcode reader beep when an item is read? What will the cashier do if it does not beep?

10. What advantages and disadvantages does the use of a digital camera have over the use of a conventional camera?

11. How can you prevent unreasonable data from being entered into a computer?

12. How does the Water Company get each customer's meter reading into his or her computer every month?

13. A barcode is a number that gives some information about the product like the country of origin.
   a) The price of the product and the description of the product are not stored in the barcode. Give a reason for this.
   b) If the price and description are not stored in the barcode, how does the cashier obtain this information by scanning the barcode?

14. For each of the following devices, list the advantages associated with it's use.
Mouse, Light pen, Optical Mark Reader (OMR), Touch Terminals, Voice Data Entry Device

15. Describe the factors that should be considered when choosing an input device.

OPERATING SYSTEMS

The **operating system (O/S)** is a set of programs that conduct communication between the various hardware devices and the application programs on the computer. It is the Master Controller. A part of the o/s called the **kernel**, lives in the computer's memory once it is loaded there. Another part is stored on the hard drive or on other secondary storage devices and is loaded into RAM when it is needed.

Functions of the Operating System

- It determines which applications can run, in what order and for how long, in multi-tasking operating systems.

- It manages the sharing of internal memory among multiple applications.

- It handles input and output to and from attached hardware devices such as hard disks, printers and dial-up ports.

- It sends messages to the applications or interactive users (or to a system operator) about the status of operations and any errors that may have occurred.

- It can off-load the management of batch jobs, e.g. printing, so that the initiating application is freed from this work.

- In a parallel-processing environment, it decides how to divide a program so that it runs on more than one processor at a time.

A computer <u>cannot work</u> or function without an operating system.

Types of Processing in Operating System

Batch Processing – Commands or jobs are collected in groups and processed in the order in which they were placed.

Time-sharing multi-processing – allows the CPU to switch rapidly between users.

Single process systems – allows only one program to use the computer at a time.

Real-time processing – used mainly in critical systems e.g. monitors nuclear plants.

Single user system – allows one person to use the computer at a time.

User Interface

A user interface is a way through which we can interact with the computer system and can be classified into two categories:- Hardware Interface and Software Interface.

Hardware Interface

This interface exists between many of the components like buses, storage and I/O devices and are defined by electromechanical and logical signals. Hardware interfaces are of two types: a) Parallel interfaces: Performance is fast. b) Serial interfaces: Distance is important.

Examples of hardware interfaces include touch screens, sensors, Braille keyboards, etc.

Software Interfaces

An operating system might need to communicate with hardware. Applications running may need to interact with the OS via streams. In object oriented programs, objects within an application may need to send messages to each other via methods. How are all these done? The best bet would be through software interfaces.

Four types of software interfaces:

1. **Menu Driven** – the user selects commands from menus.

2. **Command driven** – the user types commands at the command prompt.

3. **Graphical user interface (GUI)** – uses icons, popup and drop down menus. The mouse is used to select an icon to execute an operation.

4. **Touch** – use of finger(s) to select options or interact with the computer.

Utility programs

	Menu driven	*Command driven*	GUI
Advantages	Easy to implement and use.	Faster than menu driven and graphical user interfaces.	• User friendly. • Easier to learn • Faster than the menu driven interface.
Disadvantages	Slow, in that in order to execute a command, one has to go through a series of menus.	One has to learn all of the commands or keep referring to the user manual in order to use it. This can be difficult for a novice.	Slower than the command driven interface because of the pop-up and drop-down menus which have operations that are not executed at once.

These are programs designed to analyze, configure, optimize and maintain the computer. Some are included in the operating system while others may be purchased from off-the-shelf.

They are device drivers such as computer BIOS and device firmware that provide basic functionality to operate and control the hardware connected to or built into the computer, such as a printer.

Integrated Software

It is a kind of software written for personal computers. It combines most functions of application and system softwares into one application. These software were made necessary because of the limitations placed by software with specialized functionalities. Integrated softwares began providing users with more consistent interfaces. The very first integrated software came out in the 1980s. It was in this decade that Apple developed *AppleWorks* for the Apple II computers and *Jane* for the Commodore 128. Another integrated Software named *Context MBA* was developed which integrated spreadsheets, database, chart-making, word processing and terminal emulation functions. Since it was made to be portable, it ran slowly. This was followed by the Lotus applications. Integrated software reached its peak when Framework and Symphony were released. However these days, the integrated software is being overshadowed by software suites, most notably, Microsoft Office.

Buying general-purpose software then modifying to suit your need is called customization of general-purpose software while Custom Written Software is software written from scratch to satisfy a specific need. Teams of Programmers along with System Analysts are employed to design the software. Specialized software packages are written for a specific discipline, e.g. medicine. An example of such packages is expert systems.

Before moving on, one additional note on this topic: Although computers cannot function without operating system software, they can actually function without application software. The problem though is that without application software, computers have very little practical use for users.

Popular Operating Systems

There are many operating systems on the market. However, some popular ones are **MS-DOS**, **WINDOWS**, **UNIX** and **APPLE**.

MSDOS: a single user, single processing operating system created by Microsoft for use in personal computers and uses a command driven interface. Users have to type commands at a prompt for the computer to produce a result or do a task.

Advantage: For the experts MSDOS is the OS of choice because of the speed at which tasks can be performed once the commands are known.

Disadvantages: **MSDOS** is command driven; therefore it is not very user friendly. One has to memorize all the commands or constantly refer to a command manual. MSDOS is quickly being replaced by the friendlier graphical user interface.
It is a single user, single tasking operating system hence it only facilitates the running of one program at a time.

Some WINDOWS versions through the years

1985: Windows 1.0

- Ran on the DOS operating system

- Utilized point and click interface

- Was user friendly

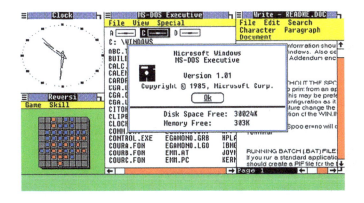

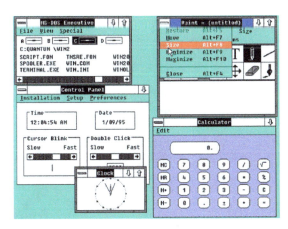

1987: Windows 2.0-2.11

- Introduced Control Panel

- The first version of Microsoft Excel and Microsoft word was able to run on this Operating System.

1990: Windows 3.0

- Faster than previous versions

- Included games like Solitaire and Hearts

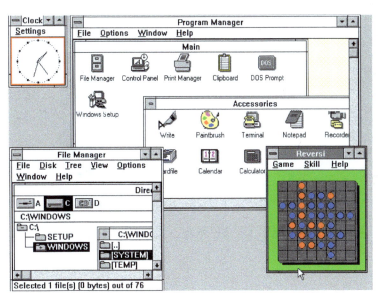

1993: Windows NT

- Included the start button

1995: Windows 95

- Featured plug and play for many peripheral devices

- Included more colours

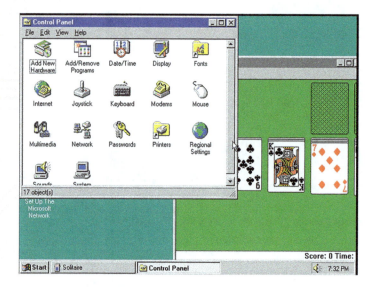

1998: Windows 98

- Featured USB support

- Featured improved games facilities

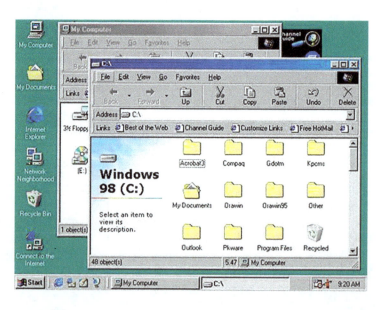

44

2000: Windows ME

- Was short-lived as it was not very user-friendly and not well-received

2001: Windows XP

- Well-received

- Facilitated 3D games

2006: Windows Vista

- Was not compatible with older systems

- Featured enhanced appearance

- Permission to activate was stricter.

2009: Windows 7

• Faster than other versions

• Included Internet Explorer 8

• Most used operating system on the internet

2012: Windows 8

• Not so user-friendly

• Included a touch screen feature which was not as flexible for users as anticipated.

2015: Windows 10

• Included an on-screen back button for ease of use with touch input.

OS/2

Operating System 2 (OS/2) is a single user, multi-tasking operating system with a graphical user interface. OS/2 needs at least 4 MB of RAM and at least 30 MB of hard disk space. It provides a dual boot feature that allows users to boot up either DOS or OS/2.

Advantages

- It is not affected by the requirement of DOS and Windows that certain device drivers must be loaded in the first 640 KB of memory. It allows long file names.

- It supports disk drives as large as 256 gigabytes.

- It's a multitasking operating system with both single user and network capabilities.

Disadvantages

- OS/2 interface is similar to that of Windows so it might take a while to adjust to some of the differences.

- Compared to Windows, there is not as much application software available to work with it.

- UNIX: UNIX was first developed in 1969 by K. Thompson, R. Canady and D. Ritchie for mini computers. UNIX is a multi-user, multi-tasking system that runs on many different computer systems from microcomputer to mainframe. UNIX is very popular in the colleges and universities.

Advantages

- UNIX is portable i.e. it can be used with many different types of computers, from microcomputer to supercomputers. The other operating systems studied cannot be used for other systems.

- It is a multi-user and multitasking operating system

- Networking is another strong feature of a UNIX operating system. UNIX can be connected through several different kind of equipment. It can share files among them.

Disadvantages

- UNIX is a difficult software for novice microcomputers to understand

- Limited amount of application program are available for UNIX.

- It is not standardized therefore an application program for one UNIX system might not work with another.

Apple

- Created by Apple for Macintosh systems. Very respected and cost more than other operating system.

- Currently Mac OS X is the version being used.

INFORMATION PROCESSING

Data and Information

Data is a collection of words, numbers, symbols, audio or symbols. Data on its own is *meaningless*. Take for example the data – John Bodden, 26, 25000, 1254 4088 6345, 945 2588. Unless we know what the various pieces of data mean, we cannot correctly use the data. However, if we know that the data is organized into Name, Age, Income per year, credit card number, telephone contact then we would be able to make sense of the data and be able to use it to make decisions or answer questions.

Information on the other hand is data that has been **organized, given meaning in a context**, and is **useful**. It is *processed* data or data that has been 'worked-on'. For example using the data for John Bodden and adding data for another customer O'Deil Duncan the computer may **process** the data to give the bank **information** on the customers' age and Income per year as follows: John Bodden age 26 earns $25000 per year and O'Deil Duncan age 30 earns $30000 per year.

The procedure of using the computer to process the data to produce information is **Information Processing**. Processing can be cutting text or numbers and placing them in a new location in a document, arranged data in order alphabetically or numerically, calculating numbers, arranged data in a table, colouring an image or arranging pictures, sounds and words to produced a video.

Sources of Data and Information

There are various sources of data and information. You may get information first-hand from another person or you may get it from the newspaper, a book, a sign or it could come from an electronic database found on a computer system or on a secondary storage device like a compact disk or even an audio tape. Information can also be accessed from a library, a museum or a company archive or from your environment.

In computer systems, digitized data may have the following sources:

1. A database which is a collection of tables which may or may not relate to each other

2. A computer file which is a collection of similar records

Data when collected and stored may be searched and "questioned" to provide information. Hence data may be used for company stock control, customer details, employee details, hospital records, for example.

Data may be **static** meaning that it does not change as in the case of a date of birth or it may be dynamic or changeable as in a person's name or a person's address. Data that is stored needs to be maintained so that it remains accurate as we may end up the old saying coming true, "garbage in equals garbage out".

Types of data stored by organizations

The types of data collected and stored are as varied as the different types of companies and organizations that exist. In all cases, it is stored so that specialized information can be output from the system. Take a look at the table that follows for examples.

Organisation	Examples of Type of information required
Hospitals	Patient records
Police	Criminal records
Immigration Department	Visitor's name, length of stay, work permit information
Credit Card Companies	Customer transactions and payments
Large Companies	Employee database, payroll
Banks	Customer account details
Stores	Stock control, customer credit card details
Schools	Student addresses, grades
Airlines	Flight information, passenger lists
Cruise Ships	Passenger lists, passengers ashore

Reasons to collect and share data

The data collected can be used by the organization to do a number of things including
- **To keep track of data** (e.g. to ensure that all passengers are on board before sailing)
- **To make decisions** (a student's grades will decide if she will graduate)

- **To find correlations** (an employer may find that employees who smoke are absent from work more often)
- **To monitor operations** (to ensure a baby's heartbeat and movements are normal)
- **To control operations** (a garden nursery may automatically control the environment– temperature, humidity, light, soil, moisture, content etc.)

Modes of Information Processing

There are different types or modes of information processing. We will examine them.

The information can be shared over **NETWORKS**, which allow users to open and work on files that are made available to workgroups. For example, the employees in a company's Accounts Department might each want to access invoice and sales files at their own workstations. When one employee changes file details, the next user sees a file that is up-to-date and consistent.

In training colleges and schools, work files and programs can be put into **shared folders**, and then accessed by any user with the correct *privileges*. This is more efficient than producing many copies of the files and handing them out, and can avoid other problems – such as losing CDs or disks that are left in rooms.

Also in schools, the main office may keep student information centrally, which can be accessed by staff in other departments. Absences, discipline records, grades etc. can be accessed and updated at different locations on the network. This leads to greater efficiency and accuracy of information.

Many organizations collect data at one workstation, and then relay that data over telephone lines to update a central database. This can be true of government organizations, police, banks, travel agents etc. The system speeds up processing of data, is more efficient and improves accuracy of information. If a user deposits cash into his account in one bank branch, he may then be able to withdraw cash at any ATM within minutes. It is also essential to have such REAL TIME PROCESSING in travel agencies, so that accurate up-to-the-minute information on flight availability, etc. is available.

Interactive Processing

This involves the user entering data, waiting for the computer to process the data entered and responding with an output then allowing the user to further input data. There is a 'back-and forth' process between the user and the computer. Airline ticket booking and online banking are examples of interactive processing.

Transaction Processing

Data for each transaction is processed very shortly after the transaction occurs. A transaction is completely processed before the next transaction. This may result in a particular transaction having to wait while an earlier one is processed. The delay will usually be short. An example might be holiday bookings where a second transaction will not be initiated until the first is completed to avoid the possibility of double booking. Transactions are processed in the order they occur. This type of processing may be (and often is) interactive. **Transaction Processing is similar to interactive processing.**

Real-Time and Pseudo Real-Time Processing

Real-time processing is when a computer responds immediately (right away) to an activity or process of the user. For example a computer that controls a plane has to respond immediately to changes in air-pressure, wind, speed and so on. An airline booking system reserves seats immediately so that nobody else can reserve or book the same seat.

A computer in a library or a supermarket performs transactions more or less immediately. A delay of a few seconds is acceptable. This is called **pseudo real-time processing**.

Batch Processing

Some transactions need to be processed straight away but others can wait to be processed along with others in a batch e.g. payment of utility and a payroll file. It is a good idea to process these transactions in batch mode because it is more economical and because you can check for errors.

In batch processing:
- The documents are collected over a period of time.
- The batch processing is scheduled for a certain time for example late at night.
- Processing can take place when computers would otherwise be idle.
- A large number of documents of the same type are widely processed together.

Stages in Batch Processing

Batch processing is therefore the processing of a group of similar transaction collected over a period of time and processed in a batch.

Stages of Batch Processing

1. Paper documents are collected into batched (e.g. of 50), they are checked, control totals/hash totals are calculated and written into a batch header document.

2. The data is keyed offline from the main computer and it is validated by a computer program. It is stored on a transaction file.

3. Data is verified by being entered a second time by a different keyboard operator.

4. The transaction file is transferred to the main computer.

5. Processing begins at a scheduled time.

6. The transaction file may be sorted into the same sequence as the master file to speed up the processing of data.

7. The master file is updated.

8. Any required reports are produced.

Criteria for Choice of Processing Mode

The following should be considered:

- Whether the information obtained needs to be completely up-to-date at all times

- The scale of the operation - batch processing is well-suited to large volumes of data.
- Cost - real-time systems are generally more expensive.

- Computer Usage - batch systems make use of spare computer capacity because they process at times when the computers would otherwise not be used.

Advantages and Disadvantages

With an online/interactive system, the data is always up-to-date and there is less need for paperwork. However, the lack of paperwork causes a problem for auditors. Checking for accuracy can be difficult.

Commercial Data Processing:

Commercial data processing involves the following:
1. A large volume of input data

2. Computational Operations – However, these are relatively few in number.

3. A large volume of output information.
   The systems which employ commercial data processing are known as Information Systems (IS).

Examples of systems which employ commercial data processing are:

1. Payroll System – Manages records of employees and the salaries paid to them.

2. Accounting System – Takes care of the accounting issues of an organization.

3. Marketing System – Manages the various marketing related activities like sales, distribution, etc.

Industrial Data Processing

This branch covers automated and embedded systems and the way they process data into information. They are used in industries which do manufacturing or construction.

Automated Systems

These systems control the operations of machinery, factory processes, telephone networks, and most other application systems which involve humans. Thus, the biggest benefit of using automated systems is that it saves labour and results are accurate and precise.

Process Control Systems

These systems are mostly used in the manufacturing facilities and factories. These systems control all the activities relating to a particular industrial process and manage them, the main purpose being to mitigate risks involved. It also saves labour and energy. The output of these systems are information which help greatly in the decision making process of any organization.

Scientific Data Processing

Unlike commercial and industrial data processing, this kind of processing involves relatively less volume of input data. It also results in relatively less volume of output information. However, the computational operations are numerous and involve mostly arithmetic and comparison operations. These systems mostly involve capturing and recording data and analyzing data

METHODS OF DATA CAPTURE

Data capture is the process of getting the data required for processing.
There are a number of different methods of data capture :

Forms and questionnaires

The design of data capture forms is important. They must:

- be clearly laid out

- have clear instructions

- have no ambiguous questions

- have examples for 'tricky' questions

- be designed to make it easy to transfer data into a computer system

Automatic Data Capture

Bar code scanners OMRs, OCRs and MICRs.

Methods which do not involve keying
in data. As little human intervention as
possible - humans generally muck
things up so this is a good thing!

Data Logging

Sensors regularly measure a physical quantity and send it to be stored on a computer. It is important that data does not have errors. Consequently lot of time is spent on methods of eliminating data errors.

Processing Different Types of Data

Numbers

Each character on the keyboard has a corresponding ASCII code, which is sufficient for input and output but not for arithmetic. Therefore, numbers, which are to be used in a calculation, are held in a different format, in binary numbers. Telephone numbers in a database are usually held in a *text* field because there is no need to calculate the telephone numbers.

Digitised Sound

Sound (music or speech) can be input via microphone, or electric keyboard and it can then be processed by the computer. An A to D converter is required (this job is done by the sound card). An A to D converter converts analogue to digital. Sound waves, which are continually variable are analogue but they have to be converted into 1s and 0s (digital format) for the benefit of the computer. The quality of the soundcard determines the quality and accuracy of the sound produced. The higher the sampling rate, the greater the quality. The resolution of the sound card (8 bit, 16 bit, 32 bit, 64 bit etc.) determines how accurately the amplitude of the sound can be measured. The sound card also has a built in synthesizer for producing music and sound effects.

MIDI (Musical Instrument Digital Interface)

MIDI is an industry standard applied to musical instruments. Adding a MIDI interface to a computer allows it to communicate with instruments like MIDI keyboards, drum pads etc. MIDI synthesised music is very compact and, therefore, small files are produced. This is because the data is stored as instructions (about pitch, length of sound etc) rather than recorded sound. The file is loaded on a computer and it can be edited e.g. pitch or speed can be altered, a keyboard solo can be converted into a guitar solo, balance between instruments can be altered etc.

Bitmapped and Vector Graphics

The screen is divided into a grid of tiny squares. Each square is called a *pixel* (picture element). High resolution screens have more pixels than low resolution screens. The pixels have to be held in memory and this is stored initially on the graphics card. WINDOWS Paint produces bitmapped graphics files (.BMP format). Scanners produce bitmapped graphics. Vector graphics are also called object orientated graphics. These consist of real geometric data rather than graphic data. A line is defined by endpoints, length, width and colour rather than by pixels. Vector graphics are produced by applications like Corel Draw.

Bitmapped Graphics and Vector Graphics

Bitmapped graphics become jagged when stretched and resized.

Do not transfer well between computers because of different screen resolutions and suffer degradation when they are zoomed in on.This is not so with Vector Graphics as their quality is maintained and they transfer well.

Information Retrieval and Management (IR)

It is an activity of obtaining data which is required for processing from a huge data pool. Years ago, when automation systems were not available to data processes, a lot of labor was involved. However with the advent of automated systems, the cost and energy associated with labor has been conserved. Information overload has also been reduced. Examples of automated systems connected with information retrieval are web search engines.

The process of information retrieval begins when the user inputs a query into the system. A query usually contains what we know as search strings. The query may return several results from which a user may select whichever result has the highest ranking or best satisfies the query.

Information retrieval is successful if the data that is given to a user as the output is:

1.   Accurate

2.   Up-to-date

3.   Structured to make searching easy.

4.   Stored on a suitable storage medium.

The data from which it is sourced can be either:

1. Human readable

Here humans read the data and not machines hence the data must be legible for the reader. Core must be taken to enter the data properly and this is more important when entering hand-written data.

2. Machine readable

There are many situations where a software is required to analyze and read the data. Humans have little to do with reading the data. In many situations the user inputs certain data and after processing, the output is printed containing the input data with extra data. For example, accounting data is added into the system and the output returns with the profit or loss added. The new updated document is a **turnaround** document.

File Organization

File organization refers to the way records are physically arranged on a storage device. **Record type** refers to whether records in a file are all the same length, are of varying length, or use other conventions to define where one record ends and another begins. **Record access** refers to the method used to read records from or write records to a file, regardless of its organization. The way a file is organized does not necessarily imply the way in which the records within that file will be accessed.

Fortran supports two kinds of file organizations: sequential and relative. The organization of a file is specified by means of the ORGANIZATION keyword in the OPEN statement. Relative files must be stored on disk. However, sequential files can be stored on either magnetic tape or disk. Other peripheral devices, such as terminals, pipes, card readers, and line printers, are treated as sequential files.

A sequentially organized file consists of records arranged in the sequence in which they are written to the file (the first record written is the first record in the file, the second record written is the second record in the file, and so on). As a result, records can be added only at the end of the file. Attempting to add records at someplace other than the end of the file will result in the file begin truncated at the end of the record just written.

There are two main methods of file access (sequential and direct) and three kinds of file structure (formatted, unformatted, and binary). Sequential-access and direct-access files can have any of the three file structures. The following kinds of files are possible:

- Formatted Sequential
- Formatted Direct
- Unformatted Sequential
- Unformatted Direct
- Binary Sequential
- Binary Direct

Each kind of file has advantages and the best choice depends on the application you are developing

Formatted Files

You create a formatted file by opening it with the FORM='FORMATTED' option, or by omitting the FORM parameter when creating a sequential file. The records of a formatted file are stored as ASCII characters; numbers that would otherwise be stored in binary form are converted to ASCII format. Each record ends with the ASCII carriage return (CR) and line feed (LF) characters.

If you need to view a data file's contents, use a formatted file. You can load a formatted file into a text editor and read its contents directly, that is, the numbers would look like numbers and the strings like character strings, whereas an unformatted or binary file looks like a set of hexadecimal characters.

Unformatted Files

You create an unformatted file by opening it with the FORM = 'UNFORMATTED' option, or by omitting the FORM parameter when creating a direct-access file. An unformatted file is a series of records composed of physical blocks. Each record contains a sequence of values stored in a representation that is close to that used in program memory. Little conversion is required during input/output. The lack of formatting makes these files quicker to access and more compact than files that store the same information in a formatted form. However, if the files contain numbers, you will not be able to read them with a text editor.

Binary Files

A binary file is created by specifying FORM = 'BINARY'. Binary files are the most compact, and good for storing large amounts of data. For binary files, a single READ or WRITE statement reads or writes as many records as needed to accommodate the number of bytes being transferred.

Sequential-Access Files

Data in sequential files must be accessed in order, one record after the other (unless you change your position in the file with the REWIND or BACKSPACE statements). Some methods of I/O are possible only with sequential files, including nonadvancing I/O, list-directed I/O, and namelist I/O. Internal files also must be sequential files. You must use sequential access for files associated with sequential devices.
A sequential device is a physical storage device that does not allow explicit motion (other than reading or writing). The keyboard, screen, and printer are all sequential devices.

Direct-Access Files

Data in direct-access files can be read or written to in any order. Records are numbered sequentially, starting with record number 1. Data in direct files is accessed by specifying the record you want within the file. If you need random access I/O, use direct-access files. A common example of a random-access application is a database. All files are composed of records. Each record is one entry in the file. It can be a line from a terminal or a logical record on a magnetic tape or disk file. All records within one file are of the same type.

Data Verification and Validation

This is the process of checking for errors when copying the data. The original is normally checked against the updated. This is known as **data verification**. **Data validation** is somewhat different in that it checks data input for errors before this data is transferred to the computer for processing. Listed below are a number of checks that can be implemented.

1. **Presence Check** –This is generally done by the data control clerk who may visually check the data as well as it can be done by a computer based system that checks the in put against known values. When finished the output should be valid in order to be passed on for further processing. For example, checking the quantity of goods ordered

2. **Type Check** – This checks the data type of entries made and accepts data based on a certain type. For example a number field accepting digits of a certain place value.

3. **Layout Check** – This checks the data based on a specific format for instance a date field wherein a data item should have one of a limited set of values. This can also be done on a logical field as well or a phone number with a set input mask.

4. **Range Check** –This checks to see if the data falls within a specified range of set values which is normally determined by the width of the data field. For example the month has to be between the numbers 1 and 12.

5. **Compatibility Checks** – This check compares data to what is stored for instance a customer's account balance on his debit card to the price of purchase.

6. **Uniqueness Check** – This is normally used in databases where the field can be used as an identifier. For example a StudentId field wherein the data stored in it must be unique so as to properly identify that student.

7. **File Lookup Check** – This could be related to the compatibility check as well where in a customer number is used to access further details on that customer. For example, accessing one's bank account information. You may use the customer number to lookup the customer's details.

SUMMARY OF IMPORTANT TERMS

Term	Description
Bistable device	a device which can exist in two discrete stable states.
Bit	the smallest memory unit. It can store either a 0 or a 1.
Byte	a group of bits (usually 7 or 8) that represents a single character.
Kilobyte	approximately one thousand bytes ($2^{10} = 1,024$)
Megabyte	approximately one million bytes ($2^{20} = 1,048,576$)
Gigabyte	approximately one thousand million bytes ($2^{30} = 1,073,741,824$)
Word	a collection of bits, treated as a single unit by the central processor.
Wordsize	the number of bits in each word e.g. 8, or 16 or 32 or 64.
Address	the *identification of a particular location* in memory where a data item or an instruction is stored.

Term	Description
CPU Type	All modern day CPU's are nothing but microprocessors. This means a CPU is contained on a single chip. Such CPU's are called single-core processors. However, recent technological advancements have led to a microprocessor revolution. Nowadays, a single integrated circuit can contain multiple CPU's. Such processors are called multi-core processors. Examples are Dual Core and Core 2 Duo processors. Recently, even quad core processors are slowly making their way into the market.
CPU Speed	Memory TypeMemory can be volatile or non-volatile. RAM is an example of a volatile memory because its contents vanish whenever a computer is restarted. Hard disks are examples of non-volatile memories. This is because it is more or less a permanent storage. I say, more or less, because there is a possibility of hard disk erase or a virus/malware attack. Hard disks are of the following types: **1.** Parallel Advanced Technology Attachment (PATA) **2.** Serial Advanced Technology Attachment (SATA) **3.** Small Computer System Interface (SCSI) **4.** Solid State Drives (SCSD)
Memory Size	The memory size is measured in bytes – usually megabytes (MB) or gigabytes (GB). RAM typically has a memory size of 512 KB to 8 GB. The costs increase with the size. The more space, better and faster the functionality of a RAM.
Memory Speed	Prior to SDRAM, memory speed was measured in terms of nano-seconds (ns). Memory speed is nothing but the amount of time it takes the module to deliver a data request. Lower the nanosecond speed, faster the processing. SDRAM speed, however, is measured in megahertz (MHz). In this case, the speed represents the time elapsed between consecutive memory clock cycles.
Word Size	A word is the natural unit of data used by a processor design. It is basically a fixed size group of digits (binary or decimal) that are handled by processor hardware. The word size is pretty much a characteristic which helps in processor selection. Word size is also known as word width or word length. Majority of the registers in a processor are word sized. Most processors usually have a word size of 8, 16, 24, 32, or 64 bit i.e. in multiples of 8. Modern processors usually have a word size of either 32 or 64 bits.
Hard Disk Capacity	Hard disks typically start with 20 GB to 1 TB. However, there has been a recent spurt in the sales of external hard disks. These have a maximum of 3 TB hard disk space. Most of these external disks support USB 2.0.

Term	Description
Hard Disk Speed	The performance of a hard disk depends upon two factors: access time and data transfer rate. The access time of a hard disk drive is the time taken by the hard drive before the actual data transfer begins. This time is mostly dependent on the mechanical nature of the disks and moving heads. To measure the access time of a disk, we consider the following components: **1. Seek Time:** It is the time taken by the head assembly to travel to the disk track where data is to be read from or written into. **2. Rotational Latency:** It is also known as rotational delay. It is the amount of time taken to wait for a disk rotation to bring the required disk sector under the read-write head. The data transfer rate is also called as throughput. It covers both the internal rate and the external rate.
Firewire Ports	It was first called **Firewire** by Apple Computers who developed it in the late 80's and the early 90's. It belongs to the IEEE 1394 interface standard. It could be compared to the USB although the USB has more market share. The firewire ports are serial buses interface standard for high speed communications and real-time data transfer. They are mostly found in Apple systems but is slowly gaining popularity with the other systems.
Expansion Slots	An expansion slot is a long narrow socket in a computer into which an expansion card can be inserted. The expansion card is a printed circuit board which is inserted into an expansion slot to add functionality to a computer system via the expansion bus.
USB Ports	USB is an acronym for Universal Serial Bus. This is an industry standard which was developed in the mid 1990s. It is used for the same purpose as the firewire ports. It has a larger market share. The most and currently used USB version is the USB 2.0. However, USB 3.0 also has evolved through faster communication between the computer system and its peripheral devices can now be achieved.

Term	Description
Hardware	The physical components of a computer system such as the input, output and storage devices.
CPU	Central Processing Unit is a single chip which contains two major subsections: the Arithmetic Logic Unit (ALU) the Control Unit (CU).
Control Unit	The Control Unit is that part of the CPU that sequences, decodes and synchronises the execution of program instructions i.e. it generates the proper timing and control signals necessary to complete the execution of the instruction. *The control unit receives instructions from the program, decodes them and then generates signals that inform the ALU what operation has been*
ALU	The ALU is that part of the CPU where Arithmetical and logical operations are performed.
Primary storage/ Main memory/ Immediate Access Storage	Semiconductor memory that is directly addressable by the CPU. A program with its associated data *can only be executed if both of them are copied into main memory.*
Backing store/secondary storage	Memory that is used for the permanent storage of data and programs.
Input device	A device that accepts data, decodes it and transmits it to the CPU in digital format.
Output device	A device that translates digital signals from the computer into a form humans can appreciate (text, graphics, sound) or into a form suitable for re-processing by the computer at a later stage.

Task 5

1. What is the difference between DATA and INFORMATION?

    (2 marks)

2. Give an example of what data may be collected:
    a) To keep track of data
    b) To make decisions
    c) To maintain and supervise operations   **(3 marks)**

3. Give one other reason for collecting data and give an example   **(2 marks)**

4. Why might a school want to use a network to share data held on its students?   **(3 marks)**

5. How could a centralized database help police in a criminal investigation?   **(3 marks)**

6. Differentiate between Batch Processing and Transaction processing.   **(3 marks)**

7. Differentiate between Data Verification and Data Validation.   **(3 marks)**

8. Explain the following:
    a) Range check   b) Type check   **(2 marks)**

SECTION 2
COMPUTER NETWORKS AND WEB TECHNOLOGIES

Data Communication

Data communication is the transfer of data from one machine to another such that the sender and receiver both interpret the data correctly. Transfer is facilitated by a computer network.

Computer Network

A computer network consists of two or more computers and peripherals that are connected for the purpose of communicating and sharing of resources.

Basic Types of Networks

(1) Local Area Network (LAN)   **(2) Wide Area Network (WAN)**

These are systems designed to connect computers together in relatively close proximity (e.g. a business office, laboratory, or college campus), usually by means of permanent link (wire - twisted pair, fibre optic, coaxial cables).

When discussing LANs, there are two things to consider:

1. LAN's topology (hardware connection method)

2. The protocol (standard set of rules describing the transfer of data between devices so they can communicate with each other.)

General components of a LAN

- Work Stations - computers that access data from the network.

- Servers (Computers that provide service to LAN users) e.g. File server, print server, communications server.

- Communication links – Fibre optic cables, telephone wires, coaxial cable, satellite, infra-red.

- Software – Consists of programs that help you establish a connection to another computer or network e.g. Network operating system

Benefits of a LAN

The connections enable users attached to the network to:

- share computer resources such as printers and modems

- share data or programs

- communicate with each other

- reduce hardware and software costs (since less equipment is needed)

- increase productivity

- enhance Security

- reduce software compatibility problems.

LAN TOPOLOGY

Topology has to do with the layout of the network.

Star Topology

All computers are connected to a central server.

Advantages:

- Adding devices is easy

- If one computer stops working, or cable is damaged, the rest of the network is unaffected

Disadvantages

- More cabling is required

- The entire network fails if the server fails.

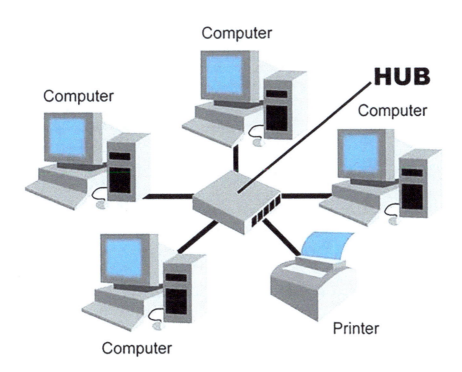

Bus Topology

A single cable forms the backbone with nodes at different points. Data is sent along the line in packets.

Advantages:
- Requires less hardware to set up
- It is easy to configure.

Disadvantages
- The entire network goes down if the cable fails.
- Collisions of data packets result in data loss.

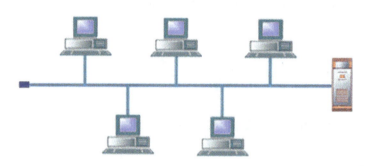

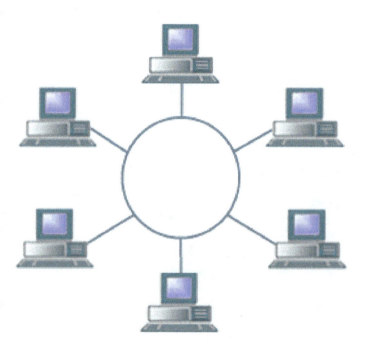

Ring Topology

Cables are connected from one computer to the next to form a loop.

Advantage
- Communication is usually faster than with a line network

Disadvantage
- If the cable is damaged the entire network goes down
- Difficult to maintain.

Wide Area Network (WAN)

Is a network in which computers are separated by large distances and therefore must be serviced via modems rather than network cards. A typical wide area network would be a local city, or county.

The largest wide-area network is the internet - a collection of networks and gateways linking millions of computer users all over the world.

Network Transmission

WANs are connected by several different types of communication systems. These communication paths are referred to as links.

a) Most users connect to the network via standard telephone lines, using dial-up modems. Dial-up connections are generally the slowest method of connecting to a network, but they are inexpensive to establish and use.

b) Other users, who require quicker data transfers, contract with the telephone company to use special, high-speed lines such as Integrated Service Digital Network (ISDN) lines. These types of links require a digital modem to conduct data transfers. Because the modem is digital, no analog conversion is required. (ISDN is an integrated services digital network which offers a high-speed digital network. It integrates voice, data and video signals on a single line. Basic Rate Interface (BRI) provides two 64Kbps channels per line. Primary Rate Interface (PRI) provides a capacity of 2Mb interface with a large quantity of multiple B channels.

COMMUNICATION MEDIA

Wired

Twisted Pair cable

Fibre Optics

Coaxial cable

Wireless

Satellite

Microwave

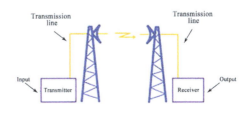

Speed

The type of medium used helps to determine the speed of transmission the speed of communication.

The speed of communication is measured in several ways:
- The Baud Rate - (the rate of Signal Change)

- The Bit Transfer Rate - (the rate at which bits are transmitted in bits per seconds (bps))

Bandwidth

This is the highest rate/speed that data can be transferred across a path.

Examples of types of bandwidths are **narrowband, voiceband, broadband**

Note also that multi-plexing technology enables the same piece of cable to carry multiple number of separate signals, forming channels. The number of channels a cable can carry is a function of the Bandwidth.

Voiceband
A channel that can transmit data at a maximum rate of about 8000 characters per second

Narrowband

A channel that transmits data at slow speeds – between 10 to 30 characters per second (e.g. telegraph system)

Broadband

A channel that transmits large volumes of data at speeds of over 100,000 characters per second.

Data flow

Simplex
Allows data to be transfered in one direction only as in a paper system - the message is sent ans cannot be responded to.

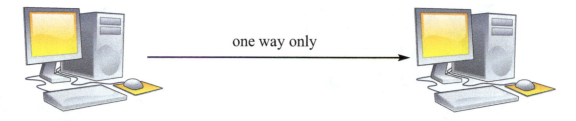

one way only

Half-duplex

Allows data to be transmitted in both directions but in one direction at a times as in a walkie-talkie radio system where one party speaks or transmits a message after which the other party may respond to the message sent.

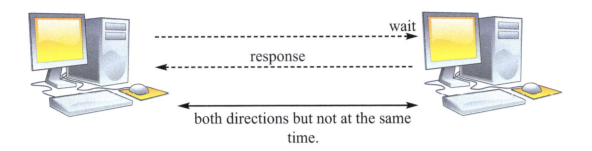

TERMS ASSOCIATED WITH COMPUTER NETWORKS

Duplex or Full Duplex

Allows data to be transmitted in both directions at the same time as in a telephone system.

Attenuation

A transmission may be in progress or have already been made, however, the data being sent is subject to electrical interference due to storms, signal loss, poor joins, or noise on the channel. This loss of the quality of the data or transmission is referred to as **attenuation**.

As the length of the cable increases, the attenuation of the data increases and the probability of correctly interpreting the data is decreased.

Point-to-point transmission computer network

Computer are set up to communicate using direct links between the computers involved.

Up-load

This is the process of reading data from a user's computer storage and transferring it to another computer via communication channels.

Down-load

This is the process whereby files are transmitted via communications channels from an external computer and stored on media located on the user's computer.

Electronic mail

Mail or messages (files) transmitted electronically by computers via communication channels. It is usual for messages to be held in central store for retrieval at the receiving user's convenience.

Bulletin Board/News group

An electronic equivalent of a conventional bulletin board. Users can post messages, read messages posted by other users, communicate with the system operator and upload or download files.

Instant messaging

Abbreviated as IM. This is a type of online chat service which allows transmission of text messages, file and graphics over the Internet.

Blogging

Blogging involves creation and maintenance of blogs. A blog is a discussion site published on a website. It sometimes acts like a personal diary. However, this depends upon the purpose of its creation. Blogs are now used heavily for advertising brands, products, and services.

File Transfer

Sharing files over the Internet. Two ways of doing file transfers are:
  1. Pull-based - Receiver initiates a file transmission request.

  2. Push-based - Sender initiates a file transmission request.

Computers which provide this service are often called **file servers**. Depending on the direction of the file transfer in relation to the user's computer, the transfer is called *uploading* or *downloading*.

Voice Over Internet Protocol

Abbreviated as VoIP. This protocol is used for sending voice and multimedia messages over the Internet. An example of an application we use in our day to day life which uses this protocol is Skype. VoIP is also available on smartphones, personal computers and on any Internet access devices.

Intranet

Intranet uses Internet Protocol just like the Internet but it operates within an organization. It is normally composed of multiple local area networks. One can term it as a private Internet.

Extranet

This can be viewed as an extension to an organization's intranet. This type of network allows controlled access from the outside for some special purposes.

Remote Log-in

Remote Login allows a user to use the resources of another computer as long as they are connected over a network. *Unix* has a software called *rlogin* which is used for such purposes. WINDOWS has a similar software called *Telnet*.

The World Wide Web

The World Wide Web or WWW as it is commonly known, is an intricate network of computers which host resources that can be used over the Internet. It is a collection of websites.

Web page

A web is an Internet resource which abides within a website.

Web browsers

A web browser is an application software which is used to display web resources. It has the following functions:

1. Find and download a web file.

2. Interpret the source code of the file.

3. Display the text and images according to the format specified in the file.

4. Manage the different hyperlinks.

Web browsers are not restricted to the Internet alone and can also be used in private networks such as the Intranet. There are many browsers on the market which include Microsoft Internet Explorer, Opera, Apple Safari, Mozilla Firefox, Google Chrome.

Web Servers

A web server may refer to a system (hardware and/or software) which stores and delivers web resources over the Internet. The most common use is to host websites. Other uses include gaming, data storage or running enterprise applications.

HTTP

HTTP stands for Hyper Text Transfer Protocol. This is an application layer protocol. This protocol is the foundation of data communication over the Internet. HTTPs is Secure HTTP which means transmission of hyper texts over the Internet is secure and safe. The integrity of HTTP transmission is maintained.

URL

URL stands for Uniform Resource Locator. When used with HTTP, it is known as a web address. It is a character string which points to a specific web resource. In most browsers, this string is displayed at the top, inside the address bar.

FTP

FTP stands for File Transfer Protocol. This protocol is used to send files over a TCP enabled network. It is based on the client-server architecture. There are two separate connections between the client and the server: data connection and control connection. Authentication is optional. Anonymous logging is allowed in certain systems. Secure transmission is now allowed with FTP being regularly associated with the SSL/TLS. The first FTP systems were command-line applications.

However, most FTP systems have now evolved to graphical user interfaces. These are intended for posting public messages. These can be compared synonymously with forums.

1. How does LAN differ from WAN? **(2 marks)**

2. What service does a modem perform? **(2 marks)**

3. What is the difference between bps and baud? **(2 marks)**

4. Describe the main types of network topologies, giving their advantages
   and disadvantages. **(4 marks each)**

5. Explain the difference between the terms data communications and
   telecommunications. **(2 marks)**

6. What is the Internet? **(2 marks)**

7. What is an e-mail? **(3 marks)**

8. If you were to send an e-mail to a friend in China, suggest what
   hardware and software you would need. **(5 marks)**

9. Differentiate between the following
   a) Simplex and duplex channels   b) Narrowband and broadband   c) LAN and WAN

   d) Half-duplex and full-duplex   e) Upload and download   **(2 marks each)**

10. Explain the terms below. Hint: if a question is allocated, give 3 points, mention 3.
    a) Telecommunication   b) Network   c) Bandwidth
    d) Wide area network   e) Voice band

    (2 marks each)

SECTION 3
SOCIAL AND ECONOMIC IMPACT OF INFORMATION AND COMMUNICATION TECHNOLOGY

Data Integrity

It is important to maintain **Data Integrity**. This means keeping the data accurate, complete and uncorrupted.

If data is held and shared digitally, there are rules concerning how it is held and there are also laws - see further along in this section.

Data should be:

Consistent
Common data held in one file should show the same information as that held in another file, and changes to one should also mean changes to the other.

Up-to-date

If a file shows there are 17 cartridges in stock, and two are used, then the data must be updated.

Complete

If there are omissions in data, this leads to inaccuracies.

Relevant

If we only want to know a person's name, date of birth and address, then we should not store data on eye colour or hobbies.

Data integrity is ensured by various tools. One such tool is **digital signature**. Digital signature is a valid way to determine whether the message is genuine or not. It is a mathematical scheme which is used to assure the recipient that the message was indeed sent by the said user. Digital signatures also ensure that message is not altered during transit. They are commonly used for software distribution, financial transactions, and in other cases. Some countries view digital signatures to be of legal significance.

USE OF INFORMATION

In this section we will take a look at how the information tapped by computer systems is effectively applied in organizations. Today, in many organizations, information about money, materials and people, has been recognized as a major resource available to managers for carrying out their work. Special systems called **information systems** have been designed to provide managers at many levels with the kind of information they need regularly.

INFORMATION SYSTEMS AND MANAGERS

Usage by Top Managers

Information Systems are used by top managers for Strategic Planning and Control as they:

- Provide information to assist in making long-range strategic decisions and future projections

- Provide summarized past and present information.

- Provide information from inside as well as outside the organization.

Example of Application: A system which provides information and tools, which helps management to decide whether a new factory should be built or if a new product should be developed.

Usage by Middle Managers

Information systems are used by middle managers for **Tactical Planning and Control** as they:

- provide information to assist in making short-term decisions on how to implement goals and objectives established by top managers

- provide fairly detailed past and current information to help managers monitor to control such things as deadlines, budgets & performance.

- Provide information from mainly inside the company and to a lesser extent from outside.

Example of Application: For a manufacturing company, a system which provides information and tools which give information about any problems during production, such as missed deadlines or cost overruns.

Usage by Low-Level Managers

Information systems are used by low-level managers for **Operational Planning and Control**
- provide information to assist in making immediate decision decisions which affect day-to-day operations

- provide detailed, current information used to assist in co-coordinating and controlling worker' activities in order to meet goals set by middle management provide internal information only.

Example of Application: For a manufacturing company, a system which provides information on current stock levels, stock due to be supplied, products to be delivered to customers, sales made, etc.

Usage by Non-Managers

Information systems are used by non-managers for **Transactional Handling**:
- support many routine tasks most of which involve some form of tedious record keeping

- focus on ensuring that data needed to make decisions at management levels are input and processed.

Example of Application: For a sales oriented company, entering sales, printing bills, updating product lists and prices, creating quotations, etc.

SECURING DATA AND INFORMATION

Security

Security refers to protecting a computer system's hardware, software and data from unintentional or malicious modification/destruction or from any type of tampering, including unauthorized access or disclosure of data. Both the physical as well as the virtual spaces are to be secured.

Cyber security is the protection of networks and computer systems from cyber attacks.

A **cyber attack** is an attempt to spoil or destroy a computer network, data or system.

Cyberspace is the electronic space which accommodates the global connection of computers or simply put, cyberspace is *the internet*.

Measures to Secure data and Maintain Data Integrity

When in charge of a vast amount of data and information, one should consider various elements including vulnerability, threats, attacks and counter measures regarding the safety and security of the data and information that are available. Protection of the data an information requires using **physical access restrictions** as well as **software access restrictions**.

Physical access restrictions

This is the first line of defence for many computer systems and cyber-systems. As the term suggests, these restrictions are implemented by using devices or strategies which restrict physical access to data and information. Some devices that are employed are:

- cables/plates to affix hardware unto the desk

- built-in locks on computers

- isolating hardware from non-users

- closed-circuit TV and alarm systems to monitor access

- computer-controlled devices that check employee badges, fingerprints or voice before un locking doors

- storing software on removable storage media which can be placed in secure areas when not use.

Computer systems are protected in a physical way not only by restricting/monitoring access but also by minimizing/preventing system failure and implementing systems for recovering from such failures if they occur. This is not only important but critical to some organizations (e.g. airline reservations, health, and national security) and is commonly accomplished by using:

- **Fault-tolerant computer systems** which are built with duplicate parts for elements that are needed to permit continuous operation and that are automatically used if the primary part fails.

- **Uninterruptible power supplies (UPS)** which permit operations to continue for a period in the event of a power cut by providing power from a battery and thus avoiding damage to hardware and software.

- **Backup procedures** which ensure that copies of important software are created on a portable or removable storage media (e.g. magnetic tapes) thereby guaranteeing recovery in the event of loss or damage.

- **Fireproof cabinets** for storing backups of software.

- **Special fire extinguishers** which minimize damage to computer systems.

Use of Smart Cards

- Smart cards are pocket sized cards with embedded integrated circuits. They are mostly made of plastic, generally polyvinyl chloride. Recently, Japanese have manufactured reusable smart cards made up of paper. Smart cards can provide identification, authentication, data storage and application processing. They also have strong security controls and used extensively by organizations.

Software Access Restriction

Unless properly secured, software can be modified, vandalized or deleted. This can be minimized or prevented by using:

1. **Passwords**
   Passwords are good ways to restrict access. They are a combination of characters which will be allowed by the system. To gain access to the system, a *secret combination* is typed in by the user and is evaluated by a disk lock software which enables users to lock their disks when they are not using them.

   Unless adequate **password** controls are used, other employees may have access to sensitive information about colleagues, and *view, edit, print, copy* or *append* to it. An untrained or disgruntled employee may even *delete* whole files either mistakenly or deliberately. Consequently, different levels of access may be given for e.g *User-level, Supervisor Level,* or *Administrator Level*.

   To prevent access altogether, the data may not even be stored on the same network system. The access can be further restricted by use of *security clearance cards, swipe cards* or even *Biometric security systems*. Passwords can also be put on individual files (e.g. Microsoft Office) to prevent unauthorized access.

2. Encryption

Encryption systems allows users to encode files so that they appear as gibberish to anyone trying to read them.

When transmitting data across telephone lines, it is often necessary to use **encryption** to make files unreadable to would-be hackers. The encryption algorithms create what we know as ciphers. The authorized recipient's computer will have the key that enables the data to be de coded. This is especially useful in credit card and banking transactions over the Internet.

There are two kinds of encryption:

a) Symmetric Encryption

Encryption and decryption keys are the same and so, the parties involved must agree on a key before they start communication.

b) Public Key Encryption

The encryption key is published for anyone to use and encrypt messages. However, the decryption key is private and is only available to the recipient.

Encryption by itself is sufficient to protect message confidentiality, but there are other techniques available to protect data integrity and authenticity like digital signature. Encryption software use many encryption algorithms like the RSA algorithm.

3. Vaccine software

Virus, Worms and other Undesirables

A virus is computer software that is designed to corrupt data or interfere with the system software in a computer. The name 'computer virus' comes from the fact that it acts just like a 'virus' an organism which multiplies within a living being by replicating itself. The computer virus, just like its living counterpart, replicates by inserting copies of itself into other computer programs, files, or the hard drive's boot sector.

Effects of Viruses

Viruses may be really harmful to the system. It can steal hard disk space, CPU time, access private information, displaying random messages on the PC screen, etc. This kind of software is written by people who are termed as **virus writers** or **virus engineers**. These people are exceptionally skilled in social engineering and have a comprehensive knowledge of networking and security protocols. Their code can identify the weak point of the default firewalls built within an operating system and through it, can enter and replicate into multiple copies.

99% of the viruses have been known to attack computers which have the Windows operating system as it is the most commonly used system and because its security infrastructure is known to be weak.

Other operating systems like UNIX, etc. possess a secure kernel making it almost invulnerable. Viruses are known to cause billions of dollars worth of **economic damage** each year by causing **system failure, wasting computer resources, corrupting data,** etc. Deliberate corruption by virus contamination can be minimized by use of VIRUS PROTECTION SOFTWARE, but this must be kept up to date, and should automatically check all disk access (including floppy disk, EMAIL and Internet downloads). However, there is no anti-virus software which can really catch all types of viruses.

Viruses are not however the only culprits. There are ransomware, worms, Trojan horses, keyloggers, spywares, etc which are as dangerous as viruses. All these softwares are grouped together under the term Malware', short for malicious software. We will now see some of these malware in brief.

Worms

A worm is actually a standalone computer program which, like a virus,replicates itself after entry into the computer system. More often than not, it uses computer networks to spread itself, relying on the loopholes that a security framework may possess. The difference between a virus and a worm lies in the fact that a worm is not a parasite. This means that it does not latch itself to an existing program. Worms are known to attack computer networks as well.

Trojan Horses

Unlike worms and viruses, this is a non-replicating computer malware.This kind of malware is typically used for data theft and possible system harm. Trojans usually present themselves like a friendly routine which make victims to install them on their computers. Once in, it starts acting like a backdoor which is under the control of the creator of the Trojan. They are not easily detectable but there will be symptoms that one can look out for. For example, the computer may run very slowly. Trojans have known to be quite a useful tool for industrial espionage and credit card frauds.

Spyware

Spyware is software that aids in gathering information about a person or organization and assert control over their computer resources. They are classified into four types: system monitors, Trojans, adware, and tracking cookies. Most spywares are installed onto one's computer system user knowledge. The installation of Spyware frequently involves Internet Explorer. Symptoms usually include unwanted CPU usage, disk usage and network traffic. Most anti-virus tools also come with anti-spyware software. If these tools are regularly updated and maintained, the chances of spyware installation on your computer can lessen.

Firewalls

A firewall is a software or hardware based network security system that controls the network traffic. It analyzes the data packets and based on a set of rules, it decides whether to allow them or not. A firewall maybe considered as a barrier between your system and the outer network. There are different types of firewalls:

1) Network layer firewalls: Operate on a low level of the TCP/IP protocol stack. They act as packet filters.

2) Application firewalls: They restrict or allow based on application.

Personal Measures

As a smart user of computer technology , one should take measures to protect self while interacting with technology.

Some personal measures should include:
- Screen of e-mails
- Using safe websites hence assessing the URLs of websites for legitimacy
- Not disclosing private information including credit card numbers online
- Restricting of information shared on social networks
- Reporting threats and attempts to intimidate via the internet
- Use of anti-viruses on devices
- Restricting access to open Wi-Fi networks

MISUSE OF DATA AND INFORMATION

Unfortunately, with the wide use of networks, the internet and with more computer literate individuals, there is *misuse of data and information* as there is wrong or malicious use or illegal use of the data available which includes violation of privacy, software piracy, electronic eavesdropping among others.

Computer Crime

This refers to the use of computers to commit unauthorized acts. Computer crime is punishable by the law. Some common crimes are listed below

- **Computer Fraud**
  This is the most common computer crime and describes premeditated or conscious effort to gain money/goods from computer systems.

- **Software Piracy**
  Propriety software is software for which an individual or organization has rights of owner ship.

  The unauthorized copying -without payment of a **software fee**, or use of a computer program or software is termed **software piracy** and is a criminal offence.

- **Electronic Eavesdropping**

This describes the intentional interception of information intended for use by others within a computer system. It is obtaining confidential data illegally by tapping into communication networks.

- **Creating and installing Computer Viruses, worms and other undesirables**

The act of create programs to damage, change, mis-represent information is a crime. They can shut-down sytems, erase data, and allow systems to generally mal-function. E-mails, Advertisements, bulkmails and often "Free Apps" are used to carry out these crimes.

- **Cyberbullying**

Threatening, intimidating or belittling another user via the internet constitutes *cyberbullying* and is punishable by the law.

- **Propaganda**

This is the use of false or distorted information meant to spread beliefs or doctrines.

- **Violation of privacy**

This occurs when there is public use of confidential information. This may be captured from e-mails, social media groups or via electronic documents stored on the system. This can give rise to **Theft of Identity/Identity Theft** where unauthorised persons access your personal data and pretend to be you.

- **Embezzlement**

This involves the use of computers to misappropriate, misuse or steal money.
Other computer crimes are electronic espionage and surveillance and phishing.

- **Surveillance**

Monitoring day-to-day activities of citizens. Data collected from a number of sources can easily be brought together to give a "picture" of the citizen (data mining) – possibly used for undesirable purposes.

RIGHTS AND LAWS

RIGHTS

Many people feel worried that "Big Brother is Watching" – that the state (or even private organisations) have access to too much information about them. The types of sensitive information which can be gathered include:

a) the racial or ethnic origin of the data subject,
b) their political opinions,
c) their religious beliefs or other beliefs of a similar nature,
d) whether they are a member of a trade union,
e) their physical or mental health or condition,
f) their sexual life,
g) the commission or alleged commission by them of any offence, or
h) any proceedings for any offence committed or alleged to have been committed by them, the disposal of such proceedings or the sentence of any court in such proceedings.

Others believe that, in order to provide a safe society, this type of information should be easily available – for example to stop terrorism or prevent serious crime.

LAWS

In many countries, DATA PROTECTION ACTS have been passed to protect the rights of individuals. Below is a brief summary of the main points of the UK"s DPA. Personal Data means data which relate to a living individual who can be identified from the data, and covers both factual information and expressions of opinion about the individual, stored electronically or manually Data Controller (a person or organisation which holds personal data) must register with the government, and treat the data in accordance with the following principles.

The main principles of the Data Protection Act

*   Personal data shall be processed fairly and lawfully and, in particular, shall not be processed unless the data subject has given their consent to the processing, or the processing is necessary in order to protect the vital interests of the data subject. The data subject must give their explicit consent to the processing of the personal data. The data subject must be given access to the information held, and must know the purposes for which the data is being held.

*   Personal data shall be obtained only for one or more specified and lawful purposes, and shall not be further processed in any manner incompatible with that purpose or those purposes.

*   Personal data shall be adequate, relevant and not excessive in relation to the purpose or purposes for which they are processed.

- Personal data shall be accurate and, where necessary, kept up to date.

- Personal data processed for any purpose or purposes shall not be kept for longer than is necessary for that purpose or those purposes.

- Appropriate technical and organisational measures shall be taken against unauthorised or unlawful processing of personal data and against accidental loss or destruction of, or damage to, personal data.

APPROPRIATE HARDWARE AND SOFTWARE

Relevant hardware and software used in business, science and technology are discussed in this section.

Hardware used in offices and organisations.

Computers come in many different types and sizes, depending on the job they have to do. In any business or organisation using computers, someone will have to decide what role information technology can play in doing the work.

The **hardware** refers to the equipment which is plugged in and switched on.

The **software** refers to the programs which are loaded into the computer, and decide what particular job the computer is going to do.

It may be that office users simply need a desktop PC (Personal Computer) with a word processing package such as Microsoft Word. The PC is the hardware, Microsoft Word is the software. Of course, the user would also need a monitor (VDU) and printer (hardware), and an Operating System such as Microsoft Windows (software).

Some businesses, such as banks, might need to share data between computers. If a customer visits different tellers, or even different branches of the bank, all his account details will still be available. In this case, a network would link a number of computers by cable. The computer terminals are linked to a central server, which stores all the information. In the building, a local area network (LAN) provides each user with shared data. If the information is shared with other branches scattered over the country, the bank would use a wide area network (WAN).

The computer processing capacity required for the diverse banking transactions is much larger than that needed on a desktop. In former times, a huge mainframe would have taken up most of an air-conditioned room. Nowadays mainframes such as the IBM System/390 are common in large businesses. These systems cost nearly 1000 times as much as a desktop PC.

Smaller businesses which required more than a simple PC would once have employed a minicomputer - a central server, with sub terminals. The terminals were not capable of any processing (i.e. dumb), but could transmit data to and receive data from the central server. Nowadays, high powered desktop-style computers provide enough power to form a network server with "intelligent" clients connected to them. A typical "mid-range" system might has a server with 2 500MHz processors, around 50 Gb of disk space and 128Mb RAM. Connected to this by network hubs or switches might be 100 or more desktop PCs. This is known today as a client/server configuration.

Automation is the term given to the computerized control of machines and processes. Some manufacturing companies may use process control to aid the production of goods. This is particularly useful in situations where it is difficult or dangerous for workers, for example in making steel.

Equipment may have sensors built in to monitor the process - e.g. to sense the temperature or the amount of a particular gas and send a signal to a processor. The signals may be analog (they may vary, such as temperature or voltage). If so, they may need to be converted into digital signals (0's or 1's), by passing them through an analog-to-digital converter. When the computer notes an awaited signal or specified time, it instructs the equipment to move on to the next step (e.g. set a switch to cut off the heat supply). Process Control is used in many different environments - Plastics, Brewing, Electrical Generating to name a few.

Systems which use computers to process data and control the source of that data are called real time systems. An example is air traffic control: here a real-time-system takes continuous data from an outside source (transmitted from the airplane) and processes the data quickly enough to be able to transmit back and change the course of the plane if necessary. Real-time-systems are also used in ground traffic control and process control applications.

Robots are widely used in **manufacturing**. Machines linked to computers can be programmed using simple programming languages e.g. CNC, or Computer Numeric Control, to complete repetitive tasks. They are commonly used in assembly lines to pick, place and weld car parts, or in engineering companies to repeatedly cut and shape the same metal parts. The design of parts can be made using a graphics package (software), and the parts then made using the computer to control the machine. The process of an engineering system allowing users to design a part, and using the data to manufacture that part is known as computer-aided-manufacture (CAM).

Supermarkets today make use of point of sale (POS) technology. This uses data communication links between computers at each cash register and a central server. The server holds a database with information on each item of stock, which can be instantly updated as it is sold. Shoppers can pay for goods using credit cards, which are automatically debited at the POS terminal, using a system called EFT (electronic funds transfer.)

Software and Organizations

An **architect or engineering draughtsman** use a computer to assist in producing drawings. The software most likely to be used is a **CAD (Computer Aided Design)** package, with output to a **plotter**. This allows large-scale plans and maps to be drawn.

Artists and printers make extensive use of a **Graphics** package, as well as **Desktop Publishing**

packages such as *Microsoft Publisher* or *Aldus PageMaker* Graphics packages to manipulate pictures in a digital format. A **scanner** is a useful item of hardware for these professionals, allowing original artwork to be digitized for use in publications.

Students and teachers may use Computer Aided Learning (CAL) or Computer Aided Instruction (CAI) packages to assist with new topics or subjects.

Desktop presentation software allows businessmen and lecturers to use graphics,animation, text and sound (MULTIMEDIA) to present information to groups. An example is Microsoft PowerPoint.

An **Expert System** also known as EPSS (Electronic Performance Support System) is an application designed to enable users to benefit from the knowledge of expert human consultants. An example is a medical system which can be used by doctors to aid in diagnosis of disease; its data can be continually updated and improved as new breakthroughs are made. The knowledge base is accessed by software called an inference engine. Answers may be given based on a series of interactive questions. Computer departments often use expert systems to log and diagnose computer faults.

Word Processing software is widely used in offices to enable easy and efficient text manipulation. Documents and letters may be saved and edited for re-use, saving valuable time. A keyboard is the normal method of data entry, but in some situations, a voice recognition system may be used. This allows users to dictate into a microphone, and uses software to create digitized patterns which can be recognized as words. The text can then be displayed as a document on screen. Improvements in natural language processing are making this type of data entry more and more popular.

Voice Synthesis is the use of digitised signals to produce human-like speech from a computer's loud-speakers or other hardware device. It can be used in a variety of applications from security systems to games.

CURRENT AND TECHNOLOGICAL TRENDS

Internet and E-Commerce

The Internet has changed our leisure and work habits. With cheaper and faster computers and transmission speeds available, the growth in Internet use has been phenomenal across the globe. It is used for everything from research to entertainment and shopping, and has become an extremely popular medium for communicating through email and chat services.

E-Commerce is perhaps the fastest growing field of all. Companies can buy and sell almost any product or service using secure transactions (with data **Encryption**). With a huge world market and increased confidence in buying over the internet, there are obvious advantages to being a "dotcommer".

Artificial Intelligence (AI)

Artificial intelligence refers to the ability of a machine to perform actions that are characteristic of human intelligence such as reasoning and learning. The first attempts at artificial intelligence were to design programs that would enable computers to rival skilled humans at games such as chess and to prove mathematical theorems. Below three main areas of AI are discussed:

Expert Systems

This is a program or computer system providing the type of advice that would be expected of a human expert:

- They capture the knowledge of experts who may not always be on hand (due to death, resignation, etc.).
- They store knowledge in such a way that it is easily retrievable and accessible
- They can train non-experts to become experts they are not affected by human constraints such as fatigue, boredom, emotion, etc.

Application
- In medicine for diagnosis of diseases
- In training and simulations
- In manufacturing for diagnosing malfunctions and effecting repairs
- In production for providing the best way to design, produce, stock and ship products.

Natural Languages

These are languages such as English, Spanish or French which are used in everyday conversation. Computer and Language experts have found the task of getting computers to listen to and respond in natural language is very challenging. Voice recognition describes the ability of computers to accept input by understanding the speech of a user. Voice Synthesis refers to the capability of computers to electronically reproduce the human voice in a recognizable manner. Computers using natural languages boast one of these capabilities.

There are some obstacles that are encountered in the use of Natural Languages:

- Interpretation - a spoken word can have different meanings depending on spelling (e.g. dear, deer).
- Tone and context accents - the same spoken word can actually sound different if the speaker has an accent
- Noise - a spoken word can sound different if there is background noise or if the speaker is ill or tired.

These problems are slowly being overcome and computers with voice recognition and voice output capabilities are now in demand.

Application
- In the military field for interpreting various commands needed to steer a ship in the medical & legal fields where doctors & lawyers use them to prepare reports by simply speaking into a microphone in the telephone services for assisting with calls, dialing, messaging, etc. more

86

and more in personal computer systems where users are being allowed to configure their computer to execute spoken commands (e.g. start a game) for language translation.

Robotics

This is the technology of creating and using programmable devices,called robots, to perform many simple repetitive tasks formerly done by human labor.

Application

In Computer Aided Manufacturing for welding, painting, assembling parts, packing and performing other routine or dangerous operations.

Computer Aided Design Systems (CAD)

These combine the use of computers and graphics to aid in the designing of products and drafting of drawings.

Examples:
- used by architects for designing buildings
- used by engineers to design bridges, buildings, etc.
- used for designing in many manufacturing industries (e.g. cars, aero planes, shoes).

Computer Aided Manufacturing systems (CAM)

These use computers to control machines in the manufacturing process.

Examples:- see examples for robotic systems.

Computer Assisted (Aided) Instruction CAI)

These are used to provide personalized teaching instruction by providing the student with sequences of instruction under the control of a program. With these systems the student and computer take part in an interactive dialog.

Examples:
- educational software
- instructional software used for on the job training.

Telemarketing

This refers to the marketing of goods or services by means of a telecommunication channel (e.g. the telephone, computer modem). In computer systems telemarketing is becoming very popular using the Internet. Using this medium users can place orders without visiting the stores.

Teleconferencing

This refers to the usage of computers and communications technology to carry on a meeting in which not all the participants need to be present at the same place or time. Teleconferencing when used on computer systems allows a conference to develop through message sent to electronic mailboxes.

Telecommuting

These technologies allow workers to remain at home or other locations and connect by telecommunications channels to other workers at other locations.

Advantages:
- increased productivity for people who don't need supervision
- saving time & expense for travel
- saving on expenses for office space & furniture.

Examples:
- Executives who normally spend many late hours working can do so in the comfort of home
- Many computer programmers tend to perform better outside of an office environment.

IMPACT OF INFORMATION AND COMMUNICATIONS TECHNOLOGY (ICT)

The development in Information and Communications Technology has social and economic impact on Job skills and Careers.

Automation and Employment

Computers are often installed as part of an initiative to automate systems which were manually done, in order to improve on productivity, e.g. CAM systems. The introduction of computers into organizations has also had the opposite effect of creating job opportunities for new as well as existing workers. New workers may be required to implement the computer system, to do repairs and maintenance, to train users, etc. Existing workers are often retrained to perform the same functions on the computer or to perform new functions created by the computer system. For example, sales persons may no longer need a secretary to prepare their quotations since the computer system may now allow them to do these from their desks. If the secretary shows the ability and interest she/he may be retrained as a salesperson.

Computer-controlled warehouses need only a handful of staff to operate them. Likewise, Computer-controlled robots are now common on production lines, replacing human workers. The old skills of workers in the printing industry are now out-of-date. Some jobs have disappeared as they can now be done automatically e.g. checking football pools coupons, marking multiple choice exam papers.

However, it is fair to say that the development of information technology has led to many new jobs such as computer technicians, programmers, web designers and systems analysts.

Job Hunting and Recruiting

These are normally facilitated by using on line services and bulletin boards like the Career network. Software is available to help to prepare the job hunter to do tasks such as resume preparation.

Computer Literacy

More and more computer literacy is becoming a prerequisite for many non-computer careers as makers of movies, videos or advertisement for television often use computers to create special effects, animation and graphics. Journalists, reporters and editors create/edit news reports using word publishers. Auto mechanics and other technicians use computer diagnostics to pinpoint problems. Travel agents book holidays by computer, not by phone or letter. Telephone banking has meant that many bank staff now work by phone in front of a computer, instead of being behind a counter.

De-skilling has taken place. Some jobs which needed a high level of skill in the past can now be done more easily. For example, print workers today can use DTP software to lay out their work. Designers now use CAD software rather than pencil and paper on a drawing board.

Teleworking

Teleworking is a welcome alternative to going into the office to work. Teleworking, sometimes called telecommuting, means working from home using modern technology to keep in touch with your business. Jobs can be relocated to places where it is more attractive, more convenient or cheaper to live. A computer, email facilities, a fax machine, a mobile phone and videoconferences equipment would be useful for teleworking.

Videoconferencing

Videoconferencing means using computers to provide a video-link between two or more people. Instead of just talking to someone by telephone, you are able to see them as well.

Better quality products

Products made with computers should be of a better quality than before. For example, car bodies are welded more accurately by robots than by humans. Robots do not get tired so the quality of work is consistent. Machines controlled by computer are much more reliable. With Miniaturisation many electrical items, such as mobile phones and video cameras, have become smaller due to developments in technology.

Social Health

Information and Communications Technology has social impact on individuals and on teams.

Many individuals experience **Technophobia**, the fear of technology which sometimes causes increased heartbeat, headaches and stress. They may not desire to work with others on a team and may resist changes which could improve their life if they were not so afraid. However, with the increased use of computers in schools and many other sectors of the society, this fear is expected to reduce dramatically as time progresses.

Excessive usage

Many individuals are guilty of spending too much time on the computer to the neglect of face-to-face interactions with others whether at home or at the place of work. This may reduce the quality of relationships if not corrected early.

ROLES OF PERSONNEL IN INFORMATION TECHNOLOGY RELATED PROFESSIONS

As the fourth generation of computing has evolved, many work roles in information technology have also evolved. Key positions in Information Technology fields are described below.

Systems Analyst

A systems analyst investigates and analyzes business problems and then designs information systems that provide a solution, in response to requests from a business or a customer. He or she gathers requirements and analyzes the costs and the time needed to implement the project.

Key Skills Required: Ability to extract and analyze information; good communication, inter-personal and presentation skills; possess a logical approach to solving problems.

Software Engineer or programmer

A programmer or computer software engineer is responsible for the design, development, testing, and deployment of the computer software used in businesses and homes every day. Two primary classifications exist for this role; software engineer and systems software engineers. The systems software engineer designs programs to run the computer; the software engineer designs software to meet the needs of users of the computer. He or she understands how both software and hardware function and spends time talking with clients and colleagues to understand solutions that are needed.

Key Skills Required: Knowledge of programming, data structure and database system concepts; software testing capabilities; attention to detail; understanding of usability concepts; strong oral and written communications capabilities; analysis; logical thinking; teamwork; attention to detail.

Database Administrator

The database administrator [DBA] oversees all aspects of the business' database structure including its architecture design, implementation, administration, monitoring, tuning, backup, migration, and support. He or she will design databases, architect data warehousing, automate and test database tasks, monitor database utilization and platforms, restore corrupted databases, install and test upgrades and patches, implement security and encryption measures, and recommend new database technologies. *Key Skills Required:* Technical and analytical abilities; an understanding of database architecture; script writing; an understanding of security; good communication skills, especially for work within the IT organization.

Network Administrator

The network administrator oversees the administration, management, and maintenance of computer network systems and data circuits. This may include upgrading, installing troubleshooting networks, network hardware devices, and software. He or she maintains hardware inventory, develops and documents standards for network operations, and recommends and schedules repairs to the network.

Key Skills Required: Technical aptitude; strong analytical skills; solid oral and written communication skills, teamwork and of confidentiality.

Computer Engineer

A computer engineer is responsible for designing, developing, and testing computer hardware, including computer systems, circuit boards, computer chips, keyboards, routers, and printers. He or she supervises the manufacturing, production, installation of the parts.

Key Skills Required: Knowledge of hardware and software component, analysis and evaluation; computerized design skills; testing skills.

IT Security Analyst

The person in an IT security analyst role maintains the security and integrity of data throughout an organization. He or she analyzes security measures and determines their effectiveness as well as implementing any training regarding taking proper security measures. This individual works with both IT professionals and the organization's management, to identify, communicate and solve system compromises. The IT security analyst also creates documentation to help prevent future security breaches.

Key Skills Required: Strong knowledge of information system security principles and practices; experience with intrusion detection systems; ability to evaluate and develop solutions; an understanding of security for the intranet and extranet; good communication skills.

Technical Sales Engineer

Technical sales is possibly one of the least hands-on technical roles, but it still requires an understanding of how IT is used in business. A technical sales person sells hardware or explains the business benefits of systems and/or services. Work involves identifying customer prospects, attending meetings and conferences, and drafting proposals. A technical sales engineer has sales targets and earns commission for completed sales.

Key Skills Required: Product knowledge; persuasion and interpersonal skills; enthusiasm, mobility, and business awareness.

Software Tester

Computer bugs can have a massive impact on the productivity and reputation of an IT firm. Testers try to anticipate all the ways an application or system might be used, and how they can fail. They don't necessarily program, but they do need a good understanding of computer code 5. Testers prepare test scripts and macros, and then analyze results for the project leader so that corrections can be made. Testers may also be involved at the early stages of projects to anticipate pitfalls before work begins.

Key Skills Required: Technical aptitude; attention to detail; creativity; good organization skills; analytical and investigative thinking; good communication skills.

Computer Forensics Expert

Forensic experts recover digital data such as email, correspondence, or erased files and preserve it for later use as evidence. They also determine how hackers or other unauthorized personnel gain access to information or computer systems, and how they navigated within those systems.

Key Skills Required: Technical skills working with operating a network systems, encryption programs and data retrieval procedures; analytical and investigational skills; communication skills both for use in court, in writing, and with the investigative organization.

Web Designer

A web designer designs, creates, and modifies websites. He or she analyzes user requirements and then designs, creates, and modifies websites, often enhancing the content with sound, pictures, graphics, and video clips.

Key Skills Required: Programming; critical thinking; system analysis; decision-making; strong oral and written communication skills.

User Interface Expert

The user interface expert partners with product managers and engineers to define, design and implement solutions for a positive user experience with webpages or a website. This often involves creating wireframes, storyboards, flowcharts, and site maps to communicate interaction and design ideas. He or she also works with end-users to evaluate the success and usability of the design. This individual will document design guidelines, best practices and standards.

Key Skills Required: Proficiency using HTML, cascading style sheets, graphics software, and languages such as JavaScript for rapid prototyping; solid visual design skills and presentation skills to share them with others; problem-solving skills, and strong communication skills.

Software Trainer

A software trainer teaches individuals how to use one or more computer programs. He or she must learn to use the software in the same manner as the user, and then determine how to present concepts and materials effectively to individuals who may have a wide variety of readiness for learning. Software trainers often partner with instructional designers, training managers, and business partners during the instructional design phase, pilot programs, and evaluation of training effectiveness.

Key Skills Required: Ability to understand concepts, workflows, and nuances of software; teaching skills; flexibility to adapt to different training settings and audiences; strong oral and written communication skills, a high degree of patience, analysis and training evaluation skills.

Help Desk or Tech Support Specialist

A help desk or tech support specialist performs troubleshooting for IT hardware, software, and communications problems. These types of specialists work for hardware manufacturers and suppliers solving the problems of business customers or consumers. Many also work for end-user companies by supporting, monitoring and maintaining workplace technology and responding to users' requests for help. Some lines of support require professionals with specific experiences and knowledge, but Tech Support can also be a good way for graduates to get into the IT industry.
Key skills required: Wide range of technical knowledge; problem solving, communication, patience and diplomacy skills.

Technical Writer

A technical writer is a professional writer who analyzes the audience and produces technical documentation for technical, business, or consumer audiences. Documentation includes manuals, user guides, white papers, design specifications and online help materials.

Key skills required: Technical proficiency with the subject matter; writing skills; analysis skills for task analysis; flexibility, especially if the subject matter is under development; the ability to collaborate with subject matter experts [SMEs] and others who may have responsibility for the successful outcome of the products delivered.

SUMMARY OF EMERGING TECHNOLOGIES

Expert systems	*Software packages that act as consultants or "experts". A KNOWLEDGE BASE is built up in specialist areas (e.g. medicine). and can be consulted by users to assist in problem solving or diagnosis.*
Robot	*A computer-controlled mechanical device which can be programmed to perform tasks such as "pick and place"*
Voice synthesiser	Output device which generate sound similar to human speech on receipt of digital signals
CADD	Computer Aided Design and Draughting is the use of computers to design construction projects and produce the blueprints. It can also calculate quantities of materials required and estimate costs.
CAM	Computer Aided Manufacture is the use of computers to control production equipment (e.g. lathes, welding machines). Can take input from CAD systems, or by direct programming such as CNC (Computer Numeric Control)
CAL/CAI	Computer Aided Learning/Instruction is the use of computers to provide instructional information to students, to pose questions and react to responses

TERMS YOU NEED TO KNOW

HARDWARE	SERVER
DESKTOP PRESENTATION	SIMULTATION
SOFTWARE	CLIENT
MULTIMEDIA	WORD PROCESSING
PC	LAN
EXPERT SYSTEM	KEYBOARD
VDU	WAN
KNOWLEDGE BASE	VOICE RECOGNITION
OS	MAINFRAME
INFERENCE ENGINE	NATURAL LANGUAGE PROCESSING
NETWOR	MINICOMPUTER
TERMINAL	VOICE SYNTHESIS
HYPERTEXT	REAL-TIME SYSTEM ROBOT
MICROCOMPUTER	GRAPHICS PACKAGE CAM
DUMB TERMINAL	POS EFT CAD
AUTOMATION PROCESS CONTROL SENSOR	PLOTTER DTP SCANNER CAL
MONITOR ANALOG DIGITAL	CAI
A to D CONVERTER	EPSS

Task 1

1. Sharing information has its hazards. Explain why and how an office should restrict access to view shared data to selected persons only?

   a) Restrict access to the server which stores shared data?

   b) Create a daily backup of the shared data?   **(6 marks)**

2. What is meant by the term CORRUPTION?

   a) State two ways Corruption can be caused.   **(3 marks)**

3. What is a computer virus?
   a) What means should be taken to avoid or repair damages caused by viruses?
                                                                       (4 marks)

4. How can data be made more secure before transmission across telephone lines? **(2 marks)**

5. What is meant by DATA INTEGRITY   **(3 marks)**

Task 2

1. Give an example of how personal data collected by an organization can be misused.

    (1 mark)

2. How have many countries attempted to protect citizens' rights? **(1 mark)**

3. State any two principles of the UK Data Protection Act **(3 marks)**

4. State one reason it may be useful for state authorities to store personal data. **(1 mark)**

Task 3

1. What are the main differences between a MAINFRAME, MINI- and MICRO-COMPUTER?

   (3 marks)

2. Describe (by use of an example) how data can be gathered in a PROCESS CONTROL application. Your answer should include the terms used in this section.
   a) Use a diagram to help explain your answer.   **(10 marks)**

3. What is meant by Computer Graphics?   **(2 marks)**

4. What is a scanner?   **(2 marks)**

5. What is a Desktop Publishing Package?   **(2 marks)**

6. What is Electronic Funds Transfer?   **(2 marks)**

7. Describe by use of an example an EXPERT SYSTEM.   **(4 marks)**

8. Explain what is meant by   **a)** CAD   **b)** CAL   **(2 marks each)**

9. Would a travel agent use a LAN or WAN to connect to the centralized database? Explain the acronyms in your answer.   **(2 marks)**

10. Explain the main feature of a REAL TIME SYSTEM, and give an example of where one might be found.   **(2 marks)**

11. What is a PLOTTER, and who would be most likely to use one in their work? **(3 marks)**

12. What is meant by the terms VOICE SYNTHESIS, VOICE RECOGNITION and NATURAL LANGUAGE PROCESSING? **(6 marks)**

13. A travel agent has recently introduced a computer system into their High Street branches. Describe two reasons why they might have introduced this system. **(4 marks)**

Task 4

1. Describe the role of **a)** Systems Analyst   **b)** a Programmer   **(4 marks)**

2. What is a DPP, and what is its purpose?   **(2 marks)**

3. List 4 jobs in the computing industry.   **(4 marks)**

4. List key skills of a computer engineer.   **(3 marks)**

5. Which profession analyze results for the project leader to do corrections.   **(1 mark)**

Task 5

1. What is the difference between DATA and INFORMATION? **(2 marks)**

2. Give an example of what data may be collected:

   a) To keep track of data

   b) to make decisions

   c) to maintain and supervise operations **(3 marks)**

3. Give one other reason for collecting data and give an example. **(2 marks)**

4. Why might a school want to use a network to share data held on its students? **(3 marks)**

5. How could a centralized database help police in a criminal investigation? **(3 marks)**

6. Differentiate between Batch Processing and Transaction Processing. **(3 marks)**

7. Differentiate between Data Verification and Data Validation. **(3 marks)**

8. Explain the following: **(3 marks)**
   a) Range check   **b)** Type check

SECTION 4
WORDPROCESSING, PRESENTATION, AND WEB DESIGN

Wordprocessing

Wordprocessing is a term we use when we create, edit, and print documents using a computer. Wordprocessing in a computer is done using a special software called a *Word Processor*. A word processor does what it is told by the user. The term 'word processor' was first coined in Germany in the early 1960s. In early days, word processor was not a computer software, it was an electronic device. Recently, there has been a rise in the web based word processors like Office Web Apps or Google Docs (now called Google Drive).

Typical functions of word processors include automatic generation of:

1. Batch mailings
2. Indices and numbers
3. Table of Contents
4. Table of Figures
5. Footnotes

There are other functions like spell checking and grammar checking. Many word processors also provide an in-built thesaurus. Other common features include review editing, comments and annotations, support for images.

Word processors are useful in various fields and sectors. Some include business (preparing legal documents, letters, memos and reference documents), home (personal blogs, diaries, etc.), and in literature (used by novelists, poets, playwrights, screenwriters, and essayists).

Microsoft Word

Microsoft Word is a word processor developed by Microsoft. It was built under some other name in 1983. However, the first version of Word for Windows came in 1989. Subsequent versions were released, each version increasing the popularity of this word processor. Prior to 1995, Word was released according to the versions of its development. However since 1995, Word has been releasing with the year of release as part of its name instead of its version. The default format for Word applications prior to 2007 was .doc. From 2007, the format has been changed to .docx.

Your employer has asked you to write a blog regarding one of its products. He has asked you to write at least a about its product and he has given you specific requirements as to how the document should look when the final draft comes to the editing department. You are now to use Microsoft Word for drafting this document.

We will be using *Microsoft Word 2007* for this particular case study.

Clicking on the Microsoft Word icon from Start->Programs->Microsoft Office will result in the opening of a new document. The new document will look like:

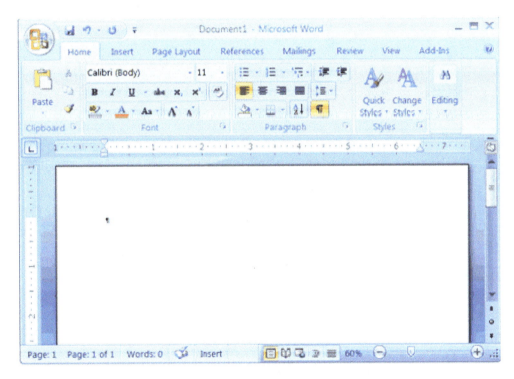

However, if you already have a document open and you want to create a new one, click on the Microsoft logo at the top left corner of the window. A menu will drop down. It will have the following menu items:

- **New:** Creates a new document.
- **Open:** Opens an existing document.
- **Save:** Save an already open document.
- **Save As:** Save a new document.
- **Print:** Send a document to the printer.
- **Prepare:** Prepare the document for inspection.
- **Send:** Send the document to Email or Fax.
- **Publish:** Publish to a blog etc.
- **Close:** Close the document.

Select **New** then select **Blank document** and then **Create**.

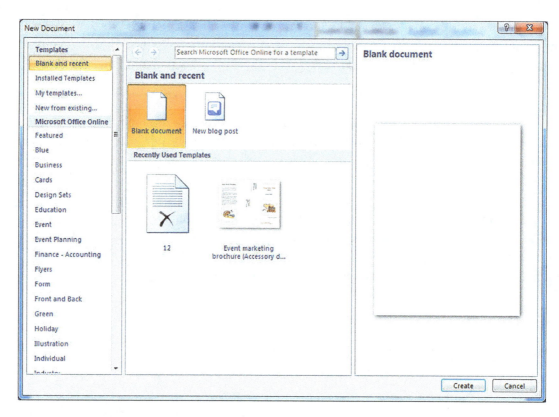

Firstly, you would want a title. In the main window, under the **Home tab**, you can see the various styles starting with **Normal** on the left and ending with **Emphasis** and some scroll buttons to the right. Since we want a title, let us click on the **Title style**.

Clicking on the **Title style** will create a blue underline. Use Font Style Cambria (Headings) and Font Size 26.

To add a title or Heading

1. Click on the **Home** tab
2. Under **Styles** click **Heading1**
3. Change the **Font** size to 26
4. Type A Sample Blog

You will notice that the text being typed for the title appears in blue font colour.

Save the Document

1. Click the **Office Button**
2. Click **Save as** or Press **CTRL + S** on the keyboard
3. Keep the Save as type as a .docx document
4. Type a name for your document – **blog**
5. Click **Save**

You will notice that the document name **blog.docx** appears at the top of the Microsoft Word document Window.

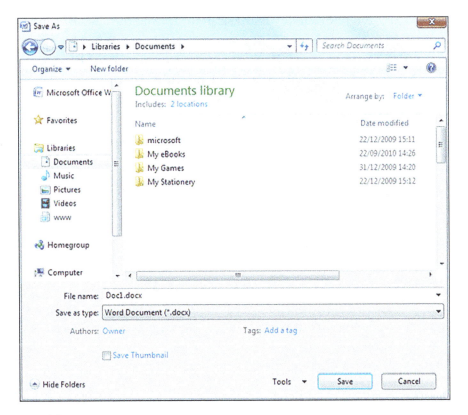

Add the body of the blog

1. **Press Enter** – the font changes to Calibri (body) and the font size to 11
2. Type the lines of information as requested by your employer. (See the screen shown)

A Sample Blog

Hello, this is John Doe. I am here to write a corporate blog of a product named 'A.S.B.T.O.S'. This is a product which is used for hair-dyeing. It is known to contain ingredients which are considered healthy to the hair follicles.

Bolding, Italicizing and Underlining Text

To enhance the appearance of your blog you will need to format selected text or pieces of information and apply **Bolding (B), Italicizing (*I*) and Underlining (U)** as you see fit.

Remember to **block** or **select** the text to be formatted then click on the **Font tab** to select the required format.

You may also use also use the relevant keyboard shortcut for the formats as follows:

CTRL + B – Bold   *CTRL + I – Italic*   CTRL + U - Underline

A Sample Blog

Hello, this is **John Doe.** I am here to write a <u>corporate blog</u> of a <u>product</u> named '**A.S.B.T.O.S**'. This is a <u>product</u> which is used for *hair-dyeing.* It is known to contain *ingredients* which are considered healthy to the hair *follicles.* This is a <u>product</u> which is used for *hair-dyeing.*

Bullets and Numbering

Microsoft Word has an extensive list of bullets and numbering features for use in creating lists and for emphasizing information in
your tables or on the pages of your document.

Bullets and numbering may be set in Microsoft Word to be inserted automatically (the default) once you begin using them as in :
- Inserting bullets
- Numbering a list of things to do
          Or
1. Insert a Title for my Blog
2. Enter the information for the blog
3. Save the blog
   You have the option to insert them when they are required – Click the relevant icon as shown.

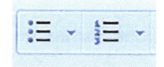

You may choose different bullet styles or different numbering formats.

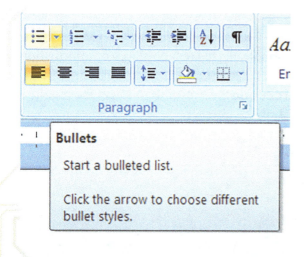

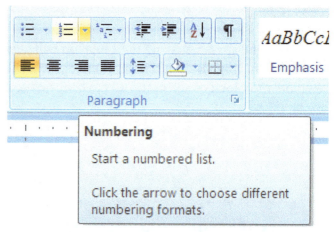

Text Alignment

You will need to "line-up" the information being presented to produce a pleasing layout for your reader. Text may be aligned or lined-up on a page as shown in the figure below. Note the keyboard shortcut for the various alignments:

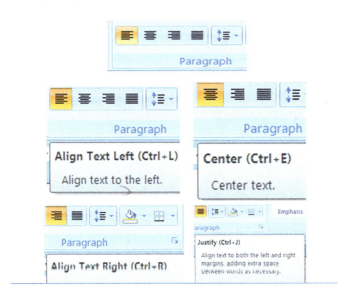

Line Spacing

This option is used to change the spacing between the lines. Using this option you can customize how much space you want before or after paragraphs.

- Click on the line spacing icon located beside the alignment icons.
- Click the selection arrow and choose from the list (1.0, 1.15, 1.5, 2.0, etc.)

Question

Your employer wants to left align the first paragraph and center align the second. Also right align the title. The paragraphs should have a line spacing of 2.0.

Solution
- Select the first paragraph and press CTRL + L.
- Then select the second paragraph and press CTRL + M.
- Select the title and press CTRL + R.
- Then click on the line spacing button and click on 2.0.

Your screen should appear like the one shown overleaf.

A Sample Blog

Hello, this is **John Doe.** I am here to write a corporate blog of a product named 'A.S.B.T.O.S'. This is a product which is used for *hair-dyeing*. It is known to contain *ingredients* which are considered healthy to the hair *follicles*. This is a product which is used for *hair-dyeing*.

It is my pleasure to say that it is one of the right products for a person of any gender.

Indentation

Indentation is often used if you want to start a new paragraph away from the margin.
Right next to icons for bullets and numbering are the indentation icons used to decrease indentation and to increase indentation.

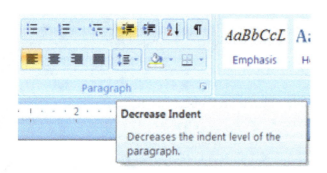
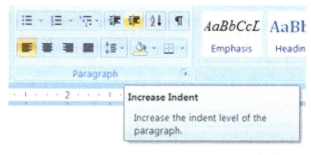

Find and Replace

Microsoft Word provides us with a **Find and Replace** feature.
To find a particular text:

1. Press CTRL + F or click **Find** on the **Home** tab.
    The screen shown will appear

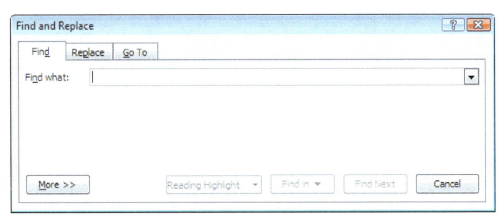

2. Enter the text in the **Find What** text box and click **Find Next.**
    The words or text matching what you typed will be selected in the body of your document.

3. Click **Find Next** again until all the text has been found.

The **Replace** tab allows you to find text and replace it. You can either replace all the texts witch match or only certain words. Clicking on the **Replace** icon will do the replacements and tell how many replacements were made.

1. Enter the text you want replaced in the **Find what** text box

2. Enter the text to be used instead in the **Replace with** text box

3. Click **Replace All** if you want all the texts that match to be replaced else
    Click **Find Next,** check if you wish for a replacement and THEN click **Replace** or keep clicking **Find Next** until all the texts are replaced to your satisfaction.

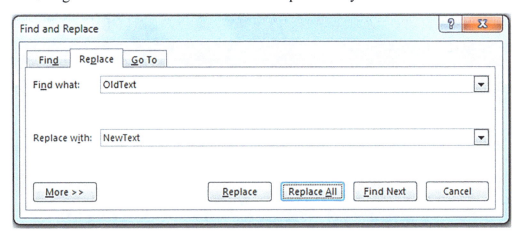

WORKING WITH THE PAGES TAB

Cover Page

Cover page is a template which you can customize. It is the first of any document and is similar to a book cover. The cover normally contains more graphics than text.

To insert a cover page:

1. Click on the Insert Tab
2. Click on the cover page icon on the **pages** tab.

Blank Page

Sometimes you may want to add a blank page.

To add a blank page:

1. Click on the insert tab
2. Click on the blank page icon which is next to the cover icon.

Page Break

Sometimes you may want to add a page at the current position in the document rather than waste spaces or lines. Use the **Page Break** option to create a page when you need to start on a new page when you have not finished all the lines on the current page.

To add a Page Break:

1. Click Insert
2. Click Page Break

Inserting a table

To insert a table:

1. Click the Insert Tab
2. Click Table
3. Drag over the rows and columns you wish to have. The maximum is 10 columns, 8 rows. You may add more at another time.
   a) Click Insert Table
   b) Type in the number of columns and the number of rows
   c) Click ok

OR

1. Click the Draw Table icon to get a border for the table
2. Insert the required rows and columns as needed.

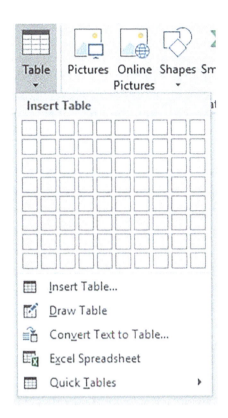

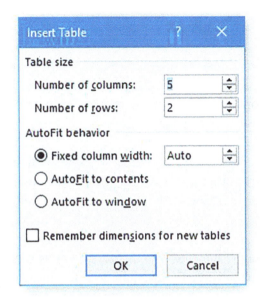

We can insert a Spreadsheet table from Microsoft Excel also and the **Quick tables** option has ready-made table templates for us to choose from.

Your employer wants you to create a table with 6 rows and 2 columns. Table headers must be bold and center aligned. Rest of table contents must be plain text and center aligned. The data given to you is:

1. Table Headers: Product Version, Color
2. Table Contents:
   Version 1, Black
   Version 2, Red
   Version 3, Yellow
   Version 4, Green
   Version 5: Brown

Solution:
The screen will look something like this.

Product Version	Price
Version 1	Black
Version 2	Red
Version 3	Yellow
Version 4	Green
Version 5	Brown

Inserting Graphics

We can easily insert images, clip arts, shapes, smart arts and charts in a Microsoft Word document. To add a picture, click on the picture button in the Illustrations menu under the Insert tab. A dialog box will open up just like the one which popped up when you clicked the open document button. You can select any image of any type.

Clip arts are drawings and other graphics which are used to illustrate certain concepts. Clicking on the ClipArt button under the Insert tab will open up a small window in the space between your text editor screen and the scroll bar. You can search for the clipart in the collections and insert it into your document.

Shapes can be inserted into the document as well. Clicking the shapes button will reveal numerous drawings which are classified under lines, basic shapes, block arrows, flowcharts, callouts, and stars and banners. Recently used shapes are available to you at the very top.

Smart art graphics are graphical tools which we can use to illustrate complex concepts like organization charts and Venn diagrams.

Charts are tools through which we can represent statistical information graphically. We can insert multiple types of charts.

Inserting Links

Hyperlinks are links which connect to a web page another page in your document or any external resource. Making a text a hyperlink causes it to be underlined in blue font colour.

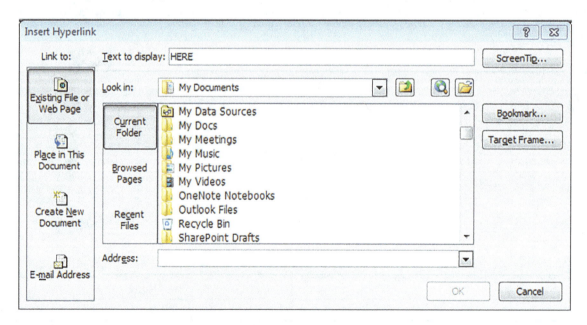

Cross-references are usually links to numbers. You can insert these in the table of contents.

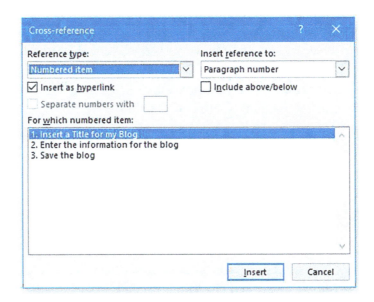

Bookmarks are used to assign a specific name to a specific point in the document.

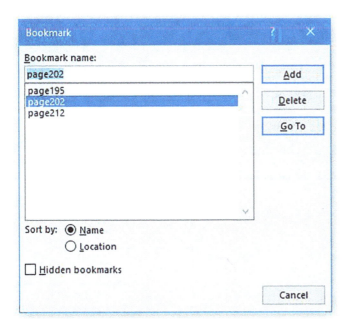

Headers and Footers

Headers are word processor elements which appear at the top of every page. To add a header, click on the header button. A list of templates will be revealed. You can edit or remove a header any time you want.

Footers appear at the bottom of every page. To add footer, click on the footer button. A list of templates will be revealed. You can edit or remove a header any time you want.
You can also include **page numbers** easily. Click on the number button. You will led to a drop down menu where you can specify whether you want the number at the top or bottom of the page, etc.

Inserting Text in text box

You can insert pre-formatted textboxes by clicking on the text box icon in the text menu. Sure, you can insert a text box using shapes too but they are normal. The Text box icon provides you with templates of text boxes which you can use.

Word Art

WordArt is used to insert decorative text in your document. This has been used in the previous versions as well but Word 2007 presents more flexibility in using them.

Your employer has given you some images.

1. Outline the steps you will take to insert them in your document.

2. Add headers and footers to your document.

3. You are required to put the title in the header and the number in the footer.

4. Add a textbox with the same text you have already typed in the document.

5. Convert the word hair-dyes into a hyperlink.

Task 2

DOCUMENT SETUP

Orientation

Setting the margins are necessary if you are writing some kind of a specialized document. For example, a resume. You can set the margins by clicking on the margins button in the setup tab. Clicking it will result in a drop down menu. The drop down men contains several options. Each option has a specific margin detail. However, you can also create custom margins. In the drop down men, click on Custom Margins.

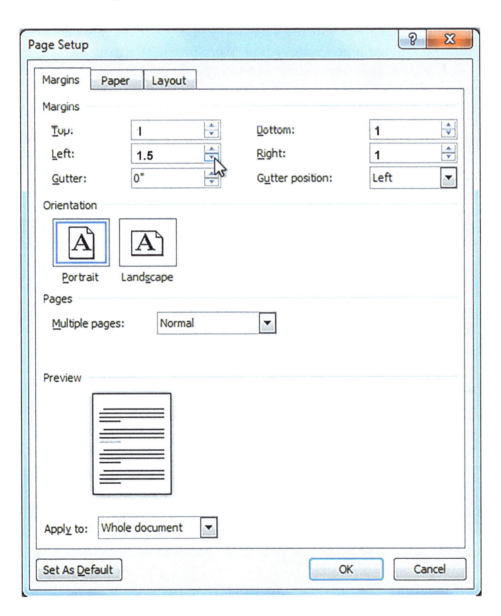

There are two kinds of orientation which you can view your document as:

1. Portrait: Portrait orientation has a narrower outlook and ideal margins.

2. Landscape: Landscape orientation increases the width.

Portrait is the default orientation when you open a new document in MS Word. The size option is also available during setup. You can choose the size you want depending upon the type of document you are penning down. There is another important feature of MS Word which is very important and that is, Mail Merge.

Spell Check and Grammar

Checking spelling and grammatical errors are automatic functionalities provided by Microsoft Word. If you make a spelling mistake you will see a red wavy line under the misspelled word. Make a grammatical error, you will see a green wavy line. Word provides alternative suggestions to the mistakes or errors, however, you may feel the need to add the words to the dictionary instead of calling them errors.

Document Layouts

There are **five methods** by which we can view a document.

1. Print Layout: This is default view. This shows exactly how the document will appear on a printed page.

2. Full Screen Reading: This enlarges the document to full screen so we get more space.

3. Web Layout: This shows exactly how the document will appear on a web page.

4. Outline: It shows the document as an outline with the outlining tools.

5. Draft: Here it shows as a quick draft. It doesn't show certain features like the header and the footer.

Comments

This feature comes in use whenever we are editing a document and is handy if we want to know what changes we have made. To add a new comment, Click on the Review tab and click on the new comment button. This will add a new comment at the current cursor position. You can have the track changes feature on if you want automatic tracking of the changes you have made.

Mail Merge

Mail Merging is useful in creating and sending out mass mail which may include letters and envelopes. The content or message of the mail is generally the same for all the recipients. There may be a few specific details that differ from one recipient to the next.

To use Mail Merge:

1. Open an **existing** Word document, or create a **new** one.

2. From the **Mailings** tab, click the **Start Mail Merge** command and select **Step by Step Mail Merge Wizard** from the drop-down menu.

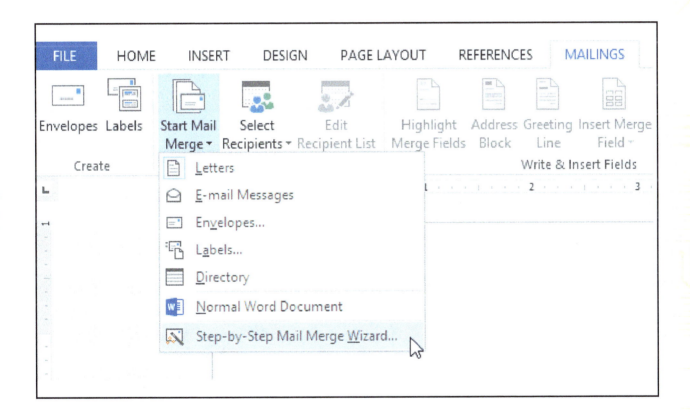

The Mail Merge pane appears and will guide you through the **six main steps** to complete a merge. The following example demonstrates how to create a form letter and merge the letter with a recipient list.

Step 1:

- Choose the **type** of document you want to create. In our example, we'll select **Letters**.

- Click **Next: Starting document** to move to Step 2.

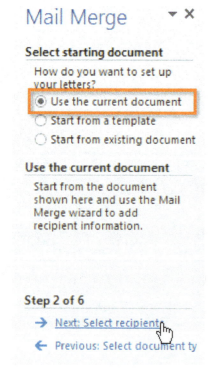

Step 2:

- Select **Use the current document**

- Click **Next: Select recipients** to move to Step 3.

Now you'll need an address list so Word can automatically place each address into the document. The list can be in an existing file, such as an **Excel workbook**, or you can **type a new address list** from within the Mail Merge Wizard.

1. From the Mail Merge task pane, select Use an existing list, then click **Browse...** to select the file.

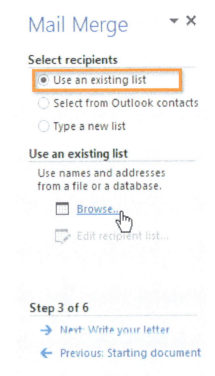

2. Locate your file and click Open.

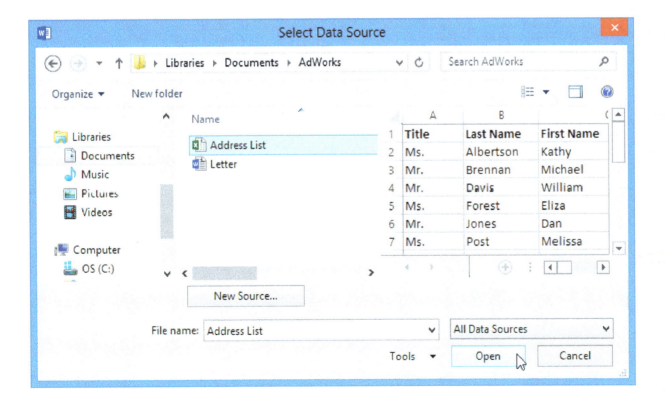

3. If the address list is in an Excel workbook, select the worksheet that contains the list and click OK.

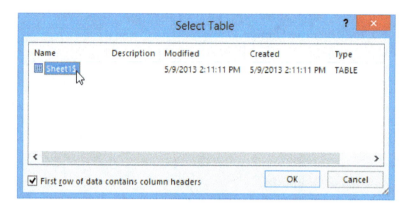

4. In the Mail Merge Recipients dialog box, you can check or uncheck each box to control which recipients are included in the merge. By default, all recipients should be selected. When you're done, click OK.

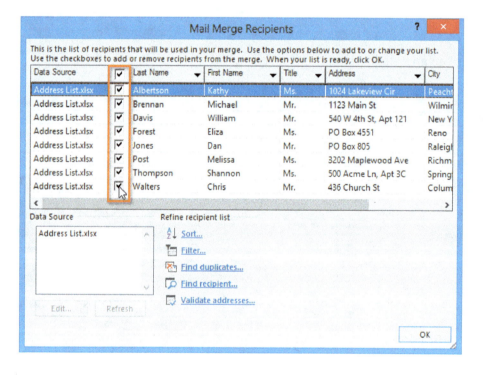

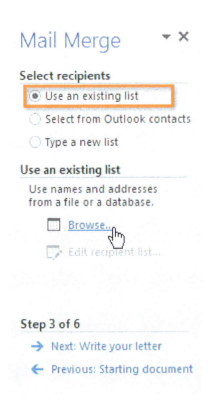

Mail Merge

Select recipients

- ⦿ Use an existing list
- ○ Select from Outlook contacts
- ○ Type a new list

Use an existing list

Use names and addresses from a file or a database.

🔲 Browse...

📝 Edit recipient list...

Step 3 of 6

→ Next: Write your letter

← Previous: Starting document

5. From the **Mail Merge** task pane, click **Next: Write your letter**.

If you don't have an existing address list, you can click the **Type a new list** button then click **Create**.

You can then type your address list.

Step 4:

Now you're ready to write your letter. When it's printed, each copy of the letter will basically be the same; only the **recipient data** (such as the **name** and **address**) will be different. You'll need to add **placeholders** for the recipient data so Mail Merge knows exactly where to add the data.

To insert recipient data:

1. Place the insertion point in the document where you want the information to appear.

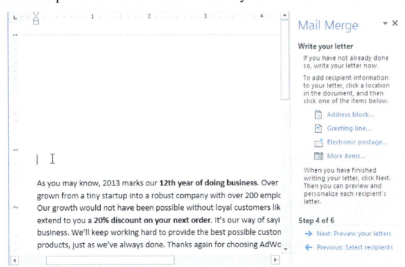

Mail Merge ▾ ✕

Write your letter

If you have not already done so, write your letter now.

To add recipient information to your letter, click a location in the document, and then click one of the items below.

📄 Address block...

📄 Greeting line...

📑 Electronic postage...

▦ More items...

When you have finished writing your letter, click Next. Then you can preview and personalize each recipient's letter.

Step 4 of 6

→ Next: Preview your letters

← Previous: Select recipients

2. Choose one of the four placeholder options: Address block, Greeting line, Electronic postage, or More items.

3. Depending on your selection, a dialog box may appear with various options. Select the desired options and click OK.

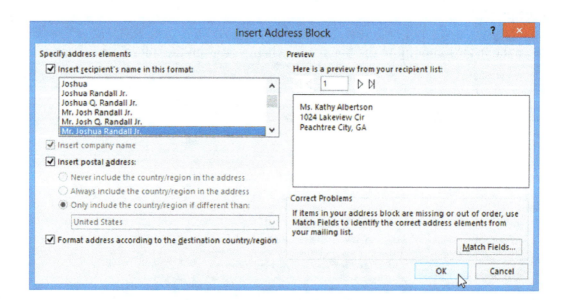

4. A placeholder will appear in your document (for example, <<AddressBlock>>).

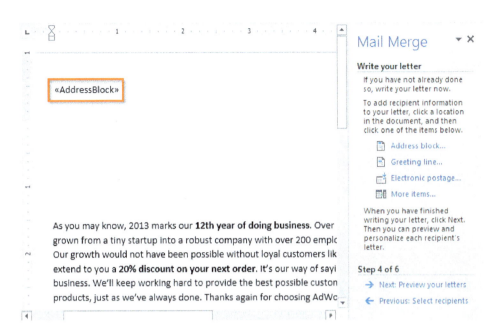

5. Repeat these steps each time you need to enter information from your data record. In our example, there is a Greeting line.

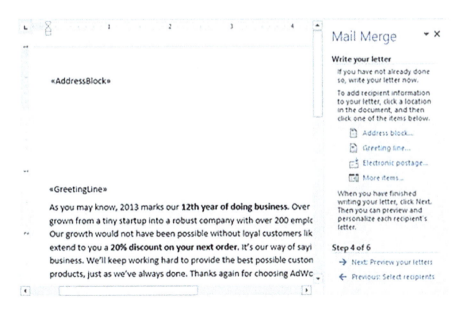

6. When you're done, click Next: Preview your letters o move to Step 5.

For some letters, you'll only need to add an **Address block** and **Greeting line**.

Sometimes, however, you may want to place **recipient data** within the body of the letter to **personalize it** even further.

Step 5:

1. Preview the letters to make sure the information from the recipient list appears correctly in the letter. You can use the left and right scroll arrows to view each document.

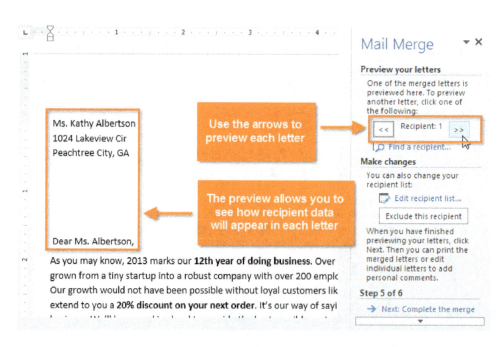

124

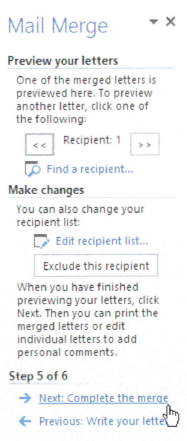

Preview your letters

One of the merged letters is previewed here. To preview another letter, click one of the following:

`<<` Recipient: 1 `>>`

🔍 Find a recipient...

Make changes

You can also change your recipient list:

📝 Edit recipient list...

Exclude this recipient

When you have finished previewing your letters, click Next. Then you can print the merged letters or edit individual letters to add personal comments.

Step 5 of 6

→ Next: Complete the merge

← Previous: Write your lette

2. Click Next: Complete the merge to move to Step 6.

Step 6:

1. Click Print... to print the letters.   2. A dialog box will appear. Click All, then click OK.

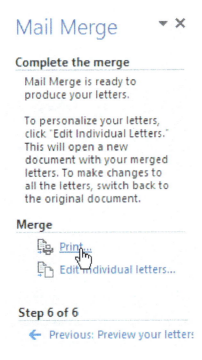

Mail Merge

Complete the merge

Mail Merge is ready to produce your letters.

To personalize your letters, click "Edit Individual Letters." This will open a new document with your merged letters. To make changes to all the letters, switch back to the original document.

Merge

🖨 Print...

📄 Edit individual letters...

Step 6 of 6

← Previous: Preview your letter:

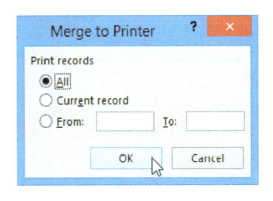

Merge to Printer ? ✕

Print records

⦿ All

○ Current record

○ From: [   ]   To: [   ]

OK   Cancel

2. The Print dialog box will appear. Adjust the print settings if needed, then click OK. The letters will be printed.

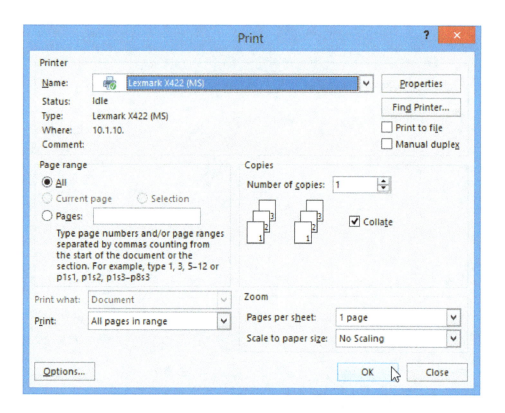

Task 3

1. View the document you have just created in: a) Web Layout
   b) Draft

2. Make a word change and then add a new comment indicating the change.

3. Change the margins of the document to:
   Top: 2" Bottom: 2" Left: 1.5" Right 1"

WORD CONTROLS

Useful keyboard shortcuts

SHORTCUT KEY	FUNCTION
CTRL + N	Opens a new document
CTRL + O	Opens existing documents
CTRL + S	Saves documents
CTRL + A	Saves documents As
CTRL + P	Prints documents
CTRL + V	Pastes previously copied text.
CTRL + X	Moves selected text
CTRL + C	Copies selected text
CTRL + SHIFT + C	Formats painter
CTRL + B	Converts text to bold
CTRL + I	Converts text to italics
CTRL + U	Underlines text
CTRL + >	Grow Font
CTRL + <	Shrink Font
CTRL + L	Left align
CTRL + E	Center align
CTRL + R	Right align
CTRL + J	Justifies text
CTRL + *	Shows/Hides paragraph marks
CTRL + F	Finds text in document
CTRL + H	Finds and replaces text in document
CTRL + Return	Inserts break
CTRL + K	Inserts hyperlink
ALT + =	Inserts equations
ALT + CTRL + F	Inserts Footnotes
ALT + CTRL + D	Inserts Endnotes
ALT + SHIFT + X	Includes selected text in the document index
F7	Checks spelling and grammar
ALT + CLICK	Opens the research task pane
SHIFT + F7	Opens the thesaurus
CTRL + SHIFT + E	Track Changes
ALT + F11	Opens the Visual Basic Editor
ALT + F8	Opens up a list of macros

Task: Masquerades

1. Create a full an advertisement for a local newspaper that informs the public about your carnival band. This must be designed on letter size paper.

2. Using a suitable feature of your word processing application, create a document which should be mailed to persons who have paid in full for their costumes. The document should inform masqueraders of the parade route, the time of assembly and departure of the band onto the parade.

    The report from the database section should be inserted into your document.
    The final paragraph should express the band leaders gratitude to masquerades for choosing to join his band for the carnival celebrations.

3. Design a suitable letterhead for your document which should be placed in a header. A suitable footer must be inserted, with the words center aligned.

4. The document should be justified. The left margin must be 1.5".

Solution:

1. Create a new document. If you have Word already opened, press CTRL + N simultaneously. If not, Word will automatically open up a new document as and when the application is opened. You are required to create a full advertisement. The design must be on letter size paper.

2. Click on Layout tab. Then click on Size. A drop down menu will open up. See whether the letter option has been selected. In most cases, it is the default one. If it is not already selected, select it.

3. Now you will see that your document size is 8.5" X 11".

Now, design the advertisement. This screenshot tells that we used Calibri Font and 11 as font size.

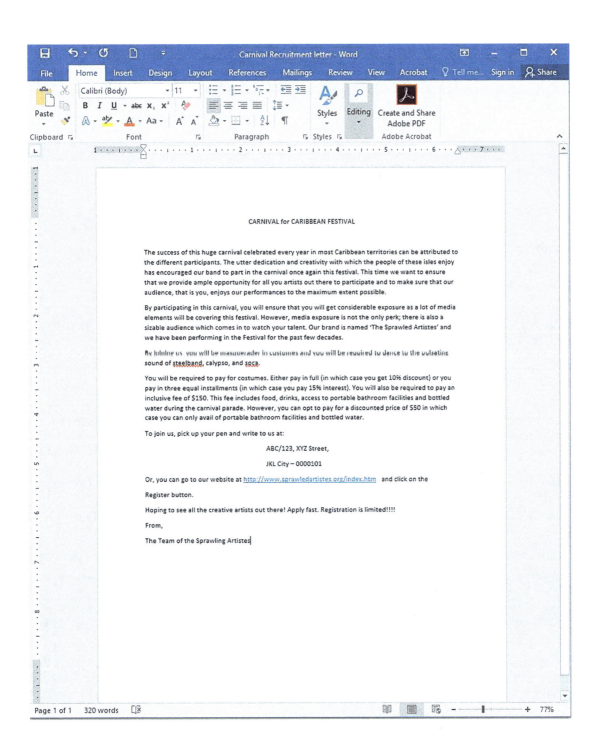

2. Using a suitable feature of your wordprocessing application, create a document which should be mailed to persons who have paid on full for their costumes. The document should inform masqueraders of the parade route, the time of assembly and departure of the band onto the parade. The report from the database section should be inserted into your document.

The final paragraph should express the band leaders' gratitude to masquerades for choosing to join his band for the carnival celebrations.

3. Design a suitable letterhead for your document which should be placed in a header. A suitable footer must be inserted, with the words center aligned.

4. The document should be justified. The left margin must be 1.5"   .

Solution:

1. Open a new document in MS Word.

2. To do the required, we would have to use the mail merge facility.

3. Go to the Mailings Tab.

4. Click on Mail Merge. Start Mail Merge. Click Letters.

5. Edit the main document with the intended letter. Mention the sender's name, company and address (right aligned).

6. Press enter three times and left align.

7. Write your whole document. Include the report generated by your **Access** database by copying from the RTF file generated.

8. Right align your salutation and below write the sender's name and company name.

9. Now the first step is to create a label main document. Start Word or press CTRL + N.

10. Click Labels after starting mail merge. In the window that emerges, click on Label options.

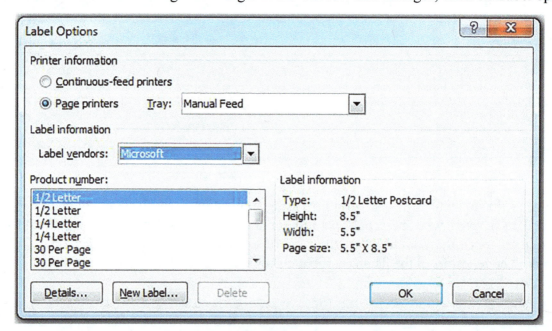

11. Click on OK.

12. Now, create Word documents for each field. You want firstname, lastname and address.

13. Create a table with the required contents (take from Access Database). Save file.

14. In the labels document, you will see labels. You will view it as a table.

15. Go to your main document. On Mailings tab, in the Start Mail Merge group, click

16. Select Recipients.

17. Click Use Existing List.

18. Find the labels document and click Open.
    To add recipients:
    1. Under Data Source, click name of your label file or data file.
    2. Click on Edit.
    3. Click New Entry and type information for that recipient. Carry on for further recipients.

19. Go to your main document. Add placeholders. After you have added the company address, press enter and left align. Click Insert Merge Fields and click Auto merge field. Repeat one more time. Here firstname and the lastname will be displayed. Next line, insert another placeholder.

20. On the next line, insert Greeting by clicking on greeting line under the Mailings tab.

21. Click Finish and Merge.

	O Duncan
	The Sprawling Artistes
	ABDCD

Elena Gilbert

MFDM

Dear Sir or Madam,

This is to notify all those masquerades who have joined and paid in full that our band will depart from ABDSEF AT 9:00 AM Sharp on 2/17/2014. You are all required to be there by 08:30 AM. The parade will take the route of ADSDSEYU through ADFGERER and stop at GDFDFDFGH at 17:00 PM sharp. The same timings are followed every other day for three months since the start date. The member details, the section and the payments details are shown below.

Report of Full Paid Masqueraders

Section_id	Member_id	Member_Gender	Bill_Amt

Now we put a suitable header to the document. Go to Insert tab and then press Header. Select appropriate format and type the title.

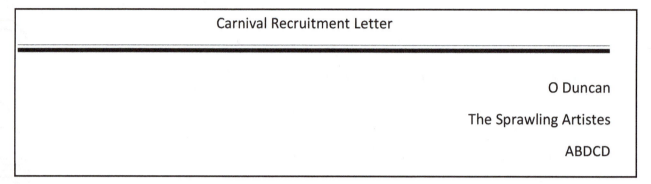

The letter head should look like the screen shown. Headers will be visible on every page.

- Now add Footer.

- Go to insert and press on Footer.

- Center align the words in the footer.

- Justify the entire document by pressing CTRL + A (selects all text) and CTRL + J (Justifies text).

- Now, change the left margin to 1.5".

- Go to layout and click on margins.

- Click on Custom margins.

- Type in 1.5 in the Left box as follows

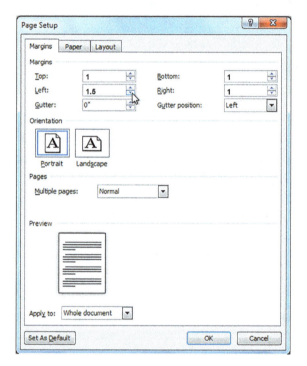

Click OK.

Your screen should look like this:

Carnival Recruitment Letter

O Duncan

The Sprawling Artistes

ABDCD

To,

Elena Gilbert

MFDM

Dear Sir or Madam,

This is to notify all those masquerades who have joined and paid in full that our band will depart from ABDSEF AT 9:00 AM Sharp on 2/17/2014. You are all required to be there by 08:30 AM. The parade will take the route of ADSDSEYU through ADFGERER and stop at GDFDFDFGH at 17:00 PM sharp. The same timings are followed every other day for three months since the start date. The member details, the section and the payment details are shown below.

Report of Full Paid Masqueraders

Section_id	Member_id	Member_Gender	Bill_Amt

WEB PAGE DESIGN

Please Learn Things to consider When Planning a Website:

1. Why do i want a web site for my business, self or organization?
   - How do i expect the web to enhance my business?
   - How would the web fit into my overall goals? An d what do I want it to do in th future?

2. Who do I want to communicate with through the website?
   - Who is my clients/audience?
   - What do I want to become to my clients/audience?
   - What does my audience need from the website? This will ultimately determine the number of webpages, content and layout of your website.

You are going to create your own web site about Sharks using Front 2003.

Please Learn Web site (or website):

A collection of interlinked underlined webpages with a related topic, usually under a single domain name, which includes an intended starting file called a "homepage". From the homepage, you can get to all the other pages on the website. Also called a "web presence".

Help

Before you ask your teacher for help click on:

Help - Microsoft Front Help? - Answer Wizard (or simply press the **F1** function key) Type your question in the Search window.

Microsoft Frontpage

Microsoft Frontpage is a HTML editor and web administration tool from Microsoft. However, it has now been discontinued and replaced by Microsoft Expression Web and Sharepoint Designer. Some of the features of Frontpage include:

1. A Split View option to allow the user to code in Code view and preview in Design View without the hassle of switching tabs.

2. Presence of interactive buttons to create web graphics.

3. Auto completion features.

4. Code snippets of commonly used code available.

5. Support for Macros.

6. Support for ASP.NET.

Creating Websites using Frontpage 2003

A new site can be created using the New button in the File menu or by clicking an empty like button on the toolbar. A new web can also be created in a similar way.

1. Creating a new web:
- Open the program Microsoft Frontpage

- Click File - New - Web

- Choose One Page Web

- Type: G:\Sharks web in the Specify location of the new web window to save it in your folder.

- Click OK

The main page (**Home page**) on a web is usually called index.htm - The main page of a <u>Website</u>. Typically, the homepage (**Index.htm**) serves as an index or table of contents to other <u>documents stored</u> at the site.

Please Learn

A **Webpage** is an individual **HTML** document. These documents are written in **HTML** (hypertext markup langauge) and are translated by your Web browser Web pages can eother be static or dynamic. Static pages show the same content each time they are viewed. Dynamic pages have content that can change each times they are accessed.

Add new blank pages to the site:
- Click File - New - Page
- Press Enter

Every time you do this, a new page will be created called "New_Page_1"etc.

Create 5 new blank pages in addition to the index.html page.

Change the colour of the pages:
- **Double** click on the **INDEX** page.
- **Right click** anywhere on the page.
- Choose **Page Properties**.
- Click the **BACKGROUND** tab.
- Change the **background colour** to **yellow**.
- Click **OK**

Now you are going to copy this background to all pages.
- Click on the folders tab to see all your pages.
- Double click on new_page_1.html to open it up.
- Right click on the page.
- Choose **Page Properties**.
- Click the **BACKGROUND** tab.
- Click on the checkbox *"Get background Information from another Page"*
- Click Browse, then double click on **Index.html**
- Click **OK**

The background colour doesn't change until you close the (click the X at the top right of the window), then re-open the by double clicking on it in the Folders list.

(Repeat the steps so that all of your pages have a yellow background).

Now let's work on your home page

- Double-click on INDEX.HTML in the folders list.

Set a Heading Style

At the top left of the screen there is a drop down menu with the text (None) in it. This is the STYLES menu.

- Click the Styles menu and choose Heading 1.
- Type in the text SHARKS
- Change the font colour of SHARKS to be red (click the A on the menu at the top of the page)
- Centre the heading by clicking the Centre icon at the top of the page.
- Press Enter to move to the next line.

Set a new heading Style

- Click the Styles menu and choose Heading 2.
- Type in the paragraph heading: Introduction
- Make the paragraph heading blue, font size 14

Type in text in normal Style

- Click the Styles menu and choose Normal
- Type in the following text:

Sharks are versatile and keen-sensed fishes, many species of which are able to hunt and eat nearly all the larger marine animals in both shallow and deep seas. The whale shark is the largest shark and also the largest fish in the sea, measuring up to 15 m (49 ft) in length; the cookie-cutter shark measures less than 50 cm (19 in) in length. Sharks are chiefly marine fishes found in all seas and are especially abundant in tropical and subtropical waters. Many species migrate up rivers, however, and one, the bull shark, reaches Lake Nicaragua in Central America. Sharks are best known as aggressive carnivores that even attack members of their own species, but two of the largest sharks - the basking shark and the whale shark, are docile feeders on plankton.

Before you move on, look at the tabs at the bottom of the page.
- All your adjustments to your web have to be carried out in the Design view.
- Preview is used to see what the site will look like in a browser.
- Look at the CODE view to see how Frontpage converts your into HTML code before it can be viewed on the web.

Saving Pages

While working in Frontpage, it is advisable to click on the save button at regular intervals. When you close down using the X button Frontpage will prompt you if saving is required.

Insert a picture from a file
- Find a picture of a hammerhead shark online

- **Right click** the picture and click **copy** twice
- Go back to your **Frontpage** document
- Paste the picture underneath the **TITLE**, but before the paragraph heading.

Saving Pages with pictures

Each time you add a new image to your Web it is sensible to save to keep all your files organised and stored in the correct location.

When you created your Web, Frontpage automatically created a folder called **images**, which is where you should store your picture files.

As you have just created a new picture file it is advisable to click the Save icon and
- In the Save Embedded Files window Click -Change Folder
- Select C:\sharks web\images
- Click OK Twice

Once you have selected this folder to save your picture files it becomes the default folder and you may not need to click on the Change folder button again in this session.

Adding Hyperlinks

A hyperlink allows you to click on a word or picture and go straight to the page or area of your web that you choose.

At the bottom of your page, type in the following text in normal paragraph style. Make the text red and centre it.

> SENSES AND FEEDING
> REPRODUCTION
> ECOLOGY
> PHYSICAL CHARACTERISTICS
> SHARK PICTURES

Now you are going to make each one of these link to a different in the web:
- Highlight SENSES AND FEEDING using the mouse
- At the top of the page, click the hyperlink icon:
- In the window which opens, double click new_page_1.html.
- Make REPRODUCTION link to new_page_2.html
- Make ECOLOGY link to new_page_3.html
- Make PHYSICAL CHARACTERISTICS link to new_page_4.html
- Make SHARK PICTURES link to new_page_5.html

SAVE YOUR PAGE AGAIN

Testing Hyperlinks

In **Preview** check your site for any errors or broken links.

NOW WE WILL WORK ON PAGE 2

In the folders list, double click on *new_page_1.html*
- Click the Styles menu and choose Heading 1.
- Type in the text SHARKS
- Change the font colour of SHARKS to be red
- Centre the heading by clicking the Centre icon at the top of the page. Press Enter to move to the next line.
- Click the Styles menu and choose Heading 2.
- Type in the paragraph heading: Senses and feeding
- Make the paragraph heading blue, font size 14
- Click the Styles menu and choose Normal
- Type in the following text:

Sharks have an acute sense of smell; they are able to detect minute substances, such as blood in water, and trace them to their source. The shark's poor eyesight only allows it to catch dim movements of shadow and light in dark waters as it approaches its prey.
Sharks are particularly sensitive to sounds of low frequency and have fine directional hearing.

Organs along their lateral lines and on the snout enable sharks to pick up weak electrical stimuli from the muscle contractions of bony fish. This combination of keen senses accounts for the evolutionary success of sharks.

When hunting in schools, sharks can incite one another into a feeding frenzy. They circle their prey and make sudden crisscrosses, frequently striking victims from below (but not turning on their backs, as is popularly believed). Considering the number of scuba divers, swimmers, and water-skiers who now venture into shark-infested waters, however, relatively few shark attacks on humans occur; of those that do, about one - third result in fatalities. Among the sharks most dangerous to humans are the great white shark, the hammerhead shark, the tiger shark, and the blue shark.

- Go back online and copy and paste any shark picture ABOVE the text you have just typed. (Remember to indicate where you got the picture).
- Reduce the size of the picture to about half its original size. Click on the corner "handle" and drag the mouse until the picture gets smaller.

Adding Bookmarks:

A bookmark is a hyperlink to an "*ANCHOR*" or placeholder on the page. To create a link to the top of the page:

- Highlight the TITLE (SHARKS) using the mouse.
- Click **INSERT** on the menu bar at the top of the page
- Click **BOOKMARK**
- Type in *TOP* and click **OK**
- Now move to the bottom of the page.
- Type in the text "Top of Page"
- Highlight the text using the mouse
- Click the hyperlink icon
- At the bottom of the pane, next to **Bookmark**: click the arrow and choose **TOP**
- Click **OK**
- Check the Hyperlink works by viewing the in *PREVIEW* mode, and clicking on it.

NOW WORK ON PAGE 3

In the folders list, double click on *new_page_2.html*

- Click the Styles menu and choose Heading 1.
- Type in the text **SHARKS**
- Change the font colour of SHARKS to be red
- Centre the heading by clicking the Centre icon at the top of the page.
- Press Enter to move to the next line.
- Click the Styles menu and choose *Heading 2*.
- Type in the paragraph heading: Reproduction
- Make the paragraph heading blue, font size 14
- Click the Styles menu and choose *Normal*
- Copy and paste some text from Encarta about shark reproduction.
- Add any picture of a shark on your page, and a bookmark to the top of your page.

In the folders list, double click on *new_page_3.html*

- Click the Styles menu and choose ***Heading 1.***
- Type in the text **SHARKS**
- Change the font colour of SHARKS to be red
- Centre the heading by clicking the Centre icon at the top of the page.
- Press Enter to move to the next line.
- Click the Styles menu and choose ***Heading 2.***
- Type in the paragraph heading: ECOLOGY
- Make the paragraph heading blue, font size 14
- Click the Styles menu and choose ***Normal***
- Copy and paste some text from Encarta about shark ecology.

Adding Hyperlinks to external sites:

You can create a link to any WWW site in the same way as you link to other pages in your site.

- Underneath your text, leave a blank line and type in normal style SHARK RESEARCH

- Highlight SHARK RESEARCH using the mouse

- Click the hyperlink icon

- On the line which starts URL (Uniform Resource Locator) type WWW.SHARK.ORG

The line should now look like this: *http://www.shark.org*

- Save the and check to see if the link works!

Please Learn Uniform Resource Locator (URL):

Abbreviation of *Uniform **R**esource Locator*, the global address of documents and other resources on the World Wide Web The first part fo the address is called *protocol identifier* and it indicated what protocl to use, and the second part is calleda resource name and it specifies the IP address or the domain name where the resource is located. The protocol identifier and the resource name are separated by a colon and two forward slashes. For example, the two URLs below point to two different files at the domain pcwebopedia.com. The first specifies and executable file that should be fetch using the FTP protocol; the second specifies a Web page that should be fetched using the HTTP protocol:

- **ftp://www.pcwebopedia.com/stuff.exe**
- **http://www.pcwebopedia.com/index.html**

COMPLETE YOUR WEBSITE

On page 5:

In the folders list, double click on *new_page_4.html*

- Click the Styles menu and choose *Heading 1*.
- Type in the text **SHARKS**
- Change the font colour of SHARKS to be red
- Centre the heading by clicking the Centre icon at the top of the page.
- Press Enter to move to the next line.
- Click the Styles menu and choose *Heading 2*.
- Type in the paragraph heading: Physical Characteristics
- Make the paragraph heading blue, font size 14
- Click the Styles menu and choose Normal
- Copy and paste some text from Encarta about the physical characteristics of sharks.

On page 6:

In the folders list, double click on *new_page_5.html*

- Click the Styles menu and choose *Heading 1*.
- Type in the text **SHARKS**
- Change the font colour of SHARKS to be red
- Centre the heading by clicking the Centre icon at the top of the page.
- Press Enter to move to the next line.
- Click the Styles menu and choose *Heading 2*.
- Type in the paragraph heading: Shark pictures
- Insert as many shark pictures as you like on this page.

Hint: You may like to place the pictures into a TABLE to position them more easily. Click TABLE...INSERT at the top of the to use this feature.

Printing your work in the browser:

To print your pages in the Browser (*Microsoft Explorer*):

- Click the PREVIEW button at the top of the page.
- Click FILE... SETUP
- Type your name in the footer
- Click OK
- Click FILE..PRINT
- Choose CURRENT PAGE
- Click PRINT
- Repeat this until all 6 of your pages are printed.

Printing your work in HTML format:

HTML (Hypertext Markup Language) is the code which produces the screen you see on a web page. When you take the examinations, you are required to print this code.

- Go back to Frontpage
- Double click the Index in Folders List.
- Click the HTML tab at the bottom of the page.
- Click FILE..SETUP
- Type HOME as the header, and your name as the footer
- Click OK
- Click FILE...PRINT
- Choose PAGES 1 to 1
- Click OK
- Repeat this for all 6 of your pages. Use a suitable header on each (e.g. REPRODUCTION, ECOLOGY etc.)

Section 5
SPREADSHEETS

A spreadsheet consists of **cells** organised in **rows** and **columns** which can contain data items such as **numbers, text** or **formula**. The spreadsheet is set out in rows and columns, similar to the format used to produce your timetable. Each data item occupies a **cell** in the table.

A **row** runs horizontally and is numbered – 1, 2, 3 4, ...104876

A **Column** runs vertically and uses letters for its name – A, B, C, AA, XFD

A **cell** is the box formed where a row and column intersect or meet.

A cell has a **cell name or cell address** formed from the name of the column and the row for example B5, M20, AA13. The column name is written before the row name as in C4 in the example below. The cell address is the location of the cell and is very useful for calculations and for making references.

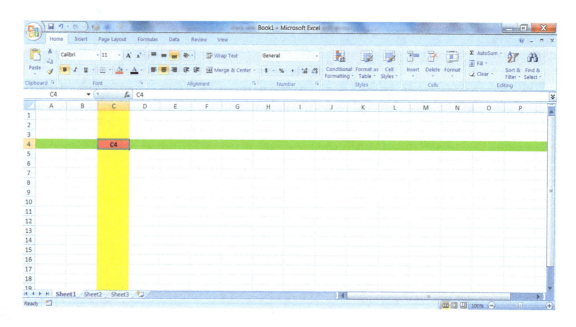

Uses of Spreadsheets

Spreadsheets are now widely used both for business and personal use. They might be used at home for family budgets, in schools and college for calculations, and in research for mathematical modeling, but their main area of use is in industry. Where they are used for accounts, stock control, sales forecasts, and planning. Their strength is that alternative plans, or costings can be tried out easily, and their consequences calculated immediately.

Spreadsheets are also useful in producing graphs, pie charts, and other statistical diagrams. Spreadsheets will be essential for some jobs and hence important to be learnt in schools.

Names of Spreadsheet software

There are several spreadsheet packages on the market including Lotus 123, OpenOffice and Microsoft Excel. We will use **Microsoft Excel** for learning about spreadsheets. The version will be **2007**.

Microsoft Excel

This is a spreadsheet application created by Microsoft. This is also one of those applications which form a part of the Office suit. It features calculations, graph tools, tables and charts, and a macro programming application.

Microsoft Excel has all the features of a spreadsheet. It uses a grid of cells divided in rows and columns to organize data. It finds great use in data manipulation by performing arithmetic functions. In addition, it can display data in graphic forms easily in the form of charts and graphs.

About Workbooks, Worksheets and Chart sheets

In Microsoft Excel, a **Workbook** is the file that stores your data. Each workbook can contain many worksheets. Hence, various kinds of related information can be organised into a single **file**.

Worksheet (also called a spreadsheet) is the primary document used in Microsoft Excel to work with data. Typically, a worksheet consists of **cells** organised into **columns** and **rows**. It forms the basic component and is always part of a workbook.

Chart sheet is a separate sheet in a workbook that consists only of a chart. Chart sheets are linked to data in the worksheet and are automatically updated when the worksheet data changes. Note also that when you create a chart, you may choose to place the chart on the worksheet with its related data.

The names of the sheets appear on tabs at the bottom of the workbook window. To move from sheet to sheet, click the sheet tabs. You may rename a sheet if you wish or if asked to do so. **When naming sheets you should use a name that indicates the kind of information contained on the sheet e.g. Budget, or use the task number e.g. Task 1**, unless you are told otherwise.

When entering

a) text data , pay attention to the case and the alignment of the text.

b) numeric data containing $, % or commas, DO NOT TYPE THESE SYMBOLS. Simply type the numbers and then use the formatting functions of the software to obtain $, % and commas.

When Printing Always

a) Check your work using the print preview option to ensure that it fits properly on one and that all data is visible. Make any adjustments in the Margins,

Orientation or Scaling Necessary, before Printing

a) Put your name, class group and the task number in the header or footer.

b) Use the spell checker to ensure accuracy.

c) Unless otherwise stated, use font size 11pts, Times New Roman for all data entry in the worksheets.

d) Save the workbook.

e) Show row and column heading when printing formulas.

f) Use appropriate buttons to place the date in the right footer and if applicable, the sheet name in the center footer.

Saving Your Worksheets

a) All work in MS Excel is done in a Workbook. When you save the workbook, ALL worksheets contained in this workbook are automatically saved.

Payroll System

Your employer requires you to create a payroll data sheet having the following columns:

1.   Employee Name
2.   Employee Salary
3.   Employee Position
4.   Employee Tenure

Your employer then requires you to enter the details of ten employees as per a list he has given to you.

Creating a new Excel Worksheet and Workbook

Opening Microsoft Excel will result in the creation of a **new Excel** sheet. However once you open the application, you will see three sheets already created for you. They are visible as tabs in the bottom.

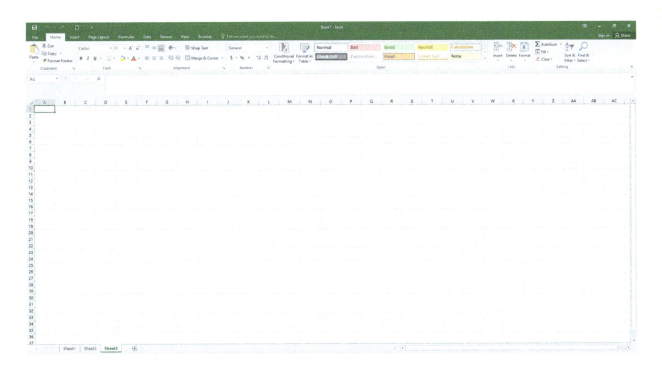

The sheets are named Sheet1, Sheet2 and Sheet3. It is good to have different sheets to capture different data within the worksheet as each sheet may be needed by different departments in an organization to carry out their processes. Separating the data into different sheet makes it easier to use and to share.

More sheets may be added by clicking the Insert Worksheet icon located next to Sheet3.

To create a new Workbook

1. Click on the Office Button

2. Select New
   Choose the type of workbook from the Templates available or choose a Blank workbook

3. Click Create

Entering Data

Enter the required data in the **cells or boxes**. You may use your cursor keys or the mouse pointer to access the cells or you may **type the cell address you wish to locate** in the **name box** at the top which displays the cell being focused on at the moment.

Enter the data for the task you have been given. Remember you may begin entering anywhere. An example is done for you as shown below.

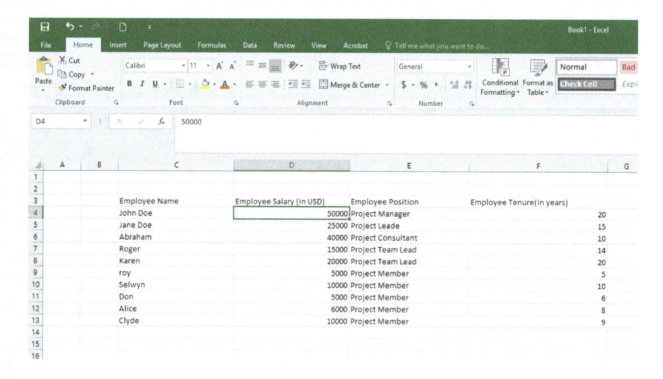

The Number Menu

This menu can be found under the Home tab. First, notice the drop down box at the top. The default selected item is General. Clicking on the down arrow you will notice a variety of options. 'General' means no specific format. However, you can apply any one of the formats to your spreadsheet.

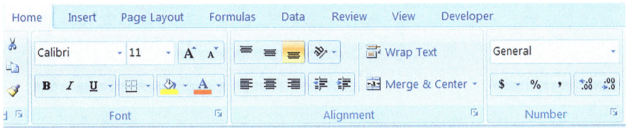

To the bottom of this drop down box, you can five buttons aligned next to each other. The first button comes handy in financial and accounting representations. By default the $ is selected. However, you can choose either of the currencies which drop down once you click on the corresponding down arrow button.

For example, clicking the $ sign will result in the following screen.

Employee Name	Employee Salary (in USD)	Employee Position	Employee Tenure(in years)
John Doe	$ 50,000.00	Project Manager	20
Jane Doe	$ 25,000.00	Project Leade	15
Abraham	$ 40,000.00	Project Consultant	10
Roger	$ 15,000.00	Project Team Lead	14
Karen	$ 20,000.00	Project Team Lead	20
roy	$ 5,000.00	Project Member	5
Selwyn	$ 10,000.00	Project Member	10
Don	$ 5,000.00	Project Member	6
Alice	$ 6,000.00	Project Member	8
Clyde	$ 10,000.00	Project Member	9

The next button has a label of '%'. The short key for this button is CTRL + SHIFT + %. Select the cell and then click on this button. It will display the cell value as a percentage. You will now select the entire tenure column by dragging the mouse upward from the last row. Remember to highlight only the last column. Also, neglect the header row.

Employee Name	Employee Salary (in USD)	Employee Position	Employee Tenure(in years)
John Doe	$ 50,000.00	Project Manager	2000%
Jane Doe	$ 25,000.00	Project Leade	1500%
Abraham	$ 40,000.00	Project Consultant	1000%
Roger	$ 15,000.00	Project Team Lead	1400%
Karen	$ 20,000.00	Project Team Lead	2000%
roy	$ 5,000.00	Project Member	500%
Selwyn	$ 10,000.00	Project Member	1000%
Don	$ 5,000.00	Project Member	600%
Alice	$ 6,000.00	Project Member	800%
Clyde	$ 10,000.00	Project Member	900%

Now undo the changes you have made so far. Pressing CTRL + Z two times should do it. The next button shows the comma button. This includes the comma after every thousandth part. Notice that in an earlier figure, the salaries had no comma in them. Now you will select the entire salary column except the column header and click on the comma button.

Employee Name	Employee Salary (in USD)	Employee Position	Employee Tenure(in years)
John Doe	50000	Project Manager	20
Jane Doe	25000	Project Leade	15
Abraham	40000	Project Consultant	10
Roger	15000	Project Team Lead	14
Karen	20000	Project Team Lead	20
roy	5000	Project Member	5
Selwyn	10000	Project Member	10
Don	5000	Project Member	6
Alice	6000	Project Member	8
Clyde	10000	Project Member	9

Conditional Formatting

In a spreadsheet you may use **Conditional Formatting** to **Format** or "fix-up" columns of data so that they standout and effectively communicate the message that is being displayed.

This feature in Microsoft Excel is located under the Home tab. See the figures below for the options that are available.

Working with Charts

A spreadsheet is popular for its use of analyzing data and creating charts. There are many types of charts found under the Insert Tab. Each type lends itself to different types of data.

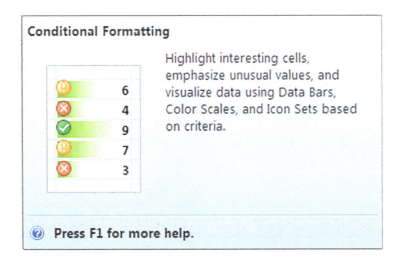

You can also format a spreadsheet as a table. Also, you can change the cell styles.

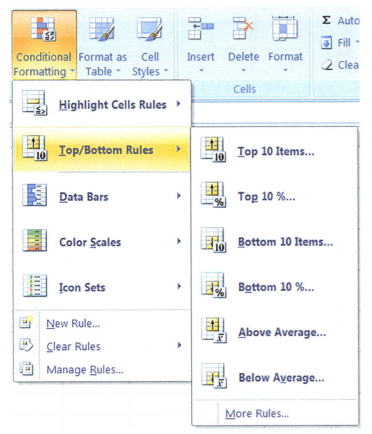

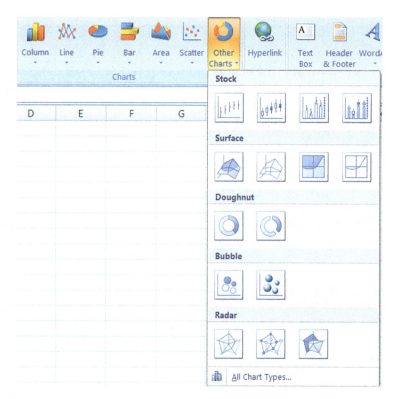

In general a chart:

- Enhances the visual impact of a presentation

- Effectively communicates comparisons and analysis of numeric data

- Provides an alternative to tables and the narration/explanation that go along with them

- Is very useful for managers in decision making as important information is easily presented in a concise manner

PIE CHARTS

A pie chart is so named because it is round like a pie and appears to have slices like a pie. Data that is arranged in one column or row in a worksheet can be represented in a pie chart. Pie charts display the size of one item proportional to the sum or whole of all of the items.

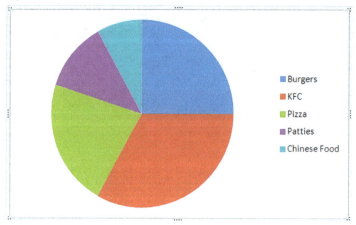

Use a pie chart if:

- All Values in the data range total 100%
- You have only one data series
- None of the values in your data are negative
- You have no more than seven data categories, all of which represent parts of the whole pie.

To create a pie chart:

- In the spreadsheet, select the **range** of data for the chart.

- On the **Insert** tab, click the **Pie Chart** icon in the **Charts** group.

- Click an option such as **2-D** or **3-D** Pie.

- **Excel** plots your selected data to produce the pie chart and applies a title which may be changed by you.

- You may change the Chart Styles, Colors of the slices or sectors and Format the Legend or key by clicking in the relevant sections and follow the menus provided.

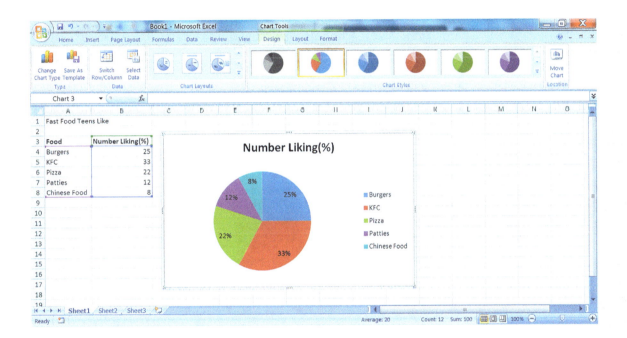

Column charts and the other charts may be created and formatted in a similar manner. You must remember to provide the data for the chart by selecting it from the spreadsheet – select first or during when you will be prompted to enter the data range.

Task 1

Your employer requires you to build a column graph using the name and salary columns.

Solution:

Select the two columns and click 2-D column from the column menu options.

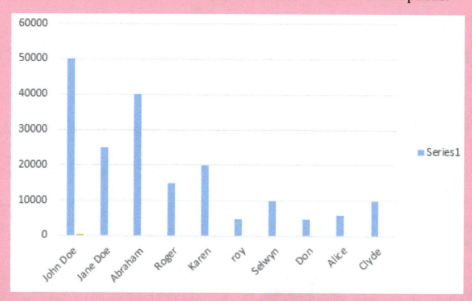

Question:

Your employer requires you to build a line graph using name and tenture columns.

Solution:

Select the two columns and click on line button.

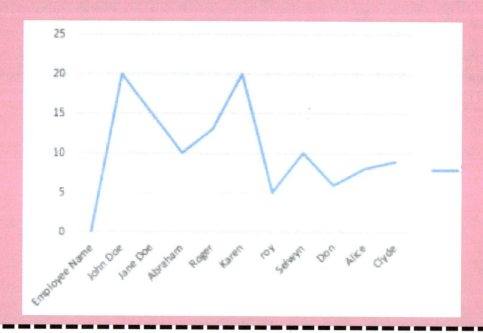

Functions and Formulae

The Insert Function button under the Formulas tab allows you to search for a specific function and use it. However, every other function can be used by selecting from the appropriate categories in the function library.

Under the Autosum menu, you can calculate the cumulative sum of the items, average, max and min of the entire column.

Task 2

Your employer requires you to calculate the summation, average of the salary column, average of the tenure column, max and min of the salary column.

Solution:

You would have added data in the worksheet from rows 5 to 14.

- Consider the salary column which is D.
- So find sum by selecting an empty cell and use function =sum (D5:D14).
- To find average, use function =average (D5:D14)
- To find max salary, use =max(D5:D14)
- To find min salary, use =min(D5:D14)
- Consider the tenure column which is F.
- Average tenure =Average(F5:F14).
- Of course, you can also click from the menu items.

Likewise, there are many functions: logical, date/time, text, etc which you can use to manipulate data. One can also import data from other sources whether it is from a database or from websites. All these are available to you in the Data tab.

Another important feature of Microsoft Excel is the ability to group and ungroup data and calculates subtotals.

EXCEL CONTROLS

SHORTCUT KEY	FUNCTION
CTRL + N	Opens a new document
CTRL + O	Opens existing documents
CTRL + S	Saves documents
CTRL + A	Saves documents As
CTRL + P	Prints documents
CTRL + V	Pastes previously copied text.
CTRL + X	Moves selected text
CTRL + C	Copies selected text
CTRL + B	Converts text to bold
CTRL + I	Converts text to italics
CTRL + U	Underlines text
CTRL + >	Grow Font
CTRL + <	Shrink Font
CTRL + L	Left align
CTRL + E	Center align
CTRL + R	Right align
CTRL + SHIFT + %	Displays cell value as percentage
CTRL + F	Finds text in document
CTRL + H	Finds and replaces text in document
CTRL + G	Go to page
CTRL + T	Insert Table
CTRL + K	Inserts hyperlink
SHIFT + F3	Inserts Function
ALT + =	Calculates sum
CTRL + F3	Opens up the name manager
CTRL + SHIFT + F3	Automatically generate names from selection
CTRL + `	Show formulas
F9	Calculate workbook now
SHIFT + F9	Calculate worksheet now
CTRL + ALT + F5	Refresh all data coming from external sources
CTRL + SHIFT + L	Filters selected cells
SHIFT + ALT + Right	Groups selected cells
SHIFT + ALT + LEFT	Ungroups selected cells
F7	Checks spelling and grammar
ALT + CLICK	Opens the research task pane
SHIFT + F7	Opens the thesaurus
SHIFT + F2	Inserts new comment
ALT + F11	Opens the Visual Basic Editor
ALT + F8	Opens up a list of macros

Masquerades

The financial records of the band are maintained using a spreadsheet application. The names of masqueraders are listed by section. Both men as well as women may register to play in each section.

There are five sections in the band. The cost of costumes is quoted in US dollars. The cost by section is $160, $220, $280, $350 and $425 respectively. Masqueraders are given the option of paying for the costume in three installments, or paying the full cost in one payment. Many people utilize the installment option. Single full payment attracts a discount of 10%, while payment by installments attracts an interest of 15%. Installments should be spread over three equal payments.

Each masquerader pays an 'Inclusive' fee. A $150 Inclusive fee entitles the masquerader to food, drinks, access to portable bathroom facilities and bottled water during the carnival parade through the streets. However, a payment of $50.00 entitles the masquerader to portable bathroom facilities and bottled water only.

Expenditure is incurred in the provision of several amenities for masqueraders during the carnival. The band leader must supply food, drinks, portable bathroom facilities, transportation, music, personnel, and artiste fees. In addition, the costs of material for the manufacture of costumes as well as labour costs are incurred. Because of the anticipated large number of masqueraders, the bandleader has decided to manage the income and expenditure of each section separately.

You are required to:
1. Design a worksheet(s) which accepts income and expenditure costs for each section.

Your worksheet must record all payments made by masqueraders, (a few persons have only made one or two of the required three installment payments on costumes), the total amount paid by each person as well as the grand total collected must be calculated. Costume payments must be made in US dollars. The total payments made by each person however, must be converted to the equivalent amount in local currency.

In an appropriate row, count the number of masqueraders in the section; calculate the total payment on costume, Inclusive fees and the total overall payment.

The expenditure incurred for each section must also be calculated. Food is $60.00 per person; drink is $40.00 per person; material is $150.00 and labour is $75.00. Other services are provided at a flat rate for the entire band. These are as follows: bathroom- $3000.00; transport $2500.00; music - $4000.00; security - $1800.00; artiste - $5000.00. The cost of each flat rate services for each section = Rate /No. of Sections.

Food and drinks are increased by 15% of the starting per person cost for each successive section, material is increased by 12% of the starting cost for each successive section, while labour is increased by 8% of the starting cost for each successive section.

The total cost of each service for each section = Cost of service X the number of masqueraders in the section.
Save your spreadsheet as **Masqueraders1**.

Solution:

Open Microsoft Excel application. We will see a new sheet opening up.
In G6, write Income Sheet in Bold.

Put down the headers as Section Name, Costume Cost Pricing, Single Payment, First, Second, third installments, inclusive costs and total price. Put these in the 10th row starting from column F to column M.

Use the arithmetic functions like Sum and Product while calculating the Total Price which is shown in column M. Calculations are done by above rules.

Calculations for single payment:
Total Price = sum (cell address of single payment-Product(0.10,cell address),cell address of inclusive payment)

Calculations for instalments:
Total Price = sum(cell range from first installment to inclusive payment columns) + Product (0.15, cell address of Costume Pricing for that row)

Put at least 12 names but not more than 15 under one section.

Income Sheet

Section 1	Costume Cost Pricing	Single Payment	First Instalment	Second Instalment	Third Instalment	Inclusive Cost	Total Price
John Doe	160	160				150	294
Jane	160		53.33	53.33	53.33	150	333.99
Roger	160	160				50	194
Laila	160		53.33	53.33		150	280.66
Eve	160	160				50	194
Adam	160	160				150	294
Rita	160	160				150	294
Margaret	160		53.33			50	127.33
Karen	160	160				50	294
Vikram	160	160				150	294
Tsin Yu	160		53.33	53.33		50	180.66
Elijah	160	160				50	195
				Count:	12	1200	2974.64

Likewise, there are four more sections created. Notice that there is the count, total inclusive fees and total price displayed.

The Expenditure Sheet

Section Name	Food	Drink	Materials	Labour	Total price
				Expenditure Sheet	
1	720	480	1800	900	3900
2	828	552	2016	970	4368
3	952.2	634.8	2257.92	1049.76	4894.68
4	1095.03	730.02	2528.8704	1133.7408	5487.6612
5	1259.2845	839.523	2832.334848	1224.440064	6155.582412
					24805.92361

Music	Bathroom	Transport	Security	Artiste	
4000	3000	2500	1800	5000	16300

			Total Expenditure	41105.92361

- The syntax of the functions is automatically shown.

- The prices in the food column increase by 15%.
Therfore, each subsequent cell in the next row is 15% higher than the previous row.
Price in next row = sum (previous cell address, product (0.15, previous cell address))

Same calculations apply for other columns depending on the rules mentioned in the problem.

- Total price is calculated as:
Total price for each row = sum (cell address of Food column for that row: cell address of labor column for that row)

Total price (Subtotal) = sum (cell address of first row in that column: cell address of fifth row in that column)

Likewise, the total price for flat rates are calculated and then the total expenditure.

Task 4

1. Modify your spreadsheet to effect the following changes:

   (a) Insert a masquerader before the last person in each of the first three sections.

   (b) Delete the third masquerader from each of the last two sections.

(c) Create a table that shows the total income and total expenditure by sections.

Solution (a)

- Click on any cell in the row next to the last record.
- Right click on that cell and press Insert.
- Then select entire row. A new row should be inserted. After the row is inserted.
- Add the details required.
- Calculate the total price for that row using either of the functions as described in the previous question depending upon the details added.

Notice the changes

Income Sheet								
Section 1		**Costume Cost Pricing**	**Single Payment**	**First Instalment**	**Second Instalment**	**Third Instalment**	**Inclusive Cost**	**Total Price**
John Doe		160	160				150	294
Jane		160		53.33	53.33	53.33	150	333.99
Roger		160	160				50	194
Laila		160		53.33	53.33		150	280.66
Eve		160	160				50	194
Adam		160	160				150	294
Rita		160	160				150	294
Margaret		160		53.33			50	127.33
Karen		160	160				50	294
Vikram		160	160				150	294
Tsin Yu		160		53.33	53.33		50	180.66
Elijah		160	160				50	195
Ruben		160		53.33			150	227.33
			Count:		12		1350	2974.64

- Make the same changes to Section 2 and 3.

- Changes will be made to the expenditure sheet also.

160

Expenditure Sheet						
Section Name	Food	Drink	Materials	Labour		Total price
1	720	520	1950	975		4225
2	897	598	2184	1053		4732
3	1031.55	687.7	2446.08	1137.24		5302.57
4	1186.2825	790.855	2739.6096	1228.2192		5944.9663
5	1364.224875	909.48325	3068.362752	1326.476736		6668.547613
						26873.08391

Music	Bathroom	Transport	Security	Artiste		
4000	3000	2500	1800	5000		16300

				Total Expenditure		41105.92361

Solution (b)

Now we will delete the third masquerader from Sections 4 and 5.

- Click on the third row of each of the mentioned sections.

- Right click and then press Delete.

- Select Entire Row and press OK. (The row should be deleted and the changes seen.) See sheet shown

	Section 5						
Harry		425	425				150
Sam		425		141.66	141.66	141.66	50
Tom		425	425				50
Skye		425		141.66	141.66		50
Molly		425		141.66			150
Arya		425	425				150
Smitha		425		141.66			50
Rajesh		425		141.66	141.66	141.66	150
Sheldon		425	425				150
Howard		425	425				50
Leonard		425		141.66	141.66		150
				Count:		11	1150

Solution (c)

- Scroll below and click on an empty cell.
- Go to the Insert tab and click on Table.
- Specify the range of the columns.
- Select three columns.
- Edit the table with the values. (See sheet shown)
- Save as Masquerades2.xlsx.

Section	Total Income	Total Expenditure
1	3201.97	4225
2	3813.96	4732
3	4485.96	5302.57
4	3617.94	5944.9663
5	5144.92	6668.547613

Task 5

3. Perform the following modifications to your worksheet.

(a) The cost of raw materials has decreased. Change the initial cost of materials from $150.00 to 135.00.

(b) Labour costs however, have increased. The starting cost of sewing costumes for the first section is now $95.00.

(c) Due to inflation, it has become necessary to increase the cost of food and drink from 15% to 20%. However, the first section has been spared this price hike.

(d) Sort the first two sections in descending order by Total Payment.

(e) Sort the third and fourth sections in ascending order by Name, then by cost.

(f) Create an appropriate chart which compares the income and expenditure of each section. Give this chart a suitable name.

(g) Create an appropriate chart, with appropriate data labels, which shows the distribution of expenditure for any one named section.

(h) Save your spreadsheet as Masqueraders3.

Solution:

(a) Change cost of material to 135.

(b) Change the labor to 95$.

(c) Make similar changes to food and drink.

Expenditure Sheet						
Section Name	Food	Drink	Materials	Labour	Total price	
1	780	520	1755	1235	4290	
2	936	624	1965.6	1333.8	4859.4	
3	1076.4	717.6	2201.472	1440.504	5435.976	
4	1237.86	825.24	2465.64864	1555.74432	6084.49296	
5	1423.539	949.026	2761.526477	1680.203866	6814.295342	
					27484.1643	
Music	Bathroom	Transport	Security	Artiste		
4000	3000	2500	1800	5000	16300	
				Total Expenditure	43784.1643	

(d) Click on the first row of each section data and press Shift + down arrow until you reach the last record.

- Right click on selection
- Sort from largest to smallest.

Section 2							
Nathan	220		733.33	733.33	733.33	150	402.99
James	220		733.33	733.33	733.33	150	402.99
Jily	220	220				150	348
Saber	220	220				150	348
Leroy	220	220				150	348
Sagnik	220	220				150	348
Neal	220		733.33	733.33		150	329.66
Roy	220	220				50	248
Hook	220	220				50	248
Emma	220	220				50	248
Jonathan	220		733.33	733.33		50	229.66
Alicia	220		733.33			50	156.33
Regina	220		733.33			50	156.33
			Count:		13	1350	3813.96

- Position the cursor as shown
- Click on Custom Sorting

Section 3							
Bonnie	280	280				150	402
Cain	280	280				150	402
Damien	280	280				50	302
Diya	280		93.33	93.33		150	378.66
Elena	280		93.33	93.33	93.33	150	471.99
Henry	280	280				50	302
Jeremy	280		93.33	93.33		50	278.66
Katherine	280		93.33			150	285.33
Lydia	280		93.33	93.35	93.33	50	371.99
Matt	280	280				150	402
Nadia	280	280				50	302
Stephen	280		93.33			150	285.33
Trisha	280	280				50	302
							4485.96
		Count:		13	1350	4485.96	

(f)   Chart showing Income and Expenditure of each section.

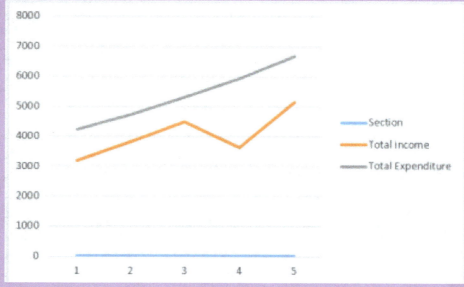

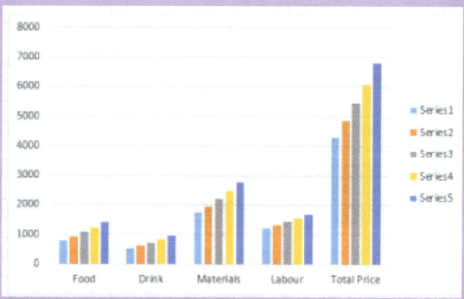

- Select the columns and the data and click on column chart.
- Edit the axis by right clicking on whatever you want to edit.
- Save the sheet as Masquerades3.xlsx

Budget

Task 6

(1)   Open Microsoft Excel.

(2)   You have an empty workbook called Book1 in front of you. Save Book1 in your folder as XX Spreadsheets where XX is your full name and class group.

3)   You are going to make a few budgets for your future life away from home. Use the information given to formulate your worksheet: **(2 marks)**

    (a)   When you are on your own, how will you spend your money? Definitely you have to spend **money** on **food** and **accommodation**, but you will also have many other expenses.

          In cells A4 to A19 type other kind of expenses you expect to have. Type at least 10 kinds.

                                                                  (2 marks)

    (b)   In column B you are going to guess how much money you will spend per month on each expense group. Type honest and sensible guesses. There is one catch, though. In column B we assume your salary is $1,000 per month, and you can not spend more than that amount. As you enter your guesses, the total sum so far is displayed in cell B20. Do not continue to (c) until your total is exactly $1,000.

                                                                   (2 marks)

    (c)   In column C we assume you earn $2,000. How will your expenses change? Will you add new expense groups? Type your amounts in the C column and do not continue to (d) until the total is exactly $2,000.   **(2 marks)**

    (d)   Do the same for columns D, E and F where your salary is $3,000, $4,000 and $5,000 respectively.   **(6 marks)**

(4)   Type your name and class group in the left section of the header.   **(3 marks)**

(5)   Change the name of the sheet from Sheet1 to Budget.   **(1 mark)**

(6)   Do a print preview of your sheet and make sure it fits on one page.   **(1 mark)**

(7)   Print the sheet with gridlines and with the sheet name in the footer.   **(3 marks)**

Music

Task 7

REF NO	TYPE	ARTIST	TITLE	QUANTITY	COST	TOTAL
A101	C	VIVALDI	FOUR SEASONS,	4	12.90	51.60
A103	T	AEROSMITH	GREATEST HITS	5	13.34	66.70
A105	T	MARLEY, BOB	LEGEND	10	15.00	150.00
A107	C	BON JOVI	SLIPPERY WHEN	2	14.00	28.00
A110	T	BON JOVI	SLIPPERY WHEN	3	11.00	33.00
A111	C	DIRE STRAITS	LOVE OVER GOLD	2	16.00	32.00
A112	C	DIRE STRAITS	DIRE STRAITS	4	16.00	64.00
A114	C	BEATLES, THE	HELP	2	15.50	31.00
A116	T	MAXI PRIEST	GREATEST HITS	3	13.89	41.67
A118	T	GEORGE	FAITH	4	15.99	63.96
					TOTAL	

A music shop is using their computer to keep track of the CDs they have in stock.

1) Enter the data shown in the table using an appropriate **FORMULA** to calculate the **TOTAL**.

2) Save the workbook as **XX MUSIC**, where **XX** is your full name and class group.

3) Here are a number of changes we would like you to make to the spreadsheet:

   i) Place a border around each cell. **(1 mark)**

   ii) Edit the cost of Aerosmith's CD to 13.00 **(1 mark)**

   iii) The column headings (top row) should be in font Times New Roman, size 18 pts and bold. **(3 marks)**

   iv) The rest of the spreadsheet should be in Times New Roman, 10 pts, normal (not bold) text. **(2 marks)**

   v) The column headings should be centred in their cells and the cells should be filled with Gray – 25%. **(2 marks)**

vi   George Michael's name should be changed to MICHAEL, GEORGE

(1 mark)

vii   Insert a row between the CDs with reference number A116 and A118 and add the following data:

A117, C, CHALICE, SI ME YA, 3, 12.99   **(4 marks)**

viii   Type a formula in an appropriate cell to calculate the total cost for CHALICE.

(1 mark)

ix   Add a formula in a suitable cell to calculate the total value of all the CDs.

(2 marks)

x   The label TOTAL VALUE should be bold.   **(1 mark)**

xi   Format all numeric cells in the columns COST and TOTAL to show a dollar sign.

(1 mark)

xii   Delete the row with Ref No A107.   **(1 mark)**

xiii   Set all column widths to fit the widest entry (this is called best-fit). **(1 mark)**

(4) Type your name and class group in the left section of the header and Task 19–Music in the right section of the header.   **(3 marks)**

(5) Print Preview the spreadsheet. Change the orientation to landscape to make the data fit on one page.   **(1 mark)**

(6) Save your workbook and print a copy of the spreadsheet showing the values.**(3 marks)**

(7) Print the spreadsheet showing formulae with row and column headings fitted to one page.

Task 8

(1) Name an empty spreadsheet **TEST RESULTS**.

The data below shows some student scores for three tests called T1, T2 and T3.

Name	T1	T2	T3
Smith Fred	10	9	7
Walter Jim	9	6	4
Ebanks Maria	10	10	9
Short Lisa	4	10	9

(2) Enter the data above in a sheet named TEST1. **(6 marks)**

(3) Set the font for all cells to Times New Roman, size 10 pts. **(2 marks)**

(4) Format the student names to bold text. **(1 mark)**

(5) Alter the T2 score for Jim to 9. **(1 mark)**

(6) Karen Jones' results should be added to the table below Lisa's. She got 8, 7 and 8 for T1, T2 and T3 respectively. Format her data the same way as the others.

(7) Right align the column headings T1, T2 and T3. **(1 mark)**

(8) Add a column with the title TOTAL right aligned. **(2 marks)**

(9) Use a function to calculate the total score for Fred. **(1 mark)**

(10) Calculate the scores for the other students using functions. **(1 mark)**

(11) Add a row with the label Average. Use the average function to calculate the average score for each test T1 to T3. **(3 marks)**

(12) Format the values in the average row to two decimal places. **(1 mark)**

(13) Add borders around every cell in the data range. **(2 marks)**

(14) Shade the top row light grey (25%). **(1 mark)**

(15) Alter the widths of the columns using _best fit'. **(1 mark)**

(16) Place your name and class group in the left section of the header. In the right section of the header type Task 5–Grades. The sheet name should show in the center section of the header. Print the sheet TEST1

(17) Copy the sheet TEST1 to a new sheet named TEST2. **(2 marks)**

Note: For the rest of the exercise you will work on the sheet TEST2.

(18) Using Test 2, appropriately insert a new column labeled T4, and add the following data:

(19) Use a function to find the average score for the test T4. **(1 mark)**

(20) Adjust the formula in the total column to include the values for T4 **(1 mark)**

(21) Remove all borders around the cells. **(1 mark)**

(22) Make sure you have used consistent formatting in the spreadsheet. Use 'best-fit'. **(2 marks)**

(23) Save the workbook.

(24) Print the sheet TEST2 displaying values, and displaying formulas. The printout should have your name and class group in the left section of the header. In the right section of the header type Task 20–Grades. The sheet name should show in the center section of the header. **(14 marks)**

Minux

Minux Computer Associates is a rapidly developing company selling computer products. They would like you to help them set up their price lists.

1. Name an empty spreadsheet **Minux**. **(1 mark)**

2. Set up the spreadsheet with the following data: **(5 marks)**

Product Name	Code	Cost
Sound Blaster	A10001	$235
Graphics Pro	A10002	$321
Ultra Max	A10003	$399
PanaSync	A10004	$211
WinTurbo	A10005	$299
Microlaser Pro	A10006	$159
Optima V	A10007	$99
Stealth Master	A10008	$299
Multimedia X5	A10009	$599
Sportster V90	A10010	$219
Clip It	A10011	$59

3. Label the sheet Minux1 **(1 mark)**

4. Right align the column headings 'Code' and 'Cost' **(1 mark)**

5. Add two more columns labeled 10 Quantity and 100 Quantity. **(2 marks)**

6. The 10 Quantity column should show a 10% reduction in cost for each item. Enter a suitable formula for the item 'Sound Blast'. Copy this formula to the other items in the same column. **(3 marks)**

NOTE: reduction in cost is Cost – (Cost * given percent)

7. The 100 Quantity should show a 20% reduction in cost for each item. Enter a suitable formula for the item 'Sound Blast'. Copy this formula to the other items in the same column. **(3 marks)**

8. Adjust all columns to 'best-fit' width.   **(1 mark**

9. Add borders around each cell.   **(1 mark)**

10. Place your name and class group in the left section of the header. In the right section of the header type Task 7–Minux Associates. The sheet name should show in the center section of the footer. Save and print the spreadsheet.

11. Copy Minux1 to another sheet labeled Minux2   **(2 marks)**

NOTE: Perform the following tasks on Minux2 ONLY

12. Insert three rows at the top of the spreadsheet.   **(1 mark)**

13. Add the title Minux Computer Associates to the top of your spreadsheet. The title should be in Times New Roman font, size 16pts, bold and centred above all the columns used.

                                                                              (3 marks)

14. The current date should be added in a row below the title Minux Computer Associates, using the TODAY() function. It should be formatted to show the day, month and year, e.g. 12-Jan-2001. Let it be in Times New Romans font, size 16pts, bold and centered across all columns.

15. Remove the borders around each cell.   **(1 mark)**

16. Type your name and class group in the left section of the header. In the right section of the header type Task 21–Minux Associates.   **(6 marks)**

17. Save and print Minux2 showing both values and formulas each on a single page.

                                                                              (8 marks)

Task 10

You are going to create a spreadsheet to record the petrol bought by a salesperson travelling around Great Britain and Europe. Do this work on a sheet named 'Task 21- Petrol' and remember to save your workbook every five minutes. Save the workbook as SP Task 21.

1.   Enter the data given in the table below.

Note that the abbreviation GBP means Pounds Sterling.

The PRICE is given per litre in the currency of the COUNTRY visited and the RATE is the rate of exchange, i.e. the number of foreign currency units to the GBP).   **(9 marks)**

COUNTRY	JANUARY	FEBRUARY	MARCH	TOTAL	PRICE	RATE	COST (GBP)
BELGIUM	90	89	92		33.33	59.27	
ENGLAND	19	20	33		0.45	1.00	
FRANCE	113	73	138		5.87	9.67	
GERMANY	56	250	40		1.44	2.87	
ITALY	200	0	190		1555.55	2160.05	
SCOTLAND	30	50	20		0.45	1.00	
SPAIN	103	110	120		94.02	181.93	
TOTAL							

2.   Use formulas to do calculations in a,b,c,d and e:

a)   The TOTAL petrol bought in JANUARY. Copy this formula to obtain the TOTAL for FEBRUARY and MARCH   **(2 marks)**

b)   The TOTAL petrol bought in BELGIUM. Copy this formula to obtain the TOTAL for other countries   **(2 marks)**

c)   The COST (GBP) for each COUNTRY using the formula:COST (GBP) = TOTAL * PRICE / RATE   **(2 marks)**

d)   Format the figures in the COST (GBP) column to integer format, i.e. zero decimal places.   **(2 Marks)**

3. The petrol bought in FEBRUARY in ITALY should have been 120 litres and in FEBRUARY in GERMANY should have been 25 litres. Make these changes.

(2 marks)

4. Expenses for ENGLAND should not have been included. Delete this row. **(1 mark)**

5. Insert a new column labelled APRIL between the MARCH and TOTAL columns. Populate this column with the data given below. (Note that you will have to calculate the TOTAL for April and edit the TOTAL formula for each country to include the APRIL figures).

COUNTRY	APRIL
BELGIUM	99
FRANCE	59
GERMANY	210
ITALY	37
SCOTLAND	37
SPAIN	117

(6 marks)

6. Calculate the total that the salesperson will be paid in GBP when the Company processes this

spreadsheet. (i.e. calculate the total for the COST (GBP) column). **(1 mark)**

7. Save the workbook and print
- the sheet 'Task22- Petrol' using gridlines. **(1 mark)**

- the formulae used. (Ensure that all data fits on one and that the row and column heading are displayed). **(3 marks)**

(Total: 30 marks)

Literature

You are asked to calculate the costs incurred by a company in sending advertising literature to European countries. Do this work in a sheet named 'Task 22 - Literature' and remember to save your workbook every five minutes. You may save the workbook as **SP Task 22**.

COUNTRY	TRANSLATOR	PRINTING	POSTAGE	TOTAL	CIRCULATION	AVERAGE COST
AUSTRIA	350	1675	910		2600	
BELGIUM	350	1330	1008		2880	
FRANCE	200	1330	1397		3990	
GERMANY	220	1700	966		2760	
HOLLAND	335	1423	910		2600	
ITALY	300	998	1085		3100	
TOTAL						

2. Use formulas to calculate:

   a) The total cost of TRANSLATOR, PRINTING and POSTAGE for each the country.
   (2 marks)

   b) The total for TRANSLATOR and all the other columns, except AVERAGE COST.
   (2 marks)

   c) In the AVERAGE COST column, use a formula to calculate the average cost per copy for each country.

   d) AVERAGE COST = TOTAL cost divided by CIRCULATION). Show two decimal places. **(3 marks)**

3. Change the entry for TRANSLATOR costs in HOLLAND to 250 and PRINTING costs in GERMANY to 1500

4. The figures for BELGIUM should not have been included. Delete the row. **(1 mark)**

a) The following country was omitted. Insert a row between FRANCE and GERMANY and enter the data:

Country	Translator	Printing	Postage	Total	Circulation	Average Cost
SPAIN	300	1280	963		2750	

5. Calculate the TOTAL for Spain.
   If necessary, edit the formulas in the TOTAL row to accommodate the addition of Spain.
   (2 marks)

6. All the labels should be set in bold and with font size 12. **(2 marks)**

7. In a row over the table, insert the label "Costs for Advertising Literature", centered over all the columns and th size 21. **(5 marks)**

8. Use comma style with no decimal places for all the numbers in the circulation column.
   (3 marks)

9. Save the workbook and print the sheet 'Task23- Literature' with gridlines on one page using best-fit. **(3 marks)**

10. Display formulas instead of values and print the spreadsheet again.
    Ensure that the data fits on one and that row and column headings are displayed.
    (3 marks)

(Total: 38 marks)

Task 12

Charts

A local newspaper has asked a reporter to check out the prices of a number of items at three computer dealers. The reporter has decided to use a spreadsheet package to help him show the editor of the paper how the results of the survey could be illustrated to the readers.

Do this work in a sheet named 'CHARTS' and remember to save your work every five minutes

1. Name a spreadsheet CHARTS and enter the data shown in the table below. **(5 marks)**

Item	outlet a	outlet b	outlet c
digitiser	140	180	165
joystick	25	30	30
mouse	45	40	40

2. Add a column labeled Average and calculate the average price for each item.

3. From the data create three charts (as shown in the diagrams overleaf). Each chart should be on a separate chart sheet.
    a) 3D pie chart
    b) Column (bar) chart
    c) Stacked column (bar) chart   **(9 marks)**

4. Create a chart to compare the cost of each item in outlet c, with the average cost of that item for all three outlets.   **(5 marks)**

5. Print the spreadsheet including all the charts, onto a single sheet of paper.   **(1 mark)**

6. Edit the data in the spreadsheet to the values shown below and print the spreadsheet including all the charts, to a single sheet of paper.   **(3 marks)**

Item	outlet a	outlet b	outlet c
digitiser	200	300	165
joystick	50	30	50
mouse	90	40	60

7. Change the title of each chart to something more appropriate(i.e. gives an indication of the purpose of the chart.   **(3 marks)**

8. Print chart A on one sheet. Include 'Chart A' as the header.   **(2 marks)**

Exam Type Question

The following data represents test scores in three subjects over the past three years. Do this work in a sheet named WORK1 and remember to save your work every five minutes

1988	Geography	Math	English
George	50	94	11
Mary	78	23	32
Joan	32	81	68
Melissa	16	89	55
1989	Geography	Math	English
George	86	76	48
Mary	86	38	80
Joan	45	97	20
Melissa	80	47	64
1990	Geography	Math	English
George	86	62	69
Mary	42	58	23
Joan	58	90	20
Melissa	35	45	70

You are required to:

1. Create a spreadsheet containing the above information beginning at Row 3 Column 2.

   (6 marks)

2. Modify the spreadsheet as follows:

   i. Add a fifth column labeled Average and calculate EACH student's average mark for EACH year. **(3 marks)**

   ii. Insert two blank rows below each year's table. In the second blank row following EACH year's table, enter suitable formulae to calculate the average mark for EACH subject. should be centered over the data. **(4 marks)**

   iii. In Row 1, column 2 of the spreadsheet, add the title 'Student Grade History'. The title **(3 mark)**

   iv. In Column 2, in each average row, enter 'Average' centered in the cell.
   In Row 3 Column 6 enter 'Average' centered in the cell. **(3 marks)**

   v. Format EACH average row and column to display 2 decimal places only.

   (2 marks)

3. Make a copy of the sheet WORK1 and name the new sheet WORK2. All subsequent changes should be made to WORK2. **(1 mark)**

4. Below the 1990 table, create a table to show the subject averages for each year as follows:

	Geography	Math	English
1988			
1989			
1990			

Enter the appropriate values in the table. **(7 marks)**

5. Change George's 1988 English score to 31. **(1 mark)**

6. Create a line chart as a separate sheet named LINE1, showing the following information:
   a. Geography averages over the 3 years.
   b. Math averages over the 3 years.
   c. English averages over the 3 years.
   d. The X-axis label is 'Year' and the Y-axis label is 'Averages'. Graph title is 'Subject Trends 1988 - 1990'. **(7 marks)**

7. Print the sheets WORK1, WORK2, LINE1 and the formula for WORK2. **(1 mark)**

(Total marks: 38)

SBA Specimen 2

Do this work in a sheet named Task 6 – XYZ and remember to save your workbook every five minutes.

The following information represents data relating to a set of members of the XYZ Over 35 Club:

NAME	AGE	ALIAS	MEMBER #	AMOUNT DUE
Egbert, R	35	Ratta	1235	$700.00
Brown, P	40	Bragga	1240	$350.00
Allan, F	45	Zacca	1245	$800.00
Allan, G	50	Gerrif	1250	$900.00
Weeks, E	75	Boss	1255	$40.00
King, P	60	Queenie	1260	$550.00
Harold, A	65	Fatman	1265	$400.00
Sangster, Z	70	Massa	1270	$710.00

You are required to:
1. Enter the data given above beginning at row 3, column 1. **(8 marks)**

2. Discounts are given to members as follows:

Groups	Discount
Age under 50 years	5%
Age 50-64 years	8%
Age 65 years and over	15%

   a. Add a column labelled Discount and use appropriate formulae to calculate the discount given to each member of the club.

   b. Use the same layout style in the new column as in the rest of the spreadsheet.
(8 marks)

3. Add a seventh column of data headed "DISCOUNTED DUES", consisting of formula which result in the following:

DISCOUNTED DUES = AMOUNT DUE - DISCOUNT

4. Modify the spreadsheet as follows:

(i) Add a report title to the spreadsheet in row 1, centred over all the columns of information. The report title is **"MEMBERS OF THE XYZ OVER 35 CLUB"**.

(4 marks)

(ii) Place a single underline border on the column headings. **(1 mark)**

(iii) Place a double underline border on the last row of data. **(1 mark)**

(iv) Sort the records in NAME sequence. **(3 marks)**

(v) Create a copy the sheet "Task 6 – XYZ" and name it "Task 6 - XYZ1".

(1 mark)

(vi) On sheet "Task 6 - XYZ1", delete row 1 and 2 and hide all columns except: NAME, AGE, AMOUNTS DUE, DISCOUNT and DISCOUNTED DUES. **(2 marks)**

5. On a new sheet called "Task 6 - XYZ2", set up a table as follows:

a)

Groups	Amount Due Subtotals
Group I: Age under 50 years	
Group II: Age 50-64 years	
Group III: Age 65 years and over	

b) Using this table, create a pie chart highlighting the sub-totals of original "AMOUNTS DUE" applicable to the three age groups. Your pie chart should clearly show the actual totals represented by each "slice" as well as a legend. The chart should be labelled "PIE". **(6 marks)**

6. Print the sheets on a separate sheets with no gridlines. Use best-fit and make sure that each sheet fits on one page. **(11 marks)**
  • Task 6 - XYZ,
  • XYZ with formulas instead of values,
  • Task 6 - XYZ1,
  • Task 6 - XYZ2
  • The pie chart

(Total: 51 marks)

Task 13

Note: Read the instructions through carefully before attempting the question.

The ABC Systems Company is nearing the beginning of a new financial year. At a special planning session all managers were asked to submit their budgets for the upcoming year. Each manager submitted his/her budget in a different form. The information has been summarised and listed below.

Personnel

Salaries	10,000,000
Stationery (US$)	25,000
New equipment (US$)	500,000
Continuing education (US$)	50,000
Staff Loans	5,000,000

Consulting

Stationery (US$)	50,000
Local Travel	1,000,000
Foreign Travel (US$)	500,000
Telephone (US$)	60,000
Electricity (US$)	10,000
New equipment (US$)	250,000
Salaries	25,000,000
Continuing Education (US$)	25,000

Marketing

Advertising (US$)	25,000
Local Travel	10,000,000
Foreign Travel (US$)	10,000
Salaries	5,000,000
Commissions	5,000,000

You will notice that some costs have been specified in US dollars (US$). The current exchange rate of local currency to the US$ is 8.33. This rate fluctuates and is liable to change in the near future.

1. Begin the work for this task on a worksheet called BUDGET1 and remember to save your workbook every five minutes.

2. Present the information given above in a suitable spreadsheet format showing clearly

   I. the individual department budgets by item   **(9 marks)**

II.	the total department budgets	(2 marks)
III.	the total company's budget by item	(2 marks)
IV.	the total company's budget	(2 marks)

All figures should be given in local currency. **(Use suitable labels)**

3. Name a new sheet BUDGET2. Copy BUDGET1 to BUDGET2. All subsequent changes in this exercise should be made to BUDGET2. **(1 mark)**

4. After seeing the list, the Personnel Manager, who is new, realized she had left out several important details. She added the following figures to her budgetary requirements:

Foreign Travel (US$)	50,000
Local Travel	50,000
Pension Payments	10,000,000
Telephone	25,000

    Amend the budget accordingly. **(2 marks)**

5. Each department forgot about books and magazines subscriptions. Add the following information to the spreadsheet. Values are in local currency.

Personnel: Books & Magazines	- 500
Consulting: Books & Magazines	- 5,000
Marketing: Books & Magazines	- 250

    (4 marks)

6. The Data Processing Department's budget arrived late and now needs to be added to the spreadsheet.

    The figures are as follows:

Local Travel	10,000
Foreign Travel (US$)	10,000
New equipment (US$)	1,000,000
Salaries	3,500,000
Accessories (US$)	500,000
Books & Magazines	2,000
Continuing education	5,000

    (7 marks)

7. The exchange rate of the local currency to the US$ has changed from 8.33 to 9.41. Make the necessary conversions.

8. The above budgets must be presented to the Board of Directors. It is felt that a graphical comparison of the needs of different departments will have a better effect. Create two graphs called GRAPH1 and GRAPH2. You should choose the type of graph or diagram that would best show the required data.

(i) GRAPH1 should show the percentages of the budget allocated to different departments.

(5 marks)

(ii) GRAPH2 should show the percentages of the budget allocated to: Salaries, New Equipment, Staff Loans, Local travel, Foreign Travel and Others. The group Others, consists of Stationery, Continuing Education, Telephone, Electricity, Advertising, Pension Payments, Books and Magazines, Accessories and Commissions.

(5 marks)

9. Save as BUDGET2.

10. Print
   (i) the worksheets BUDGET1, BUDGET2 and the formulae used.
   (ii) the graphs GRAPH1 and GRAPH2.

(Total: 41 marks)

PROCEDURES

Expanding column width

. Position cursor in appropriate column

. Select Format, Column Width

. Change to appropriate width

. Select OK

Inserting column/row

. Position the cellpointer in desired column/row

. Select Insert, Columns/Rows

Deleting a Row

. Position cellpointer in appropriate cell

. Select Edit, Delete, Entire Row, OK

Alternatively copy formula using Copy & Paste

. Position the cellpointer in desired cell

. Select Edit, Copy or click on the copy icon

. Block the desired range to be copied to

. Select Edit, Paste or click the paste icon.

Unlocking input data area

. Block desired range

. Select Format, Cell, Protection

. Remove check mark from locked

. Select OK

Enabling Spreadsheet Protection

. Select Tool, Protection, Protect Sheet, OK

Searching and replacing data

. Position the cursor at the top of the document

184

. Select Edit, Replace

. Enter relevant information

. Select Replace All

. Replace the other words with their codes
{Position cellpointer at top of document after each replacement}

Inserting border line beneath first table

. Block desired range

. Select Format, Cell, Border

. Make appropriate selections

. Select OK

Inserting functions for calculations

. Position cellpointer in desired cell

. Select Insert; (choose desired function)

. Select Finish

. Delete the present function argument

. Enter the function argument

. Press Enter

Printing the entire spreadsheet on a single page.

. Select File, Setup

. Change orientation to Landscape

. Adjust the scaling to 70%, data fits on one page

. Select Print

. Select OK

. Select Print Preview

Section 6
DATABASE MANAGEMENT

*A **database*** *is a collection of data organized in tables that are related to each other.*

Databases generally store data composed of text and numbers but there are modern databases that store pictures and sounds as well.

Since the data stored is organized, electronic databases allow for quick, easy retrieval, extraction and manipulation of the data with the help of a **Database Management System Software (DBMSS)**.

Database Management System Software

A **Database management software system** is a specially designed software application that interacts with the user, other applications, and the database itself to capture and analyze data. A general-purpose DBMS is a software system designed to allow the creation, querying, updating, and maintenance of databases.

Examples of DBMSs

Well-known large-scale contemporary DBMSs include Microsoft SQL Server, Oracle, and SAP. Typically these types of systems utilize servers to store the database tables, systems and reports. Users access the database from a desktop or laptop PC or a mobile device such as a tablet or smartphone.

Applications such as Microsoft Access, LibreOffice Base, FoxPro, and FileMaker Pro are not usually developed on such a large scale, but are useful to many individuals and businesses who do not require giant enterprise-wide systems.

Microsoft Access is a good application that can be used to learn the basics of a database management system. It runs on a desktop or laptop computer, or through the Internet, has learning support tools, and is cost-effective.

Uses of Databases and DBMSs

In **Microsoft Excel**, you can create and manipulate data tables stored in columns and rows. However, Excel does not provide relational capabilities. With a DBMS, you can create and link tables with greater flexibility and efficiency in terms of how the data is stored, connected, and accessed.

Using a database such as **Microsoft Access**, you can:
- Add new information to a database, such as a new item in an inventory list
- Edit data in the database, such as changing the current location of an item
- Delete information, perhaps if an item is sold or discarded
- Organize or sort and view the data in different ways
- Generate forms and reports to share the data with others.

Major worldwide retailers such as Amazon.com, Microsoft, and Walmart all perform these tasks and activities with very sophisticated databases, providing certain screens to customers on the "front end" while also managing their large-scale businesses on the "back end". Other institutions such as government, hospitals, manufacturing companies, accounting firms, and virtually any other type of business of which you can think also depend on database systems to run their businesses.

Setting up a Database

When setting up a database, it is important to plan its use in advance. This is particularly important if you are setting one up which will be used by other people. Among the things which you should consider are:

- What data you will need to store
- What information you want to get out
- Who the data is intended for and how other users will use it
- Whether you want to restrict access to parts of the data to some users only
- Who is allowed to add or change data
- If your data refers to actual people, it may need to be registered under the *Data Protection Act* (though this doesn't apply to a personal database of family and friends)

Although you can change the specifications of your database as you develop it, you will save yourself a lot of work if as much as possible is planned in advance.

Microsoft Access is a relational database management system (which allows you to link together data stored in more than one table). It is fully supported by IT Services and is available for personal purchase as part of the Ultimate Steal and for departmental installation under the *Microsoft Select Agreement.*

Understanding Key elements for working with a Database

A **Field** - This is the smallest component in a database. It holds one piece of data for an element - person, place, event, thing or an idea. There are usually several fields.
Example: LastName or Firstname or Age or shoesize

A **Record** -All fields with data for one element
Example: Allen, Mark, 25, 6 (All data for student named Mark Allen)

A **Table** - All the Records for all the elements
Example: Allen, Mark, 25, 9
         Smith, Samantha, 24, 7
         Brown, Tricia, 24, 9

A **File** - All the Tables, Forms and other objects that make up the entire Database. There can be one or several tables.
Example: Students, Payments, StudAwards

TIP:

If you right click on the Microsoft Access entry in the menu and choose Send To then Desktop (create shortcut) you'll have an icon on the Desktop for future easy access. You can also do this with any Access file.

Creating a New Database

You will create a database that tracks the training needs of students. The first table will store data about the students. Later, you'll add to the database, and manipulate the database.
First, create a new blank database.

- Load **Access 2007 or 2010**
- Click **Blank database**.
- In the **File Name** box, delete the name that appears and type the file name for the new database, **Training**. [Access automatically adds the proper file extension.]
- To save the database in a location other than the default folder, click the folder icon noted by the blue arrow below, and navigate to the folder you want as you would with any other Microsoft Windows application.
- Click **Create**.
  Notice the new database opens with a new default table named Table1 displayed on the left in area known as **the navigation pane**.

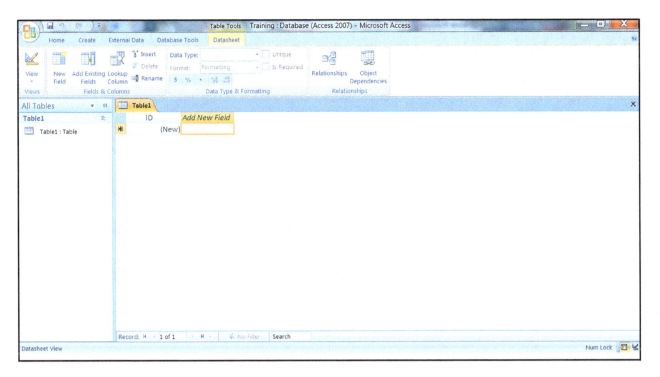

The Navigation Pane controls access to the various entities or **objects** within a database. This database has one object displayed (Table 1) but there are other objects available but not yet created.

The list of objects are:
- **Tables** - hold the raw data
- **Queries** - extract part of the raw data to produce dynasets - dynamic sets of data which can change each time the query is run (to reflect any changes to the data in the tables)
- **Forms** - user-friendly layouts to display data on the screen (either in a table or from a query)
- **Reports** - output files, ready for printing
- **Pages** - for creating/editing WWW pages
- **Macros** - lists of commands to perform particular functions
- **Modules** - programs which expert users write in a programming language called Access Basic to perform tailor-made functions not generally available.

The objects are accessed from the Navigation Pane. Pages, Macros and Modules are not dealt with in this course. As you use the different objects, the tabs on the Ribbon change appropriately.

1. Click on a double arrow on the right to show or hide the objects in a particular group
2. Click on the single arrow at the top of the Navigation Pane to view further display options

Working with Tables

Begin by creating the table named *students*. This contains data relating to students in a department in a University.

The **structure** of our table will involve the name of each field (**Fieldname**), a description of what will be stored in the field (**Description**) and the type of data to be stored in each field (**Data type**). We will also define the **Field Properties for each Field (Field size, Format).**

Structuring the Table

There are two view options for tables in **Access; Datasheet** and **Design**.

- **Datasheet**. Datasheet view allows you to display and change data in the table, including field names. This is the default view in Access.

- **Design**. In design view, Access shows the structure of the table so it can be modified. Design view also makes it easier to work with attributes such as field names, field sizes, and data types.

We'll use the **design** view to set up our field names, data types, and field descriptions. Click the **View** icon and select **Design View** .

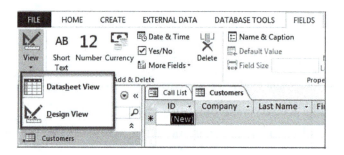

Because we haven't saved anything yet, Access will prompt us to name the table. Type Students, then click OK.

Access displays the table in design view, ready for the user to declare the fieldnames, data types, description etc..

Field Names

We want to track several fields in the **Student** table. The field and properties are listed below. Note that some of the fields which contain two words have been put together **without any spaces** in their **Field names**. This is standard practice for naming database fields that contain more than one word.

The fields (and properties) are as follows:

StudNo: A text field containing each student's personal id, as allocated by the University Registrar's Office. Text fields are the commonest type of fields and can be used to store any characters (letters, punctuation, numbers etc). Numbers should be stored as text if not being used in calculations. This field is set up to hold up to 10 characters and a Caption is used to expand the field name. This number uniquely identifies each student -the Required property has been set to **Yes** and Indexed is set to **Yes (No Duplicates)**. This field has also been used to set up a Primary Key, which you will learn more about later.

Tip: It's good practice not to include spaces in field names (or in the names of tables / queries /forms /etc). Instead, make use of Captions to expand the field name (to include any spaces). Not only do you have less characters to type but it makes manipulation of the data much easier if you find you need to use more advanced database features.

Press **<down arrow>** to move to the next field (then repeat this for each field)

- **Surname:** A text field containing the Family Name of each student. This field is required,can hold up to 25 characters and is Indexed as Yes (Duplicates OK)

- **Title:** Another text field but this time for up to 4 characters. Here, we know the possible values (Mr/Mrs/Miss/Ms) and can set up a Validation Rule to check that the data entered is correct - if it is not, the Validation Text is displayed. A Default Value (Mr) has also been set

- **FirstName:** Another text field for student's first name - up to 20 characters

- **OtherInitials:** A text field for any other initials - up to 6 characters

- **EntryYear:** A number field recording the student's year of entry. Numbers can be stored using different field sizes; here, an integer is used - see the data type table provided for a full explanation.This could also be stored as a text or date/time field, depending on how it is to be used.

- **Hall:** Another textfield where the values are known (there are only certain Halls of Residence) so a Validation Rule has been set- up to15 characters. A Default Value (Private) has also been set

- **Userid:** This is the student's computer username, which can also be used for the student's email address (see next field) - a text field for up to 8 characters

- **DOB:** The data type here is Date/Time, which has been set up in Medium Date format. Note that a Caption is used to expand the field name.

- **Address1:** First line of the student's home address - a text field storing up to 50 characters

- **Address2:** Second line of the student's home address - a text field storing up to 20 characters

- **PostCode:** The student's home post code - a text string storing up to 10 characters

- **Phone:** The student's home telephone number - note that even though this is a number it is stored as text (you won't be doing any mathematical calculations with it!)

- Overseas: A Yes/No(or logical) field storing whether the student is from an EEC country or not. The Default Value is set to No.

- Notes: For any other pieces of information - for longer pieces of text, a memo is used

- Photograph: Digital data (eg a passport photograph) are stored as OLE Objects

See the Table shown with some Data Types that are available. We may not need to use all of then when creating a Table.

Data Type	Use	Size
Short Text [formerly know as "Text']	Alphanumeric data [names, titles, etc.]	Up to 255 characters.
Long Text [formerly known as "Memo"]	Large amounts of alphanumeric data: sentences and paragraphs.	Up to about 1 gigabyte [GB], but controls to display a long text are limited to the first 64,000 characters.
Number	Numeric data.	1, 2, 4, 8, or 16 bytes.
Date/Time	Dates and times.	8 bytes.
Currency	Monetary data, stored with 4 decimal places of precision.	8 bytes.
AutoNumber	Unique value generated by Access for each new record.	4 bytes [16 bytes for ReplicationID].
Yes/No	Boolean [true/false] data; Access stores the numeric value zero [0] for false, and -1 for true.	1 byte.
OLE Object	Pictures, graphs, or other ActiveX objects from another Windows-based application.	Up to about 2 GB.
Hyperlink	A link address to a document or file on the Internet, on an intranet, on a local area network [LAN], or local computer Up to 8,192 [each part of a Hyperlink	data type can contain up to 2048 characters].

Attachment	You can attach files such as pictures, documents, spreadsheets, or charts; each Attachment field cancontain an unlimited number of attachments per record, up to the storage limit of the size of a database file.	Up to about 2 GB.
Calculated	You can create an expression that uses data from one or more fields. You can designate different result data types from the expression.	Dependent on the data type of the Result Type property. Short Text data type result can have up to 243 characters. Long Text, Number, Yes/No, and Date/Time should match their respective data types.
Lookup Wizard	The Lookup Wizard entry in the Data Type column in Design view is not actually a data type. When you choose this entry, a wizard starts to help you define either a simple or complex lookup field. A simple lookup field uses the contents of another table or a value list to validate the contents of a single value per row. A complex lookup field allows you to store multiple values of the same data type in each row.	Dependent on the data type of the lookup field.

Tip:

Note that the student's surname is stored separately from the first name (similarly each line of the address is in a separate field). You can then, for example, sort by surname then first name, or reference the students formally (ie Mr X) or informally (by their first name).

Fill in the details pressing Tab or the cursor keys to move from one column to another and from one row to another.

Your Screen should look similarly to the one below.

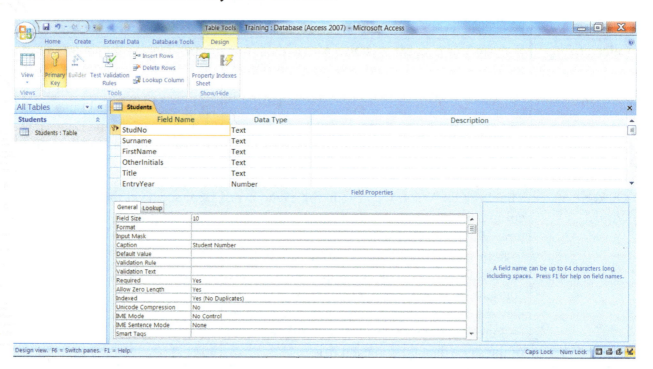

Close the Table Design pane – Click the "X" just above the right of "Description". Respond "yes" to **Save** the changes to the design of the Table .

We are now ready to populate our Table with data one record at a time.

Enter 7 records as shown. Fill in the other data on your own. Be creative.

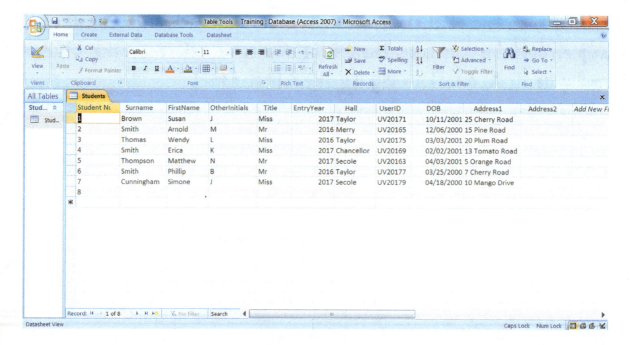

Searching for a Specific Record

To search for a specific record (ie down a field), you should first move to the field you want to search:

1. Press **<Tab>** to move to the Surname field
2. Click on the **[Find]** icon on the right hand side of the Home tab on the Ribbon (or press **Ctrl + F**) and a Find and Replace window will appear
3. The cursor is already positioned in the **Find What:** box - type in smith

The default options should already be set correctly. The **Look In:** box shows the search is restricted to the current *Surname* field (alternatively, you can search the whole table). In the Match: box, you can choose to match the **Whole Field,** *Any Part of Field or the Start of Field. Search:* is set to *All records.*

The other options are Up and Down. *Match Case* lets you distinguish capitals from lower case (if you need to). Finally, *Search Fields* as *Formatted* is useful for finding data as displayed (a date format, for example).Note that you also have access to a Replace tab for editing data.

4. Press **<Enter>** for [Find Next] and the search should be carried out
5. Press **<Enter>** again and another Smith will be found
6. Keep pressing **<Enter>** until you get the message that the search item is not found

Obviously, this is not a very elegant way of retrieving information from the database - but it works! To close both the warning message and *Find* window:

7. Press the **<Esc>** key twice or click on **[Cancel]** (or on the red **[Close]** button)
8. Finally, press**<Ctrl Home>**to move back to the first record (or use the first button on the record indicator bar)

Sorting

Sorting is arranging data in a specified order using one or more specified fields. The result of the sort will allow you to easily make decisions as the more important data you require will be made prominent for analysis.

Sorting using **Access** is quicker than you could have done manually as it is a great task to scroll through screens of data and to compare them to decide where each is to be placed in comparison to the other. It is also definitely more accurate.

We can sort data alphabetically or numerically in Ascending or Descending order.
We may use the **Quick Sort icons** featured on the **Sort Filter** tab as shown.

Ascending ![AZ icon]   Descending ![ZA icon]   Clear All Sorts

To sort data using a selected field:

1. Click the column with the fieldname required (Surname)

2. Click the icon for the order required (Ascending)
   The data is automatically re-ordered or sorted. Notice that we now have Brown, Cunningham, Smith Arnold, Smith Erica, Smith Phillip, Thomas,Thompson.

Follow the order of the screens below to see how the sort was done.

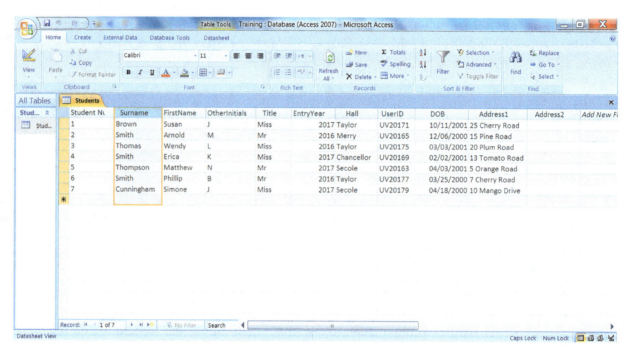

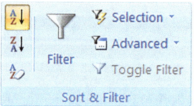

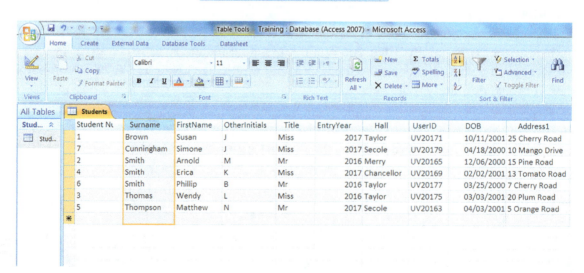

Changing the Default Display Order for Sorting

If you want to keep the new display order for the next time you open the table, all you have to do is close the table, saving the changes to its design. Try this next:

1. Move to the field you want sorted (eg Surname)
2. Click on **[Ascending]** (or **[Descending]** if you want the data in reverse order)
3. Close the table by clicking on its [Close] button
4. Save the changes to the table design when asked - press <Enter> or click on [Yes]
5. Now press <Enter> again to reopen the table - you should find it in the new order

BEWARE: it's very easy to accidentally save unwanted changes to the table design (if you perform a quick sort on another field, for example). Sort on the correct field again (then close and save) to get back your original table order.

Sorting in a Query

Sorts can also be carried out and stored in a *query*. Moreover, within a query you must set an explicit sort otherwise the records are displayed in their original order of entry. Queries are particularly useful where you have more than one field you need sorted - a simple quick sort only lets you sort on the one field (you can't for example sort by surname then firstname). By using a query you can produce a display sorted on any of the fields and can even create complex sorts within sorts. You will be looking at queries shortly, and carrying out sorts in them, so there is no need to carry out an example here.

Indexes

An **index** in a database can be likened to an index in a book which adds just a few extra pages but is invaluable if you want to look up something. In a database an **index** is used to **speed up searching**, **sorting** and **grouping data** - one should be set on any field used frequently in these ways. **Access** records the sort order in a hidden object so that it doesn't need to repeat the sort each time.

Indexes also perform a second useful function in that they can be used to guard against **duplicate data entry**. They are always used when a field is set up as a *Primary Key*.
Try setting up an index on another field:

1. Click on the [View] button to switch back to Design View

2. Note that the StudNo field already has an index - set to Yes (No Duplicates). As this is used as the Primary Key, it must have this setting

Adding, Editing and Deleting Records

New Record   Delete Record

Whenever you make any changes (additions, deletions or edits) to a table, it is the original data file that you are altering. Unlike most other applications, a database does not make a working copy of the file first. For this reason, it is essential to keep a back-up copy of your file (to which you can always return), just in case you make mistakes when carrying out amendments.

To Add a New Record

To add a new record to the database, use the **[New]** button (on the status bar or in the *Records* group on the **Home** tab of the *Ribbon*) – you can also press **<Ctrl +>**. New records are always added at the end of the existing data. As soon as you start to type, Access creates a new empty record (marked with an asterisk), while the current record indicator changes from an arrow to a pencil:

1. Click on the **[New]** button - you should now be on Record 391
2. Type in a number for the StudNo (type in your own or just **99**) then press **<Enter>** (or **<rightarrow>** or **<Tab>**) to move to Surname
3. Type in your own name then move to Title (press **<Tab>**, **<Enter>** or **<right arrow>**)
4. Repeat step 3 until you have filled out most of the record (at least the columns up to Hall)

Note that some fields already have a default value. To change a value in a field you simply type in a new one. Note also that some fields (eg *Hall and Option*) can only accept certain values, others (eg StudNo, Surname and FirstName) cannot be left blank. Calculated fields, such as email,cannot be edited.

The *Photograph* field can hold a *picture*. The best way to add one is via the Clipboard (i.e. **Copy** and **Paste**). If you right click on the field and choose **Insert Object**... then it may appear as an icon which you then have to double click to open. As pictures cannot be displayed in tables anyway, don't try filling out this field here.

To delete a record

*   Click on the **[Delete]** button below **[New]** on the Ribbon and choose **Delete Record** (alternatively, select the record by clicking at the far left then simply press the **<Delete>** key)

Deleting records from a database is potentially very dangerous as they are erased once and for all, hence you are given one final chance to change your mind:

*   Press **<Enter>** for **[Yes]** to confirm the deletion
    Note that you can't now use **[Undo]** to recover the record. If you have several records to delete:
*   Using the mouse, point to the left-hand edge of the first record to delete - you will find that the mouse cursor changes to an arrow
*   Hold down the mouse button - the record id marked - then drag through the records required
*   To delete them. press the **<Delete>** key (or use the **[Delete]** button)
*   When asked to confirm the deletions, this time click on **[No]** and the records will reappear

Note: Records must be next to each other in order to delete them (you cannot use *<Ctrl>* click like you can in other Microsoft software, though *<Shift>* click can be used to select a block of records). You will see next how to select a subset of non-contiguous records, which you could then delete.

Selecting Records

Databases offer you the facility of extracting sub-sets of records according to some pre-set conditions. In the Library, for example, you can search for the books written by a particular author or those dealing with a given subject. Access offers you two methods for selection, *QuickSelect using aFilter and Selection using a Query.*

Quick Select and Filter

Selection  Toggle Filter  Filter

Simple selections can be made directly on the table itself, using a **filter**. ACCESS 2010 provides two mechanisms for this, as you will see:

1. Press **<Ctrl Home>** to move to the first record (press **<Enter>** first if this didn't work)

2. Move across to the Hall field - to find all the students living in a particular hall

3. Using the *<down arrow>* key, move to a record showing the Hall of Residence you require (or click on it using the mouse or you could use **[Find]** to search for a particular Hall)

4. Click on the **[Selection]** button (in the *Sort & Filter group*) and choose **Equals**…
   Note that at the bottom of the screen it says Record 1 of XX and Filtered. To turn off the filter:

5. Click on the highlighted **[Toggle Filter]** button (below **[Selection]**)
   You can also filter on part of a field - for example, you might want all students with a May birthday:

6. *Double click* on any occurrence of May in the *DOBfield* (or drag through the word) to select it

7. Click on the **[Selection]** button and choose **Contains "May"** to carry out the filter
   If you now also wanted to find the first year students born in May (we'll use the other method of filtering this time):

8. Click on the **[Filter]** button at the top of the Year of *Entry field*

9. Untick the Select All check box and tick the year required (here, 2011) – press **<Enter>** for
   [OK]
   Note that this method is more flexible in that it allows you to set more than one criterion:

10. Click on the **[Filter]** button again and tick a second year – press **<Enter>** for **[OK]**

You now have the **May** birthday students in two of the years. If you wanted the July birthday students instead, use the **Date Filters** option followed by **All Dates in Period** in the *Filter* button window. Note that you can also open the filter selection by clicking on the filter icon shown on the right at the top of each column.

Having made your required selection, there are several things you might want to do next. For example, you might want to delete these records - even though they are not next to each other in the full data set, you could drag through them here and delete them as before (but don't do so here).

Another thing you might want to do is to print off the data. However, you probably wouldn't want all of the fields, so you'll see next how to hide unwanted columns.window. Note that you can also open the filter selection by clicking on the filter icon shown on the right at the top of each column.

Changing the Fields Displayed

Tables often contain a lot of data, only some of which may be required. You can control which fields are shown and which hidden. Here, you may want just the student name and hall:

1. Right click on the *StudNo* column heading and choose **Hide Fields**
   To hide several adjacent columns in one go:
2. Click on the *Userid* column heading
3. Scroll to the right then hold down **<Shift>** and click on the *Photograph* column heading
4. Right click on the selected columns and again choose **Hide Fields**

   If you want to change the order of the fields on the screen, you can either use *cut and paste* or, more simply, *drag and drop*. Both these techniques should be familiar to the Microsoft Office user. To list the students starting with their full name (including title) in the correct order:

1. Click on the Surname column heading to select the column
2. Move the mouse cursor back into the column heading, hold down the mouse button then (with the button still depressed) drag the column to the right to a position immediately before the Year field
3. Release the mouse button to drop the field in its new position

   Note: you are only changing the screen display - the data is still stored in its original order. Finally, you might want to print your list. First, it's a good idea to preview it:

1. Click on the **File** tab, choose **Print** then **Print Preview**

   You will notice that Access automatically adds a header and footer to your page, which you may or may not want. Normally you would now print your list, but here:

1. Click on **[Close Print Preview]** on the far right of the new **Print Preview** tab to turn off the preview To redisplay any of the hidden fields:

2. Right click on any column heading and choose **UnHide Fields**

3. Click in the box against the required hidden column to redisplay it then press **<Esc>** for **[Close]**

Advanced Filters

The relationship between queries and filters is a very close one. You can in fact save a filter as a query by turning on the advanced filter option. This can be a useful aid in designing a query. As an introduction to queries, save the current filter (students born in May who came in a particular year):

1. Click on the **[Advanced]** button in the Sort & Filter group and choose Advanced Filter/Sort...

   A *Filter* Design pane appears.This is very similar to the Query Design pane, which you will be using next. Examine how the criteria have been set up.

2. Move to the **File** tab and choose **Save** – the Save As Query dialog box appears

3. Save the filter as **MayBirthdays** (press **<Enter>** for **[OK]**), then [Close] the filter window

4. Close the **students** table - *don't save the changes to the design* (click on **[No]**)

   Tip: The simplest way to redisplay all the fields if some are hidden is to close the table without saving the changes to its design. When you reopen it, it will appear in its original format.

To rerun the filter:

- Select **May Birthdays** from the new *Queries* category in the *Objects* list and press **<Enter>** to open it You'll find that all the fields are displayed. You'll see later how to specify particular fields in a query.

- End by closing the query - click on its [Close] button

   Once a filter has been saved as a query,it's easy to modify its design if necessary.

   Using a filter in this way is straightforward but a little limited. To do more complicated selections you have to use a *Query*. Queries also offer various other facilities, including sorts within sorts. In fact you may always want to view your data through a query – here, for example, you might want to see the students listed alphabetically by *Surname* then by *First Name*.

Working with Querries

To introduce you to queries (which may look a little complicated at first, but which are in fact very easy), try carrying out a sort within a sort. There are two ways to start a query:

- You can choose **[Query Wizard]** on the **Create** tab of the Ribbon to get help
- You can choose **[Query Design**] on the **Create** tab

The Query Wizard isn't very useful here, so try the second method instead:

1. Move to the **Create** tab on the *Ribbon* then click on **[Query Design]** in the *Queries* group

2. In the *Show Table* window, select the **students** table then press **<Enter>** to **[Add]** it

3. Press **<Esc>** to **[Close]** the *Show Table* window

Note: If you ever wanted to add a different table, click on the [Show Table] button in the Query Setup group on the new Query Tools Design tab on the Ribbon.

The *Select Query* pane may look a little confusing, but in fact it's very simple to use. The cursor should be flashing in the Field: row in the lower part of the screen waiting for you to define the fields to be displayed. Earlier, you sorted the *students* table by students' surnames but you couldn't then also sort by their first name. Here in a query, you can:

1. Click on the *list* arrow on the right of the *Field*: cell and choose **students.**

The asterisk notation means all the fields in the students table (if you only want certain fields displayed you must choose them individually). If you were to run the query as it stands, you would see the data in its original unsorted format (i.e. the sort you set when the table is opened isn't carried across – instead you have to set up explicit sorting in the query).

2. Click on the *list* arrow in the *Field*: cell in the second column and choose **Surname**
3. Repeat step 2 in the third column but choose **FirstName**
4. Move down to the *Sort:* (third) row and type a (for **Ascending**) in *both* columns **2** and **3**
5. In the *Show:* (fourth) row, untick the check boxes in *both* columns **2** and **3** (you can click anywhere in the cell) - if you don't, the *names* will appear twice as they are already included in **students.**
6. To carry out the query, click on the [Run] button on the far left of the Ribbon (or you can use **[View]** to move from Design View to Datasheet View)

You should find that the students are now listed in their correct order (look at the Smiths) and that this query should be used whenever you want to look at the complete set of data.

7. Click on the query's **[Close]** button
8. When asked, press **<Enter>** or click on **[Yes]** to save the query
9. Save the query as SortedStudents - press **<Enter>** or click on **[OK]**

Selection using a Query

Next, you are going to repeat the filter you carried out earlier to list all students from a particular hall. This time your new query will be making use of the fact that you already have the students sorted by name (a query can be based either on a table or another query):

1. Click on the **[Query Design]** button on the **Create** tab
2. In the Show Table window, click on the **Queries** tab and select the **SortedStudents** query
3. Press **<Enter>** to **[Add]** the sorted students then press **<Esc>** to **[Close]** the Show Table window
4. Set the Field: in the first column to **Surname** and that in the second column to **FirstName**

You now need the **Hall field** in a separate column to set up the selection criteria. Another way to fill up a field is to double click on it in the field list in the top half of the Select Query window. You can try this next:

5. *Double click* on the **Hall** – it should be added to the next empty column in the query
6. Move down to *Criteria:* in column 3 and type the name of the required hall - eg Wessex
7. To carry out the query, click on the **[Run]** button on the far left of the *Ribbon* (or use **[View]** to move from *Design View to Datasheet View*) or right click on the Query design and choose **Datasheet View**

The difference between this query and the earlier filter is that you can save it directly for future use.

8. Click on the query's **[Close]** button
9. When asked, press **<Enter>** or click on **[Yes]** to save the query
10. Save the query as Hall - press **<Enter>** or click on **[OK]** **Note:** You can't give a table and query the same name.

Now try re-running the query:

11. Double *click* on the **Hall** query in the *Objects* list - you have your results again

Parameter Queries

The selections you have carried out so far have only met fixed criteria - in this case: Show me the students who live in Wessex (or whichever) Hall. With a query, however, you can change the criteria each time you run it by making it a *parameter query*. The design is very similar to what you have already seen except that instead of setting a fixed criteria, Access asks for the information at run time. Modify the Hall query to do this:

1. With the *Hall* query still open, click on the **[View]** button to change to the *Design View*
2. Click in the *Criteria:* field in the third (*Hall*) column and **<Delete>** the current criteria
3. Type in a new criteria saying: **[Which Hall?]**

Note: square brackets tell Access that this is a question, to be displayed at run time.

4. Click on the **[Run]** button (or on **[View]** to switch to *Datasheet View*)
5. When asked the question *Which Hall?* type in the required hall of residence - eg. Sibly
6. Press **<Enter>** or click on **[OK]** and the query will be run

Normally, you would run the query each time from the Objects list (or from a user-friendly interface - a form called a switch board). Here, however, to run the query again:

1. Click on the [View] button to change to the Design View
2. Click on the [Run] (or [View]) button again
3. Type in the name of a different hall - eg. **Windsor** - and press <Enter> or click on [OK]

As you can see, this query is much more useful than when it only worked for a fixed hall. The same mechanism is used when you look up a book in the Library. Here, the query picks up the parameter from a box on the screen (where you have typed in the author's name or the subject you are searching for).

More Complex Queries

Next, try some more complicated queries. What if you want to have an alternative criteria in a parameter query? For example, you might want a list of students living in *either* one hall or another. To do this, you have to set up criteria on two different lines.

1. Click on the [View] button to change to *Query Design*
2. In the *second* line of the Criteria: in column 3, type: [or?] for a second question
3. Click on the [Run] button (or on [View] to switch to Datasheet View)
4. When asked Which *Hall*? type in the name of the first hall - eg **Wantage** (press <Enter>)
5. When *asked or*? type in the name of another hall - eg **Wessex** (press <Enter>)
6. You now have the students from both halls - [Close] the query, saving the new design

You have seen how to match values in a query but you can also use criteria such as greater than, less than, not equal to, between one value and another, or matching part of a field. For example, how do you set up a query to pick out just the female students? The answer is that you can use a special called Like.

The **Like** notation indicates that the words which follow must be embedded within the data in that field for a record to be selected - wildcards (* or ?) can be used to denote characters which may precede or follow the required text. ? represents a single character whereas * represents any number of characters. For example, **Like C*** could be used to give you all the students with names beginning with the letter C, while **Like *son** would match students whose names end with son. For the female students:

1. Click on the [Query Design] button on the Create tab
2. In the Show Table window, click on the Queries tab, select **SortedStudents** and [Add] it
3. Press <Esc> or click on [Close] to close the Show Table window
4. Set the Field: in the first column to **SortedStudents.*** (ie double click on the *)
5. Set the Field: in the second column to **Title**
6. In Criteria: in the second column type: *s (this covers Miss, Ms and Mrs) and press <Enter>(Access automatically changes this to **Like "*s"** for you)
7. Turn off *Show*: by unticking the box
8. Click on the [Run] button to run the query - or switch to Datasheet View

To set up a second condition on this subset of data (eg female students who have a particular tutor) is very easy. Whereas alternative conditions are set up on different lines, simultaneous conditions must be set up on the same criteria line:

1. Click on the **[View]** button to move back to Design View
2. Set the *Field*: in the third column to **Tutor**
3. Turn off Show: by unticking the box
4. In *Criteria*: in the third column, top line, type: **[Which Tutor?]** - or set a fixed value
5. Click on the **[Run]** button to run the query - or switch to *Datasheet View*
6. When asked *Which Tutor?* type in the name of a tutor (eg Foot) - press **<Enter>** for **[OK]**
7. **[Close]** the query, saving it as **Females**

Adding New (Calculated) Fields

Earlier, you did a very simple selection to show just the student's name and hall of residence. One fault with the original example was that the students' names (first name and surname) were printed in separate columns. In a query you can calculate a new field, joining these together:

1. Click on the **[Query Design]** button on the **Create** tab of the Ribbon
2. In the *Show Table window*, select the **Students** table and **[Add]** it   press <Esc> to **[Close]** the window
3. In *Field*: in column one, type: **FullName: FirstName & " " & Surname**
   (don't forget the space between the double quotes) - press **<Enter>**

Tip: You should always use an ampersand (&) rather than plus (+) sign when joining text together. Though both appear to work, plus signs can occasionally cause problems.

4. Set the *Field*: in the second column to **Hall**
5. Set the *Field*: in the third column to **StudNo**
6. Set the *Field*: in the fourth column to **Surname** and set Sort: to **Ascending** and turn off Show
7. In the fifth column, repeat step 6 but set the *Field*: to **FirstName**
8. Click on the **[Run]** button (or on **[View]** for Datasheet View) to run the query
9. *Double click* on the dividing lines between the column headings to widen the FullName column
10. *Right click* on the **StudNo** heading and choose **Hide Fields** (this field is needed later but doesn't need to be displayed here)
11. **[Close]** the query, saving it as Names

A calculated field also occurred in the original *students* table – you can add such fields both to queries and tables. To see how it was calculated

1. Open the **Students** table and click on the **[View]** button to move to Design View

2. Click on the **Email** *Field Name* and take note of the *Expression* in the *Field Properties*

3. You'll find the email address is defined as: **[Userid] & "@reading.ac.uk"**

Note that the *Result Type* of this email field is *Text* and not *Hyperlink*. This means it has not created an active hyperlink (ie you wouldn't be able to click on it to send a message).
Finally, [**Close**] the *students* table

Tip: When creating complicated calculations, it'suseful to evoke the Expression Builder. This appears if you right click in the Field: row (or, indeed in Criteria:) and choose **Build**.... There's also a [**Builder**] button on the Ribbon. You then have access not just to the field names but also to built-in functions. Even more importantly, a Criteria: can be set to pick up values held on forms.

WORKING WITH FORMS

The next object to investigate is a Form. Forms offer a friendly way of viewing the data in that they show a single record at a time. Forms can also be used to display results from queries. They are also used to facilitate data input.

Modifying a Form

To modify a form, you view the form design:

1. Click on the [**View**] button (or *right click* and choose **Design View**)

   Note that ACCESS provides you with three new tabs on the Ribbon to help you with the design. You are not going to modify the design of this form - you will see how to later, in Part 2 of these notes.

2. Click on the [**View**] button to move back to *Form View*

Forms and Filter

If you want to select a subset of the records using a filter, you can still use the [**Selection**] button as before. This isn't very convenient, however, if you want to base the filter on information not displayed on the current form. Here, you might want to search for students living in Wessex Hall (which isn't on the current record). You can do this using the [**Filter**] button as before, but Access also provides a special filter for use with forms.

1. Click on the [**Advanced**] button and choose **Filter by Form**

2. Click on the *list arrow* attached to the Ha*ll* field and select **Wessex**

3. Click on the [**Toggle Filter**] button - you should have just 9 records (use <**Page Down**> see them)

4. Click on the [**Toggle Filter**] button again to see all the records

Though this exercise could have been carried out using the **[Filter]** button, this next one can't:

5. Again. click on **[Advanced]** and choose **Filter by Form**– your previous filter is shown
6. Click on the *list arrow* attached to the *Title* field and select **Mr**
7. Now click on the *Or* tab at the bottom of the filter pane for a second filter
8. Select a *Title* of **Miss** and a *Hall* of **Windsor**
9. Click on the **[Toggle Filter]** button - you now have 19 records (press <Page Down> to see them)
10. Close the form by clicking on its **[Close]** button

Note: You can also use [Filter by Form] on a table (a blank record appears for you to type in the criteria).

Tables and Relationships

A relationship can exist when there are two or more tables. The tables must have **at least one field in common** in order for them to be **linked** to form a **"relationship"**.

We will create another table called **HoR** for **Hall of Residence** in order to work with relationships.

We will be using the table below to complete the fields for HoR.

Field Name	Data Type	Field Size Property	Description
Name	Text		
Warden	Text		
Phone	Text		
Road	Text		
Town	Text		
Rooms	Number	Integer	
Meals	Yes/No		Are meals provided

1. Click on the **[Table Design]** icon

2. The first field is for the *name of the hall* - type in **Name** and press **<Enter>**

A warning message appears telling you that *Name* is a *reserved word* and could cause problems later. Other reserved words include Date and Year. There's a problem here in that it's necessary for this field to be called Name in order to import the Halls' data in the later exercise. Indeed, it's important that you name the *fields exactly as specified in these notes for this exercise to work.*

3. Press **<Enter>** for **[OK]** to cancel the warning and accept the field name
4. The *Data Type* is Text by default - press **<Enter>** as this is what you want for this field
5. The *Description* is optional - type in **Name of Hall of Residence** if you want
6. Move down to the Field Properties

Tip:
Key <F6> can be used to switch panes - or you can use the mouse.

7. Set a *Field Size* of 15 and press **<Enter>**

   If you need to increase the field size at some time in the future there should be no problem (any existing data stays exactly the same). However, if you ever choose to decrease it then you could lose some data. This is called truncation.

8. Set up a Caption of **Name of Hall** then *Required* to **Yes**

9. Set *Indexed* to **Yes (No Duplicates)**- it's important to put an *index* on this field since it will be used to link up the students' data and it also insures that the data for a particular hall is not entered twice

10. Move to the second row - use the mouse this time

11. Set the *Field Name* to **Warden** and the *Data Type* to **Text**

A relational database management system lets you store data in many tables which can then be linked together. This is particularly useful when you have information which is either heavily duplicated or sparse (many records having empty fields). This improves both performance and scalability.

For example, if you have an inventory of equipment, it's better to record information about the suppliers (the name, address, phone/fax numbers, contact etc) in a separate table. Then, in your inventory, you need only record the name of the supplier to find out the other information. As each supplier will be supplying several pieces of equipment, this avoids massive data duplication.

It's the same situation here with the students. There is no need to store information about Halls of Residence for each student - that can be picked up from the **HoR** table. You'll see next how this is done. The aim of the exercise is to create a list of students, living in hall, such that you can send a letter to them to their University address.

1. Move to the **Create** tab and click on **[Query Design]** in the *Other* group on the right of the *Ribbon*
2. **[Add]** both the **HoR** and **students** tables and the **Names** query - press **<Esc>** or click on **[Close]**

You next have to join the three tables together on common fields. Joins can be created between tables when you design the database (in a special *Relationships* window), or made in a query (in which case they only apply to that particular query).

Tables are automatically joined in a query if two fields have the same name. Here, the StudentID field in the *Names* query has been joined to the equivalent field in the students table. The other common field (the Hall of Residence) is called *Hall* in the *students* table but *Name* in the **HoR** table and has not been linked. In this case you have to create the join manually by dragging the field name from one table/query over to the corresponding name in the other table/query.

3. Position the cursor over the **Hall** field in the **students** table
4. Hold down the mouse button and drag the field over the **Name** field in the **Halls** table

When you release the mouse button, a join line appears. If you made a mistake, simply click on the join line to select it then press <Delete> and try again. Now you need to set up your query:

5. In column 1, set the *Field*: to **FullName** from the **Names** query (*double click* on it)
6. In column 2, set the *Field*: to **Hall** from the **students** query
7. In column 3, set the *Field*: to **Road** from the **HoR** table
8. In column 4, set the *Field*: to **Town** from the **HoR** table
9. Click on **[Run]** to run the query - you should find 265 records are displayed (if you spelt *Wessex* and *Windsor* correctly - the 125 students living in private accommodation are excluded)
10. Click on the query window's **[Close]** button, saving it as **Addresses**

Setting up a Primary Key

Primary Key

Whenever you design a new table, it's a good idea to set up a Primary Key on one of the fields. **Primary Keys** help ACCESS uniquely identify each individual record in a table and hence work more efficiently. If a table doesn't contain a unique identifier then ACCESS will ask to set up an ID field for you. Here, the Halls of Residence table already has a unique field - the name of the hall:

1. Click on the **Name** field (row 1)
2. Click on the **[Primary Key]** button - a key symbol appears in the *field indicator* column
3. Click on the **[View]** button to move to *Datasheet View*

4. When asked (press <Enter> for [Yes]), save the table as **HoR** - press <Enter> for **[OK]**

You'll find you have an extra column labelled *Add New Field*. To hide this:
5. *Right click* on the column heading and choose **Hide Fields**

You could now type in your data, if you wanted to. Using a datasheet isn't very friendly, however, so try setting up a special *data-entry form*. A form gives you more control over what data is entered and can be designed to cut down on typing mistakes, as you saw with the students form.

Creating a Data Entry Form

There are two simple ways of creating a form; you can either use a *Form Wizard* or *AutoForm*.

AutoForm is a very quick and easy way to produce a form - it does so at the click of a button:

1. With the **HoR** table still open, click on the Create tab then on **[Form]** - the form appears instantaneously in a new window

2. Click on its **[Close]** button to **Close** the form - don't save it this time (click on **[No]**) as you will be creating the form using a *Wizard*.

    The *Form Wizard* is equally easy to use and offers you various additional options.
3. Still on the **Create** tab, click on **[More Forms]** then choose **Form Wizard**

As you already had the *HOR* table open, that is chosen automatically. If you start up the *Wizard* without a table or query open (or if you wish to base the form on a different set of data) then you would select it here. You are now asked which fields you want to appear on your form (here you have the choice - *AutoForm* gave you them all). As it happens, for a data entry form, you need all the fields:

4. Click on the double arrow **[>>]** to move them all (alternatively select individual fields in the order you want and use the **[>]** button) - press **<Enter>** or click on **[Next>]**

5. Choose a layout for your form (explore the alternatives, if you like); **Columnar** is best so choose that then press **<Enter>** or click on **[Next>]**

6. Set a style for your form - choose **None** (press **<Enter>** or click on **[Next>]**)

7. Add a title - type **Halls of Residence** (press <Enter> to **[Finish]**)

    The form is now opened for you to use. As it stands it is neat and simple, but a little boring - in fact it's almost exactly the same as that produced using AutoForm. To improve it

8. Right click on the form (or use the arrow attached to the base of the [View] button) and choose **Design View** to move to Design View

    Forms have three (sometimes more) sections - a header, footer and the detail. The data itself is entered into the detail section; the header and footer can be used for titles etc. To add a footer:

9. Position the mouse over the bottom border of the Form Footer - the cursor should change shape to a double-headed arrow. Hold the mouse button down and drag the border down one unit (there's a scale on the left-hand side)

10. Click once on the **[Label]** tool in the Controls group - the mouse pointer now has an 'A' attached.

11. Move the pointer into the form footer (top left corner) and click once

12. A small label box is drawn - type your form footer: **The University of Reading**

13. Press **<Enter>** and the label box is completed

14. Change the **[Font Size]** (eg to **14** point) and click on **[Bold]** to make the title more imposing To display the enlarged label:

15. Right click on the label box and choose **Size** then To **Fit**

16. Right click on the label box and choose **Font/Fore Color**- pick a colour to apply to your footer

17. Right click on the header background (away from the label) and choose a **Fill/Back Color**

Note: If you wanted to add a picture to the form (eg the University identity) then simply click on the [Logo] tool, choose where you want the picture, click the mouse button then browse for the required picture file. You can also amend the design of a form (just the position of objects and their colour) in Layout View:

18. *Right click* on the tab at the top of the form and choose **Layout View**

19. Click on the detail area on the far right – the detail area is outlined in orange

20. Use the **[Fill/Back Color]** button on the *Ribbon* to change the colour of the detail background

Tip:

Use the [Format Painter] to copy the colour scheme of one label or text box to the others - this speeds things up and gives a better overall design. Double click on the button if you want to paint the format to more than one object (then click on it again to turn it off when you have finished).

21. Press **<Ctrl s>** (or click on the **[Save]** button) to save the changes to the design of the form - the name of the form is picked up automatically as **Halls of Residence**

22. Click on the **[View]** button to move to *Form View*
    The form is now ready for you to type in the data. Note how large the boxes are for the *Warden, Phone* etc compared to the Name box. This is because you left the Field Size at 255 (whereas for Name you set it at 15).

Entering Data Using the Form

You are now going to use the form to enter a couple of data records:

1. For the first record, type in the following:

> Name: **Wessex** (and press <Tab> - if you **press <Enter>** by mistake, press
> <**Backspace**>) Warden:**Dr R.P.B. Smith**(<Tab>)
> Phone: **x8643** (<Tab>)
> Road: **Whiteknights Road**
> (<Tab>) Town: **Reading RG6 6BQ**
> (<Tab>)Rooms: **196** (<Tab>)
> Meals: the *option box* is already set on for **Yes**

2. Press <Tab> or <Enter> to move on to the second record, which is as follows: Name: Windsor (and press <Tab>)

> Warden: **Prof A.L. Jones** (<Tab>)
> Phone: **x8800** (<Tab>)
> Road: **Upper Redlands Road**
> (<Tab>) Town: **Reading RG1 5JL**
> (<Tab>) Rooms: **353** (<Tab>)

Meals: aga,   .   uiin, the *option box* is already set on for Yes

This is all you are going to enter explicitly; the remaining records are going to be *imported* from a data file created using another package.

3. Close the *Form window* by clicking on **the [Close]** button (save any changes to the design)

4. Also, close the *HoR* table by clicking on its **[Close]** button (saving any design changes)

You may be wondering why the records you entered weren't shown in the table (remember, the form is used as a friendly way to enter data into the table). The reason is that the screen wasn't refreshed. To see the data:

5. *Double click* on the HoR table in the *Objects* list then [Close] it again once you have seen the data

WORKING WITH REPORTS

Earlier you viewed an existing report; now, try to generate some yourself. Reports are saved within the database - you can then modify them at some later date if you need to tidy up the layout, for example. Note that you can also export data to Word or Excel via **Export** on the **External Data** tab.

ACCESS gives you the opportunity of designing your own reports from scratch (using *Design View*), however, unless you are an expert, don't even attempt this. It's much easier to use AutoReport or a *Report Wizard* and then modify the design if you need to.

Creating a Report Using Auto Report

Begin by creating a report for the *HoR* table using *AutoReport*.

1. Click on the **HoR** table in the *Objects* list – there's no need to open it
2. Move to the **Create** tab and click on **[Report]**

   Access shows you the results in *Layout View*. The dashed lines show the breaks, but it's much easier to see the layout in *Print Preview*:

3. *Right click* on the report tab (or use the arrow below the **[View]** button) and choose **Print Preview**
4. In the *Zoom* group, click on **[Two Pages]**

   You'll find that the information stretches over two pages, with the paper portrait (upright). It should be possible to display all the information on one sideways sheet. To do this:

5. *Right click* on the report tab again and this time choose **Layout View**
6. Move to the *Report Layout Tools* Setup tab and click on **[Landscape]**
   You'll find the report still doesn't quite fit onto a single page; next, you have to manually shrink the columns:
7. Position the mouse cursor on the border between the Phone and Warden columns (it becomes a two- headed arrow)
8. Hold down the mouse button and drag the border to the left - release the mouse button when the column is properly sized
9. Repeat steps **6** and **7** on the other columns until all columns fit on the one page
10. Repeat step 3 to **Print Preview** the page
    There are still some problems with the report – Access doesn't seem to have realised the paper has been changed to Landscape (the date and number are in the wrong position). To rectify this:

11. *Right click* on the report tab and choose **Design View**
12. Click on the Date placeholder (where it says = Date()) in the *Report Header* then hold down the **<right arrow>** key to move it to the far right of the (or *drag* it to the right with the mouse)

13. Repeat step 12 for the **Time** and **Page Number** placeholders, moving the latter to the centre
14. *Next, click* on the **Count(*)** placeholder in the *Report Footer* and **<Delete>** it
15. *Right click* on the report tab again and choose **Print Preview** to check your changes
16. Finally, close the report (click on the **[Close]** button) and, when asked, **[Save]** it as **HoR**

With AutoReport, you have no say in the way the report is produced. By using the *Report Wizard* instead, however, you can set various other options (as you found with the *Form Wizard*). You'll look at this next.

Using Report Wizards

To demonstrate the Report Wizard, you are going to produce a report listing the students by their hall of residence, with the hall address only appearing once for each group of students. You'll see how, at each step of the wizard, you have control over which fields appear and also over the layout of the report:

1. Click on the **Addresses** query in the *Objects* list
2. Move to the **Create** tab and click on **[Report Wizard]**
3. The *Report Wizard* now goes through six steps:
   a. Move across the fields you want on your report. Here, you just want the **Full Name** and Hall (select each in turn then click on **[>]**) - press **<Enter>** or click on **[Next]**

Importing Data

Access allows you to bring in information from other sources - this is called importing. Databases vary on how they bring in the data and on which sort of files they can import. If you have a really large dataset, it is a good idea to try importing a small section to a new table first and only if that works successfully to try to import it all.

Access can import data in various formats, including Dbase (another widely-used database) and HTML (from web pages). Microsoft Excel spreadsheet files can be imported directly. Here, the data has been saved as *tab separated values*, which is a standard format which any spreadsheet (or indeed word processor) should be able to produce. Other basic formats include *comma separated* values and just plain text. One thing to note when importing a file is that the first line may contain headings - Access has an option to cope with this and can use them for field names.

To *add* the data to an existing table (or create a *new* table) from a file:

1. Move to the **External Data** tab then click on **[Text File]** in the **Import** group
2. Click on **[Browse]** to search for the required file
3. Check that the current directory is set to **Training** on the **D:** drive (if using a lab PC; if not, the file can be downloaded from the WWW via the hyperlink at step 4)
4. Select the file called **halls2010.txt** then press **<Enter>** to **[Open]** it The default is to create a new table, but here:
5. Choose the **Append a copy of the records to the table** option and select **HoR** Click on **[OK]**

6. The *Import Text Wizard* now starts up. This has several stages, as follows:
   a. Choose whether the data is *Delimited* (eg tab, comma or space) or *Fixed Width* (where extra spaces have been used to line up the data in columns) - press **<Enter>** or click on **[Next>]** for *Delimited*
   b. Choose the delimiter (here, Tab is correctly chosen) and whether or not the *First Row Contains* Field Names (**here, it does, so click to set it**) - press **<Enter>** for **[Next]**

Tip:

If you are adding to an existing table and the first row doesn't match the table field names then import them as an extra record, which you later delete

   c. The final step of the wizard confirms the table name (or asks you for a one if creating a new table) - press **<Enter>** for **[Finish]**
   d. Don't bother saving the import steps – press **<Esc>** for **[Close]**

You should have imported 11 new records – if a message appears press **<Enter>** for **[OK]** to cancel it.

7. *Double click* on the **HoR** table in the *Objects* list to see the new records
8. Resize the columns by *double clicking* on the column heading dividers
9. End by closing the table - click on its **[Close]** button, saving the changes to the layout of the table (press **<Enter>** for **[Yes]**)
Note: you can also export data from Access for another package via the Export buttons on the External Data tab. Amongst the formats available are *Excel, Word and Text File* (suitable for many applications, including SAS, SPSS and Mini tab).

To demonstrate the Report Wizard, you are going to produce a report listing the students by their hall of residence, with the hall address only appearing once for each group of students. You'll see how, at each step of the wizard, you have control over which fields appear and also over the layout of the report:

1. Click on the **Addresses** query in the *Object* list.
2. Move to the **Create** tab and click on **[Report Wizard]**
3. *The Report Wizard* now goes through six steps:
   a. Move across the fields you want on your report. Here, you just want the **FullName** and **Hall** (select each in turn then click on **[>]**) - press **<Enter>** or click on **[Next>]**
   b. Step two allows you to set grouping levels. You only need a list of names for each hall, so move across Hall (using **[>]**) then press **<Enter>** or click on **[Next>]**
   c. Sort by: **FullName** (*Ascending*) - press **<Enter>** or click on **[Next>]**
   d. Choose a *Layout*: **Outline** is fine - press **<Enter>** or click on **[Next>]**
   e. Choose a *Style* for your report (or, better still, **None**) - press **<Enter>** or click on **[Next>]**
   f. Call your report **Addresses** - press **<Enter>** or click on **[Finish]**
      The resultant report may not be exactly what you want but it's easier to modify the design than to create one from scratch.
4. Right click on the report tab and choose **Design View**

5. Widen the *FullName* field by clicking on the box in the *Detail* and dragging the right border to the right
6. Minimise the height of the *Detail* by positioning the mouse on the border between it and the *Page Footer* and dragging it up a little
7. Next, click on the **[Property Sheet]** button – every object on a Report (or Form) has properties
8. Click on the **Hall** label on the left and, on the Format tab, set the **Visible property** to No
9. Repeat step **8** for the **FullName** label in the

Detail section To force each hall onto a separate page:

10. Click on the **Hall Header** and set **Force New** to **Before Section** then **[Close]** the Property *Sheet*
11. Finally, right click and choose **Print Preview** to see the changes you have made
12. Click on the window's **[Close]** button, saving the changes to the design of the report next, try using a special wizard to generate address labels for the students.
13. Click on the Addresses query in the Objects list
14. Move to the Create tab and click on **[Labels]**
15. The Label Wizard now goes through five steps:

    a. Setup the size for your labels - check Filter by manufacturer: is set to Avery, change the Units of Measure to English and select 5160 as the Product number: - press **<Enter>** or click on **[Next>]**

    b. Setup the Font name and Font size etc which you require (here leave them as they are) - press **<Enter>**or click on **[Next>]**

    c. Move the fields across to a Prototype Label by clicking on the arrow provided:
        - move across FullName then press **<Enter>**
        - move across Hall then press **<spacebar>** and type Hall - press **<Enter>**
        - move across Road - press **<Enter>**
        - move across Town - click on **[Next>]**

    d. Sort by: Hall and then Full Name- press **<Enter>** or click on **[Next>]**

    e. Call your report Labels Addresses - press **<Enter>** or click on **[Finish]**

16. Press **<Enter>** (for **[OK]**) to cancel the warning message
17. View the report then click on its **[Close]** button to close it

Tip:

Getting Access reports looking exactly the way you want can be very time-consuming. It maybe easier to do the formatting in Excel or Word. On the External Data tab, the [Excel] button lets you send data to an Excel spreadsheet, while the [Word] button creates a Rich TextFormat (.rtf) file. Using the [More] button you can export in various other formats or carry out a mail merge in Microsoft Word.

Leaving ACCESS

You should now be back at the *Navigation Pane*, where you could continue to work on the students database, adding further tables and queries and producing more reports. When you have completely finished your work:

1. Click on the **[Office Button]** and choose **Close Database**

    This closes any opened tables etc. and ensures that the database file is properly shut down. You could now go on to use or create another database, but the course is now over so

2. Click on the **[Office Button]** and choose **Exit ACCESS**

3. Finally, on the public machines, don't forget to **Log Off**

SECTION 7
PROBLEM SOLVING AND PROGRAM DESIGN

There are always problems which confront us in our daily undertakings. The smartest way to get out of a problem is to find a solution for it.

Problems can manifest in many forms. Sometimes, they arise out of bad decisions; most other times, these problems are circumstantial. When problems are circumstantial, it means that there is no fault of ours but still a problem is a problem. So, when we encounter a problem, how do we approach it? How do we solve it? Let us consider a simple scenario for example. We are given a mathematical problem to solve. What do we do here?

The **first step in any problem solving procedure is to define the problem**. In this scenario, we state word to word what the question demands - we **define what the problem is**.

The next step is For to **analyze the problem**. This means we understand what we have stated. For example, in this scenario, we understand what the question is, we note down the data that is given to us, and then we look at how this data is going to be used in solving a problem. Once this data is assimilated, we need to **process it** and every process requires a step-by-step execution.

However, we must remember that there are many possible solutions to a given problem. For example, consider the mathematics problem we have been given. The textbook book is just one possible way of solving the problem. If we search anywhere else, we may find other ways to do the same thing. How then do we decide which way is the best way to deal with the problem? The answer is simple. We analyze which solution is difficult for us to understand. Sometimes, a textbook solution would be the one we fail to understand.

However, we may find some other way which would seem easier to us than the one we have been taught in the classroom. Once we find the easier way, we choose that solution. Once we have chosen the way, we solve the problem. Use the data in the way that is required. Once done, we verify whether the result is what is expected by the teacher. If it is, then we know that we have committed no mistakes. The same concept applies to every mundane activity of our life. **Problem-solving** is an art but it also requires a **logical mind**.

PROBLEM SOLVING USING COMPUTERS

Computers were invented to supplement the human mind. A computer is faster, more efficient, and less prone to errors. Not to mention, it is versatile.

STEPS IN PROBLEM SOLVING

Step 1: Define the problem

The first step is to be clear on what we want. So, define the problem. If there is no clear and concise definition of the problem we are about to solve then there can be no possible solution. Everything will be murky and chaotic.

For example: Problem: An array is given to us with as many as ten elements. We are required to find a specific element within the array and display its position. Now that we have defined the problem, let us now go to the next step.

Step 2: Analyze the problem

The next step is to analyze the problem. Here we see what data we have been given and how we can use that data to achieve the goal.

Data: The ten elements in the array and the element we require to be searched.

Step 3: Find possible solutions and choose the best solution

The next step is to source out possible solutions, evaluate them and then choose the best solution. To choose a solution for a problem we are going to solve using computers, we need to look at the complexity of the solution. This is done by using the Big O Notation. The Big O notation analyses the solution by predicting how much memory the solution will use and how much faster the solution will compute.

Solution:

We find that there are two possible ways to search for an element in an array. They are:
1.   Linear Search
2.   Binary Search

So we have come across two search methods. Depending on complexity analysis, we choose a solution. For many, linear search would be an easier way of searching through the array.

Step 4: Create algorithm

Now that we have chosen our solution, we will now create a way to implement this in the form of an algorithm.

An algorithm is a step by step method of performing calculations and operations. Algorithms are used in:
- Calculation
- Data Processing
- Automated Reasoning

An algorithm is an effective way and consists of well-defined instructions. The process of creating an algorithm involves three stages:
  1. Determining the input data.
  2. Processing the input.
  3. Giving or "outputting" the processed input.

Input. This is data that needs to be entered by the user in order to solve the problem.Input data is known by the user, hence something which is unknown and is to be determined through processing, cannot be part of the input.

How do I look for the input?

(a) Check for key words or phrases e.g. **read, enter, accept, prompt the user** etc.
(b) Determine whether the processing or the output is dependent on an input. If so, then the input is necessary. If an input is required, count the number of different input entities and determine whether an entity has to be entered more than once. Assign a **variable** name to each type of input.

> **Processing.** This involves
>   - calculations
>   - repeating program instructions and
>   - selecting segments of the program at times.

How do I know if calculations are required?

a) Check for the key phrases such as **calculate, percentages, discounts, Totals and averages, counting values - determine the number of times, determine the frequency etc.**

b) Check for the need to **add, subtract, divide** and/or **multiply.**

N.B. These calculations may be implied by the output that is required.
> **Output.** This is information that will be generated as a result of

i. solving the problem

ii. Or it may be messages - called prompts that appear on the screen to facilitate processing.

Example:

1. Write a program that <u>prompts</u> the user for <u>three numbers</u> and *outputs* the *sum* of *these numbers*. (Note that the keywords in the question are underlined)

Analysis

Code:

What is the input?	Processing:	What is the output?
three numbers - stored in the variables Num1, Num2 and Num3.	Input values Calculation: the sum i.e. add A, B and C Output results	sum of the numbers inputted - stored in the variable Sum.

Print "Enter the first number"   {Prompt the user}
Read Num1   {Input values into the program}
Print "Enter the second number"   {Prompt the user}
Read Num2   {Input values into the program}
Print "Enter the third number"   {Prompt the user}
Read Num3   {Input values into the program}
Sum = Num1 + Num2 + Num3   {Processing or calculation statement}
Print "The sum of the three numbers is ", Sum   {Statement and output}

Characteristics of an algorithm:

We should take care of the following characteristics before getting to designing any algorithm:

1. **Finiteness:** An algorithm must end after a finite number of steps. Each step of an algorithm must only take a measurable amount of time.

2. **Definiteness:** Each step must be precisely defined. The action must be rigorous and unambiguous for every case of input data.

3. **Input:** An algorithm can have zero input. It can also have one or more inputs but the number has to be a finite number.

4. **Output:** An algorithm can have one or more outputs. However, the requirement of one output is compulsory. Zero output means we cannot know the solution provided by the algorithm.

5. **Effectiveness:** An algorithm should be effective. Each operation performed in an algorithm must be basic and simple.

Step 5: Test and Validate the Algorithm

Once we have created the algorithm, we manually work for logic and consistency. We want to know whether the algorithm we have created is giving the result we require. In our scenario, we want to know whether the element we want searched in an array is really being returned.

Testing the algorithm is done by creating test cases. Test cases include sample data which we assign to the elements of an algorithm and check it by manually tracing through it to see if the resultant output is what we require.

Step 6: Implement the algorithm in a programming language

The next step is we convert this algorithm into a coded language. The language is chosen depending upon the environment the program is going to be used and many other factors. When an algorithm is written in a programming language, the result is called as a program.

Examples of programming languages include C, Pascal, C++, Java, etc.

Step 7: Run the program

The program, once written, is now sent to a compiler. A compiler is a system software which converts the program written in a programming language into an executable file which can then be run.

Step 8: Document and maintain the program

Documentation of a program is very important. There are two kinds of documentation:

1. External Documentation: Involves user manuals, etc.

2. Internal Documentation: Involves comments, etc.

IPO Diagrams:

IPO is an acronym for **Input-Process-Output**. These diagrams find usage in the analysis of a problem. It is a functional model and acts like a conceptual schema of a general system. This diagram helps in the identification of the inputs given to an algorithm, the outputs generated by the algorithm and the process required to convert the input into the refined output.

Input	Process	Output

BASIC ELEMENTS OF AN ALGORITHM

Variables

A **variable** is a name associated with a **particular location in memory** used to **store data**. Variable names should be meaningful. Examples: arg, firstname, sum.

Some variables are reserved by the software used to write the program and hence cannot be used.

Data Type

A variable has the ability to store different types of data.

There are four important data types that we must know about:

1. Long (integer, number with no decimal point)
2. Double (real number, number with decimal point)
3. String (text)
4. Boolean (true or false)

Declaring Variables

We declare variables in order to reserve space for the data in the memory unit and to inform the computer system what kind of data will be stored.

Initializing a variable

Variables have to be initialized so it gets the correct starting variable. However, it is not compulsory for all variables.

Example: Sum:=0, Counter:=0.

Constants

Constants are usually fixed values. Examples: 5, 'abc', etc. They are normally assigned to variables or used in computational operations.

Literals:
A literal is a notation for representing a constant in the source code of a programming language or an algorithm. They are often used to initialize variables.
For example:
Int a = 1;
A:=1;

Ways to Represent Algorithms

There are many ways to represent algorithms. However, these four are the most prominent:

1. Narrative
2. Pseudocode
3. Flowchart
4. Data Flow Diagrams

Narrative

A narrative is a way of representing an algorithm in precise English language. For example, let us consider doing a linear search for an array:

Narrative Example for linear search:

1. Declare Array A of type Integer with 10 elements.
2. Declare Num and found of type Integer.
3. Declare counter I of type Integer and initialize to 0.
4. While I is less than 10, read array element A [I].
5. Increment I by 1 and goto step 4.
6. Read Num.
7. Initialize I to 0.
8. While I less than 10, perform the following step:
9. If A [I] is equal to Num then Initialize found to 1 otherwise increment I by 1.
10. Goto step 8.
11. If found = 1 print "Element found" otherwise print "Element not found."
12. Stop.

Pseudocode

Pseudocode can be termed as an informal high level description of an algorithm. It uses the same conventions as a computer program but its purpose is to be easily understood by humans rather than a machine. People usually find pseudocode to be easily readable and understandable than programming language code. It follows all the key principles of algorithm design.

Example:

Write a program that will allow *input the name and price* of an item in a supermarket. The program will *calculate* and *output* the *name of the item* and the *newprice* after a 15% discount is given.

224

What is the input?	Processing:	What is the output?
• The name of the item - stored in the variable **Name.**	Calculations: • the discount given - stored in the variable **Discount**.	• The name of the item
• The price of the item - stored in the variable **Price.**	• The discounted price of the item – stored in the variable **NewPrice**	• The discounted price of the item

Pseudocode:

Print "Enter the name of the item"
Read Name
Print "Enter the price of the item"
Read Price
Discount = Price * 0.15
NewPrice = Price – Discount
Print "The name of the item is", **Name**, "and the new price of the item is", NewPrice

1. Write a program that asks the user for her name and gives the response: "<the given name> is a beautiful name."

Plan:

declare the variables
ask for name (input)
give the response (output)
end the program

Code:

var NameGiven: string;
readln(NameGiven);
writeln(NameGiven,' is a beautiful name');
End.

Task 4

2. Write a program that asks the user for her age and responds: —You are only <the age given>! I thought you were at least <the age given + 2>."

Plan:	Code:
declare the variables	var Age,NewAge: Integer;
ask for age (input)	readln(Age);
calculate new age	NewAge = Age + 2
(processing)	Writeln('You are only', +Age+, _
give response (output)	'I thought you were at least' +NewAge+ '.')
	End.

end the program

3. Write a program that asks the user for an amount in CI dollars and outputs the equivalent in US dollars. (NB: To convert CI dollars to US dollars, multiply the CI amount by 1.20.) **Required format of output:** if the amount in CI dollars is 60, then the output would be: "60 CI dollars is equivalent to 72 US dollars."

4. Write an algorithm which prompts the user to enter the price of an item and which calculates and prints the new price after a discount of 12%.

5. Write a program that asks for the radius of a circle and prints out the area and circumference. Note that area = pi * r * r, circumference = 2 * pi * r and pi = 3.14159. Required format of output if the radius is 5: "The area is 78.53975 and the circumference is 31.4159 when the radius is 5."

6. Write a program that first asks for the first name and then asks for the last name of the user. The program should print out the last name followed by a comma, a space and the first name. So, if the user type "Elvis" and "Presley", the program should output "Presley, Elvis".

7. A certain account at a bank earns compound interest on a yearly basis, and has no deposits or withdrawals. The balance after a year has passed is given by the formula: This Year's Balance = Last Year's Balance * $(1 + \text{Interest Rate})^N$, where Interest Rate is given as a decimal fraction. (For example, 25% must be entered as 0.25.)

Write a structured algorithm to do the following:
(a) Request the user to provide the interest rate as a decimal, the number of years to compute interest for, and the starting balance.
(b) Read in the interest rate R, and the value N which is the number of years to compute interest for.
(c) Read in the starting balance.
(d) Compute and display the balance, including the interest, after N years have passed.

8. Write pseudo code to interchange the values in two variables A and B.

9. Write a program that asks the user for her first name, age, favourite colour and favourite food. The program should output a full sentence on this form "I agree with you Susan, blue is a beautiful colour. When I was 17 I ate a lot of pizza too."

Selection/Decision Statement

Example of a Selection or decision statement:

IF statement
- A statement for testing conditions to allow for decision making. The IF statement conditionally executes a statement based upon the truth value of a condition.

The **IF** part is executed if the condition (*information that should be kept in mind when making a decision*) is true, the **ELSE** part (*if present*), is executed if the condition is *false*.

In programming, conditions are written as Mathematical expressions. See table below.

Condition	Mathematical Expression
Single Conditions A is greater than B price is less than or equal to 25.00	A > B price <– 25.00
Multiple conditions First name is equal to John and age is less than 17 Mark is between 50 and 80	FirstName = "John" and Age <17 Mark > 50 and Mark < 80

Format: this form of the IF statement is used when the problem definition gives two distinct options to choose from.

Note that:

IF <condition> **THEN**
      Option 1 (program statements)
Statements are executed when the given condition is **true.**
ELSE
      Option2 (program statements)
Statements are executed when the given condition is **false.**
ENDIF

Example 1:
Write a program which accepts the price of an item. The program should calculate and print the discounted price of the item. A **15% discount is given for prices above $100.00 and a 10% discount for all other prices.**

Analysis:

INPUT	PROCESSING	OUTPUT
Price of an item (to be stored in the variable Price)	1. **Two** choices are presented implying that an IF statement is required. The **condition** for selection is: **Prices above $100.00 i.e. Price > 100.00; Price > 100, 15% discount given;Other prices, 10% discount given;** 2. Calculate the discounted price	Discounted price of the item (to be stored in a variable called **DiscountPrice**)

Solution written in pseudocode:

Writeln („The price of the item after discount is', DiscountPrice);
ReadIn (Price);

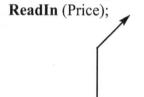

Condition

IF Price > 100.00   **THEN**
          Discount := Price * 0.15
ELSE
          Discount := Price * 0.10
ENDIF
DiscountPrice := Price - Discount;

WriteIn('The price of the item after discount is', DiscountPrice);

Example 2

A bonus of $1500.00 is given to employees who were absent for less than 4 days in a year. The bonus is added to the salary to arrive at the total income. Read the days absent and salary and output the employee's income.

Analysis

INPUT	PROCESSING	OUTPUT
1. Number of days absent (to be stored in the variable called **DaysAbsent**) 2. Salary of the employee (stored in a variable called **Salary**)	1. IF statement: The **condition** for selection is: Days absent less than 4 **DaysAbsent < 4, bonus given;** **Otherwise, no bonus given** 2. Calculate the Total Income	1. The employee's income (stored in a variable called **Income**)

Solution written in pseudocode:

Writeln ('Enter the salary of the employee');
Readln (Salary);
Writeln ('Enter the number of days absent');
Readln (DaysAbsent);

Condition

     IF (DaysAbsent < 4) **THEN**

             Income := Salary + Bonus
     ELSE
             Income := Salary
     ENDIF

     writeln('The employee's income is', Income);

Note that if more than two options are given, then we can use a combination of **IF** statements called **embedded IF statements (to be discussed)**.

Programming Worksheet

Topic: Selection/decision statements

1. So far we have looked at three program statements. One of them is an input statement.
Identify the other two.

1. _____

2. _____

2. Program statements can be categorized into one of the following groups: input; process; output; For each of the following statements, identify its category:

Statement	Category
Writeln(Newprice);	
A = 2 * P + Q	
Readln(Score);	
Discount := Price * 0.5	

3. Write the condition for the following statements:

• A day is considered hot when the temperature is above 32°C and normal otherwise. Output the appropriate message.

_____

• Output the message tall for boys with heights of at least 5'9".

_____

4. Write the selection statement for the following scenario:

• If A is bigger than B, output the difference between A and B. In all other cases, output the sum of A and B

5. Write the analysis and algorithms (in pseudocode) to solve the following problems:-

A credit union pays 4% interest on shares that are greater than $25,000.00 and 3% on all other shares. No interest is paid on deposits.
a)   Read a share and a deposit.
b)   Calculate the interest amount
c)   Calculate the total savings (**total savings := shares + deposit +interest amount**).
d)   Output the interest amount and total savings.

Analysis:

Inputs:	Processing:	Outputs:

Write Pseudocode for the algorithm below.

_____

_____

_____

_____

_____

_____

_____

_____

_____

_____

_____

_____

Analysis:

Inputs:	Processing:	Outputs:

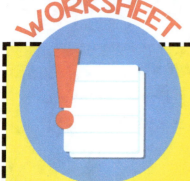

2. Input the mark that a student obtained for each of three subjects. If the average mark is less than 60, output "fail" otherwise output "pass".

Pseudocode:

_____

_____

_____

_____

_____

_____

_____

_____

3. Read the quantity sold and unit price for an item and the money received. Calculate the total cost. If the money received is greater than or equal to the total cost, output the amount of money due to the customer. Otherwise, output the comment "Account receivable".

Inputs:	Processing:	Outputs:

Pseudocode:

Concepts you should know in order to do the tasks that follow: logical terms, logical expressions, if-then-else-endif, if-then-elseif-elseif-else-endif, indenting if-statements.

1. Write a program that asks the user for his name and gives the response "David is a beautiful name" if the name is "David" and otherwise gives the response "X is an ugly name", where X is the name given.

Plan:	Code:
Declare variables	var NameGiven: string;
	Begin
Input name	readln(NameGiven);
	If NameGiven = "David" then
Compare input with "David"	Writeln(NameGiven, 'is a beautiful name')
If same as David	Else
print "input" is a beautiful name	Writeln(NameGiven, 'is an ugly name')
Otherwise	Endif
print "input" is an ugly name"	End;
End program	

2. Write a pseudocode algorithm to read two numbers and print the lower value. (Assume the numbers are not equal)

3. Write a structured algorithm to read in two numbers and print the higher value. (Assume the numbers are not equal)

4. Write an algorithm to read in TWO numbers into A and B. The algorithm should store the smaller in A and the larger in B, and then print A and B. (5 marks)

5. Write an algorithm to read an integer value for SCORE and print the appropriate grade based on the following:

SCORE	GRADE
80 or more	A
less than 80 but 65 or more	B
less than 65 but 50 or more	C
less than 50	

Write a program that asks the user for the capital of Venezuela. If the right answer is given, it should respond: "Yes, you are right! Caracas is the capital of Venezuela." If the answer is wrong, it should say: "No X is not the capital of Venezuela." where X is the answer given.

Programming

Task 2

1. A hired car is charged at $25.00 per mile for the first 100 miles and $10.00 for the rest, plus a fixed charge of $17.75. Write a structured algorithm which prompts the user to input the distance traveled. The program should calculate and print the total charge.

2. Write an algorithm to read the amount of sales made by a salesman. He is paid $500.00 plus a commission of 10% of sales. Calculate his commission and output his sales, commission and total pay.

3. Write an algorithm which prompts the user to input the length and width of a room. Calculate and print the total cost of carpeting the room. One square metre of carpet costs $45.00.

4. Write a structured algorithm which prompts the user to input two numbers which are stored in A and B. If B is 0, output the message - You cannot divide by zero‖, otherwise divide A by B and output the result.

5. An examination consists of two papers. A student fails if his or her percentage for either paper is less than 50. It should output the information with the words "Pass" or "Fail" as appropriate.

6. Write a structured algorithm which prompts the user to enter the price of an item and the discount percentage given on the item. The program should print the discounted price of the item.

7. Write a structured algorithm which prompts the user to input two unequal numbers which are stored in A and B. It should subtract the smaller number from the bigger number and print the result.

8. Write a structured algorithm which prompts the user to input two unequal numbers which are stored in A and B. The algorithm should store the larger number in A and print both A and B with suitable comments.

9. Write a structured algorithm which prompts the user to input two unequal numbers which are stored in A and B. The algorithm should print the smaller number.

Programming

Research and answer the following questions in the space provided.

1.   Explain the following terms:
        (a) Compiler

        _____
        _____
        _____

        (b) Source Code

        _____
        _____
        _____

        (c) Object Code

        _____
        _____
        _____

2.   What is produced as a result of the compilation process?

        _____
        _____
        _____

3.   Name two programming languages that have to be compiled before the code can be executed.

        _____

4.   State one benefit of the compilation process.

        _____
        _____
        _____

LOOP STRUCTURES

There are times when writing programs, that we want the computer to execute a set of statement several times. To do this, we need a loop structure to instruct the computer
- what to repeat and
- how often to repeat these steps

There are basically two types of loop structures/statements

Note: *Use this statement when the problem that you are solving gives a condition for stopping/ terminating the repetitions.*

I. The WHILE Statement
- Executes a series of statements as long as a given condition is True.

Format of the while statement:	Explanation of terms: condition
While <condition> do begin } Program statements END	an expression that evaluates to **True** or **False** **Program statements** One or more statements that can be executed *while the condition is* **True**

How does the while statement work?

When a while statement is encountered by the computer, it checks the truth value of the condition. If condition is True, all program statements (as shown above) are executed until the End (endwhile) statement is encountered. Control then returns to the While statement and condition is again checked. If condition is still True, the process is repeated. If it is not True, execution resumes with the statement following the end statement.

Example 1:
Write a program to input a set of prices. The list will stop <u>when the user enters -1</u>.

Solution:

Writeln ('Enter the price of the item');
Readln (Price);
WHILE Price <> -1 do begin
        Writeln ('Enter the price of the i tem');
        Readln (Price);
END;

Terminating condition

238

The following examples illustrate use of the While statement:

Write a program that accepts the price of a set of items <u>terminated by an entry of 9999</u>. The program output the total price paid by the customer. It should also output the highest price entered.

```
Writeln('Enter the price of the items');  }Input the first item in the list
Readln(Item);
Largest := Price; -------------------- }Initialize variable - gives the variable a starting value
Sum := 0;        -------------------- } Initialize variable sum
WHILE price < > 9999 DO
       Begin
                     Sum := Sum + Price           }Accumate te total/sum
These steps are    IF Price > Largest  THEN
repeated until     ENDIF
9999 is entered    Readln(Price);                }Input the next item in the list

              END;                        }Ends while loop when Price = 9999
       Writeln('The largest value in the list is', Largest, 'and the total is', sum);
```

Example 3:

Write a program that accepts the mark a student got in five subject areas.
The program should output the average mark obtained by the student.

```
       Counter := 0                          {Initialize variable.}
       Sum := 0

       While  Counter < 5 do begin           {Test value of Counter.}
              Writeln('Enter the mark');
              Readln(mark);

              Readln(Mark);                   {Input an item in the list.}
                     Counter = Counter + 1;   {Increments the Counter.}
                     Sum := Sum + Mark;       {Adds the marks.}

       End;                                   {End While loop when Counter = 5.}
       Average := Sum/ Counter;
       Writeln('The average score obtained by the student is', Average);
```

2. FOR Statement

Repeats a group of statements a specified number of times.
Use this statement when you are told exactly how many repetitions there are.

Format	Terminology
	counter
	Numeric variable used as a loop counter. The variable can't be an array element or an element of a user-defined type.
For *counter* = *start* **To** *end*	
	start
[Program statements]	Initial value of *counter*.
	end
End;{ Endfor)	Final value of *counter*.
	statements
	One or more statements between **For** and **End {Endfor}** that are executed the specified number of times

Comments:

Once the loop starts and all statements in the loop have executed, the counter is increased by 1. At this point, either the statements in the loop execute again (based on the same test that caused the loop to execute initially), or the loop is exited and execution continues with the statement following the **Next** statement. **Note** Changing the value of counter while inside a loop can make it more difficult to read and debug your code.

Example 1
Write a program that accepts the mark a student got in five subject areas.
The program should output the average mark obtained by the student.

```
Sum := 0                          {Initialize variable.}
For Counter = 1 To 5 Do begin     {Increment and Test value of Counter.}

    Writeln('Enter the mark');
    Readln(Mark)   {Input an item in the list.}

    Sum := Sum + Mark             {Adds the marks.}
    Sum := 0
    For counter = 1 To 5 Do

End;   {Ends For loop when Counter = 5.}

Average := Sum / counter

Writeln('The average score obtained by the student is', Average);
```

Definite Loop) For Next Loop	In Pascal you can find the sum of the first 100 numbers like this: Sum := 0 For Counter := 1 to 100 do begin Sum = Sum + Counter End; Writeln('The sum of the first 100 numbers is', Sum);

While loop	In Pascal you can ask the name of students in a class in a while loop:
	Sum := 0
	Readln(number);
	While number <> 999 do begin
	     Sum := Sum + number
	     Readln(number);
	End;
	Writeln('The sum of the first 100 numbers is', Sum);

logical operators and statements	<> stands for not equal to, >= stands for greater or equal to Example of a logical statement (a sentence that is either true or false): FirstName = "John" and (Age <> 37 or Hobby = "Sailing)

1. **Write a program the calculates and prints the square of the first five integers.**

Pseudocode:

12 *Begin*
    Counter = 0

    While counter < 5 **do**
    Square = counter ^ 2
    Counter = counter + 1

Endwhile

End

9
10
11
12
13
14 Pascal

Counter := 0; ' **Initialize variable.**

While Counter < 20 do begin **'Test value of Counter.**
    square := Counter ^ 2;
    writeln('the square of', Counter, 'is',square); **'Outputs the square**
    Counter = Counter + 1; ' Increment Counter to go to the next integer.
End;   ' **End While loop when Counter => 20.**

2.   **Write a program the reads a list of numbers terminated by an entry of -1 and prints the average and sum of the list.**

```
Begin
    Sum = 0 Counter = 0
    Print " Enter a number",
    Read number
    While number < > -1 do
            Sum = Sum + number
            Counter = Counter + 1
            Print "Enter a number",
            Read number
            End while
    Average = Sum / Counter
    Print "The sum of the numbers entered is", Sum
    Print "The average of the numbers entered is", Average
End;
```

Programming

Topic: Loops, IF statements, finding the maximum and minimum value in a list.

Task 4

Maximum and minimum using the **FOR** loop

1. Write a program that will accept a list of ten scores. The program should print out the maximum score.

2. Write a program that will accept a list of fifteen temperatures occurring during the month of May. The program should print out the minimum temperature for that month.

3. Write a program that will accept a list of twenty scores for the students in a class. The program should print out the maximum and minimum scores obtained by the students.

4. Write a program that will accept the price of fifteen items from supermarket and output the lowest price entered. The program should also output the total price of the items entered.

Maximum and minimum using the **WHILE** loop

1. Write a program that will accept a list of scores terminated by an entry of 999. The program should print out the maximum score in the list.

2. Write a program that will accept a set of temperatures occurring during the month of May. The list is terminated by an entry of –1. The program should print out the minimum temperature for that month.

3. Write a program that will accept a set of scores terminated by an entry of 9999 for the students in a class. The program should print out the maximum and minimum scores obtained by the students.

4. Write a program that will accept a set price of items from supermarket and output the lowest price entered. The list is terminated when the price –1 is entered. The program should also output the total price of the items entered.

Task

1. Write an algorithm that reads one hundred numbers and finds their sum.

2. Write an algorithm to read a sequence of numbers terminated by 0 and print their sum. It should also print the amount of numbers entered.

Task 5

3. Write an algorithm to read a sequence of numbers terminated by 999. The algorithm should count and print the number of negative values (i.e. values less than zero) and the number of zero values.

4. Write an algorithm to read the name and test scores for ten students. Each student does three tests. The algorithm must print the name of the student along with his/her average score.

5. Write an algorithm to read a set of integers terminated by 0 and print their average.

6. Write an algorithm to read a sequence of numbers terminated by 999 and print
    a. the sum of the positive numbers
    b. the sum of the negative numbers and
    c. the product of the sums.

7. The following data represent some sample scores obtained by students in a test:
    5, 4, 7, 10. 0, 6, 0, 1, 9, 8, 999
    999 is a the dummy value which terminates the data. Write an algorithm to read any data in the above format and print the number of students scoring 0 and the number scoring 10.

8. Write an algorithm to read a sequence of fifteen numbers and pint the sum of all the even numbers.

9. Write an algorithm to read the names of a sequence of products and their price. The data terminates when a 0 price is entered for a product. Print the number of items purchased and the grand total.

FLOW CHARTS

What is a Flow chart?

Step-form and pseudocode program designs are both text- based, the statements are written. Flow charts are a graphical method of designing programs and once the rules are learned are very easy to draw. A well-drawn flow chart is also very easy to read since it basically uses just two symbols, two decision constructs. and two iteration constructs: the sequence symbol, the decision symbol, the decision construct if ... then the decision construct if ... then ... else the repetition construct - repeat, the repetition construct - while, there are other symbols but the real work is depicted by the two symbols and the constructs. This shouldn't come as a surprise since in the step-form and pseudocode that is what you have been learning.

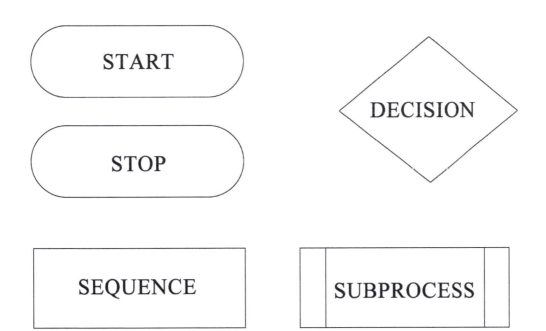

The language of flow charts

The major symbols are the **DECISION** (also known as selection) and the **SEQUENCE** (or process) symbols. The **START** and **STOP** symbols are called the terminals. The **SUBPROCESS** symbol is a variation on the sequence symbol. There are also connectors drawn between the symbols and you will see these used in the examples below. There is at least one other sequence symbol which is used to represent input/output processes but I think it is unnecessary so I don't use it. There are some important rules concerning the symbols and these rules apply also to other ways of stating algorithms: Processes have only one entry point and one exit point. Decisions have only one entry point, one **TRUE** exit point and one **FALSE** exit point. Repeat loop. Note that the repeat loop has the process preceding the decision. This means that a repeat loop will always execute the process part at least once. This is an important point to remember because it may not be what you want to do. For instance are world powers in control of nuclear weapons and have written a launch missiles in the event of an program contains a loop which assume you arsenal of program to attack. You launch a missile each time you are struck by an enemy missile, for example:

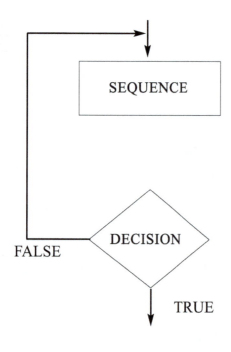

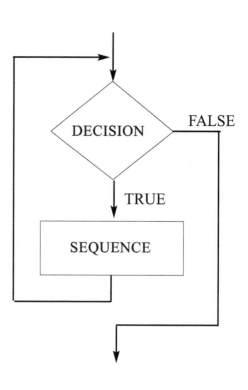

Repeat Launch Missile Until Enemy Stops

Is a repeat loop a good idea in this case? Probably not since, if we assume you are not under attack and you run the program, the repeat loop executes the process at least once and you will probably start the next world war. A while loop would be a safer and more humane choice **While loop**. The while loop is basically the reverse of the repeat loop, the decision comes first, followed by the process. The while loop is usually written so that it iterates while the condition is true, the repeat iterates until the condition becomes true.

An interesting question is: When should a repeat loop be used rather than a while loop? and vice-versa. The while loop should be used when it is possible that the process or processes which are in the scope of the decision (that is, in the loop) may not need to execute.

For example assume you have a designed an air-conditioner controller program and the program turn on the compressor while the ambient temperature is above the desired temperature.

A while loop is a good choice here since the ambient temperature may be at the desired level before the compressor part of the program is executed.

If a repeat loop was used then the compressor would be turned on but it wouldn't be necessary. That would be wickedly ignorant of green sensitivities.

A repeat loop would be a good candidate for the kind of situation in which a program needs to check for an external event at least once.

For example: assume you have now written a program for a video cassette recorder and it has a menu for doing things like tuning TV channels, setting the date and time, programming events and so on. When the menu is displayed it is a **QUIT** option along with all the others, the VCR doesn't know which option will be chosen so it stays in the menu mode, that is repeats it, until **QUIT** is selected.

The IF ... THEN construct is shown here and is also known as the NULL ELSE, meaning that there is no ELSE part. I have use lines with arrow-heads (connectors) to indicate the flow of sequence. Although this is important in flow charts once you have gained some skill in using them and if you draw them carefully you will find that determining the sequence is straight forward. A typical rule is to use arrow-heads on connectors where flow direction may not be obvious.

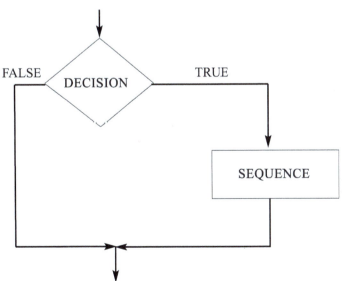

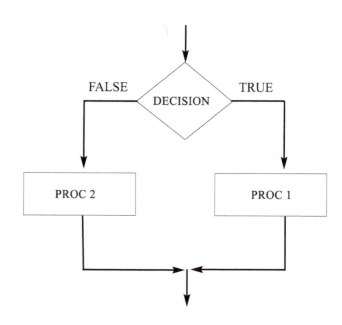

The IF ... THEN ... ELSE ... Construct has a process at each branch of the decision symbol. The only difference here is that each value of the decision (TRUE/FALSE) has a process associated with it.

Using flow charts to design programs

With other topics I've explained the use of technique with an example. There is something of a precedent there. This flow chart example uses all the symbols except the sub process symbol. The algorithm sums all the even numbers between 1 and 20 inclusive and then displays the sum. It uses a repeat loop and contains a null else within the repeat loop.

The equivalent pseudocode is: sum = 0
count = 1
REPEAT
IF count is
even THEN
sum = sum + count
count = count + 1
UNTIL count > 20
DISPLAY sum

You can see quite clearly from this example what the price of flow charting is. There is quite a bit of drawing to do in addition to writing the legend in the symbols. The pseudocode is quite simple by comparison so why would you use flow charts?

The major reasons are that the flow chart. is easier to read more closely follows a standard, this is not the case with pseudocode probably lends itself more readily to computer-aided techniques of program design

Some rules for flow charts
Well-drawn flow charts are easy to read. What must you do to draw well-drawn flow charts? Here are a few rules:
• Every flow chart has a START symbol and a STOP symbol
• The flow of sequence is generally from the top of the to the bottom of the page.
• This can vary with loops which need to flow back to an entry point.

- Use arrow-heads on connectors where flow direction may not be obvious.
- There should be only one flow chart per page
- A flow chart on one page should not break and jump to another page
- A page should have a page num,ber and a title
- A flow chart should have no more than around 15 symbols (not including START and STOP)

Exercise 1

Now it's time for you to try your hand at designing a program using a flow chart.
Draw a flow chart and trace table for the following problem:
Fred sells bunches of flowers at the local shopping centre. One day Fred's boss, Joe, tells
Fred that at any time during the day he (Joe) will need to know:
How many bunches of flowers have been sold.
What was the value of the most expensive bunch sold?
What was the value of the least expensive bunch sold?
What is the average value of bunches sold?

Flow charts and sub processes

There is one last topic to do while we are running hot on flow charts - dealing with subprocesses.
Remember that when you studied pseudocode you learned about subprocesses and the benefits of using them. The subprocess is useful because:

- it provides a means of simplifying programs by making common processes available to a wide number of programs.

- it permits the modularisation of complex programs.

- it makes for more reliable programs since once it is shown that a process works then it can be made a subprocess and need not be tested again.

- In flow charts subprocesses are also useful in dealing with the flow charting rule that a flow chart should have no more than 15 or so symbols on a page. Here is an example of the use of subprocesses in flow charts:

This is the main flow chart and it contains two subprocess symbols. Each symbol contains some legend which describes briefly what the subprocess does. Each symbol also contains a reference which indicates where the subprocess flow chart is.

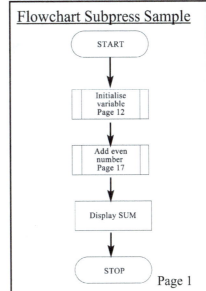

Flowchart Subpress Sample

START

Initialise variable Page 12

Add even number Page 17

Display SUM

STOP

Page 1

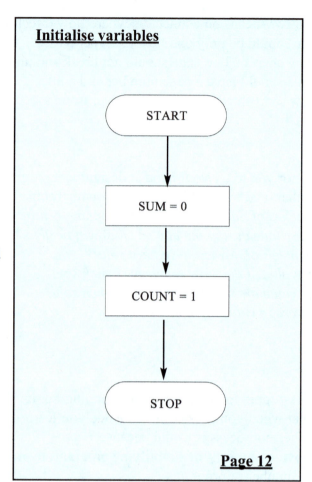

Note that the flow chart has a title and a number and here is 12!

START

SUM = 0

COUNT = 1

STOP

Page 12

Add even number

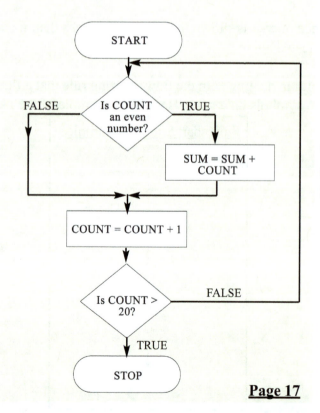

START

FALSE | Is COUNT an even number? | TRUE

SUM = SUM + COUNT

COUNT = COUNT + 1

Is COUNT > 20?

FALSE

TRUE

STOP

The *Add even number* subprocess appears on its own as indicated by the main flow chart on 1.

Page 17

A subprocess flow chart can contain other subprocesses, there is no limit to how deeply these could be nested.

Exercise 2

With your answer for Exercise 1 modify the flow chart so that it has a main flow chart and shows each of the following as subprocess flow charts:

- *the initialisation of the variables*

- *the process or processes for calculating how many bunches of flowers have been sold the process or processes for calculating what was the value of the most expensive bunch sold the process or processes for calculating what was the value of the least expensive bunch sold*

- *the process or processes for calculating what is the average value of bunches sold the display of all the result*

Using nested loops in flow charts

The nested while loop is shown here. This example is much simplified, it doesn't show any initialisation of either of the loops, the outer loop doesn't do any processing apart from the processing the inner loop, neither loop shows any statements which will lead to the termination of the loops.
Each single step through the outer loop will lead to the complete iteration of the inner loop. Assume that the outre loop counts through 10 steps and the inner loop through 100 steps. The sequence in the inner loop will be executed 10 * 100 times. Nested loops will do a lot of work.

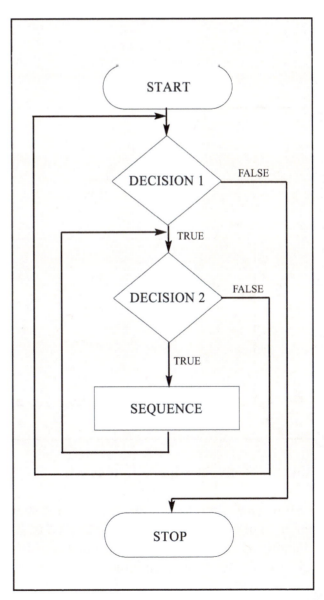

The repeat loop shown here, like the while loop example, is much simplified. It does show two processes, sequence 1 and sequence 2, one process in the outer loop and one process in the inner loop.

Like the while loop the nested repeat loop will see a great deal of work done. If the outer loop does a thousand iterations and the inner loops does a thousand iterations then sequence 2 will be executed 1000 * 1000 times.

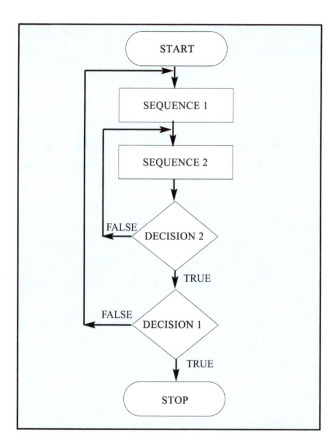

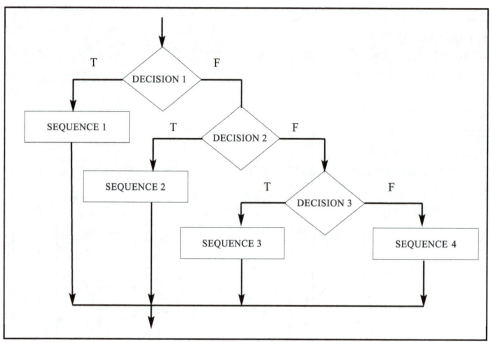

Using multiway selection in flow charts

The flow chart form of multiway selection is shown here. You can see it how it shows quite clearly the notion of decisions nested within decisions. If decision 1 is true then sequence 1 is executed and the multiway selection is finished. If decision 1 is false then decision 2 is tested, if this is true then sequence 2 is done and the multiway selection is finished. If decision 2 is false, you get the picture.

252

Task 6

Assume you have the following data stored somewhere:

Fred, Joan, Brian, Bert, Selie, Sue, Jack, Ng, Jacques, CLASS, Chris, Cheryl, Pam, Allan, CLASS, END

and it represents students in different classes. Design a program using flow charts which:
- reads the data and displays the names of the students in the class
- counts the number of students in each class
- counts the number of classes

Case Study 2: Event Management System:

The system has the following functions:
1.   Maintains Customer details
2.   Maintains Event and Facility details
3.   Maintains Employee information
4.   Handles payments and enquiries
5.   Reports and administration.

Section 8
PROGRAM IMPLEMENTATION

Programming Languages

Programming languages are used to create software/programs which communicate with the computer system. Studying programming languages help us to write and understand programs.

What is a program?

A program is a set of instructions written in a format which follows the rules of a prescribed computer language.

Whenever a program is executed, the computer system will carry out the tasks outlined in the program. To program a computer is to tell it what to do.

A computer is a human's slave - Humans command, the computer obeys.

The person who writes a program is known as a **programmer**. A programmer needs to have key qualities in order to be efficient and successful. Some key qualities of a good programmer are:

1. Must be **curious** to know more about the language and **willing** to go into the depth of the language.
2. Needs to come up with **creative** solutions.
3. Needs to be **bold** in front of the mammoth tasks which will inevitably arise as the programmer learns more.
4. Needs to be **humble**. A programmer needs to know that writing a program is difficult. He/she should accept that fact.
5. Must be **stubborn**. If any error persists, the programmer should not easily give up.
6. Should have a **logical** mind. The ability to reason is a quality which is looked for the most in programmers.

Building a program involves the following steps:

1. The problem is discovered first.
2. A step by step solution is found. In other words, an algorithm is developed.
3. Translate the algorithm into a program written in a suitable computer programming language.
4. Test the program on a computer.
5. If test reveals errors then fix it or improve the solution.
6. Write the user documentation.

What does a good program look like?

- **Easy to use** with limited training and support.
- **Robust** to cope with errors without producing wrong results or stopping.
- **Flexible** so it can be easily customised for use in a
- **Reliable** so it won't stop due to design faults.
- **Portable** so it can be used on different computer hardware.
- **Easily maintained** so errors can be corrected, new modules can be introduced, and performance can be enhanced.

Programming languages are classified into two categories:

1. **High Level Languages:** High level languages are very close to the English language and hence easily understandable. They can be easily debugged and rendered error-free.

2. **Low Level Languages:** They are machine level code and hence understood properly only by the computer system. They are tough to debug. Depending upon the time in which the language was invented, programming languages have been classified into generations.

Programming Language Generations:

Programming instructions are written in accordance with a **programming language** e.g. Visual Basic. Each programming language has its own **rules** and **commands**. A **command** is a word, which tells the computer to perform a specific action. Programming languages are classified as:-

i. Machine language.
ii. Assembly language.
iii. High-level language.
iv. Fourth generation languages.

(a) **Machine language (First generation language)**
A microprocessor can understand only instructions represented by binary digits--machine language. Any instructions issued to a machine, either by the user or a program, must be converted to machine language for execution.

Characteristics of Machine Language:
- Is written using **0s** and **1s** only.
- Programs are **tedious** to write and it is therefore easy for the programmer to make mistakes.

- These programs are machine dependent i.e. they may not work on computers other than those for which they were written.
- Programs execute faster than programs written in other languages.
- The machine/processor understands this language therefore no translation or further coding is required as is the case with other languages.

(b) Assembly language (Second generation language)
- A series of mnemonic statements that can be "assembled" (translated) into low-level machine language using a program called an assembler. This language is fast and efficient, but very difficult to read or write.

Characteristics:
- Is written using short codes (mnemonics) e.g. ADD, STO, SUB.
- Programs are machine dependent i.e. they may not work on computers that they were not specifically written for.
- Programmers have to focus on both machine and software.
- Programs do not execute as fast as machine language programs.
- Translation to machine code is required.

(c)   High-level language(s) (Third generation language)
- Is a machine-independent, procedural language that uses human words and symbols to program diverse computer systems e.g. Cobol, Fortran, Pascal, Basic, C

Characteristics of High Level Language:
- Is **not machine dependent**.
- Use **English like statements**.
- Is **easier** to write than earlier generation languages.
- Were developed with particular objectives in mind:
  - **Cobol** was developed for processing large volumes of data e.g. Billing, accounts, inventory.
  - **Fortran** was developed for solving complex mathematical problems.
  - **Pascal** was developed to assist students in understanding programming.
  - **Basic** was developed for solving math and business problems.
  - **C** was developed for writing operating systems and business software.

(d)   High-level language(s) - Fourth generation language (4GL)
A programming language that contains constructs that allow a programmer to express system logic to a computer system in a manner that is closer to the natural language that he/she uses than earlier generation computer languages. One statement in a fourth generation language such as **Progress** typically corresponds to many lines of code in a third generation language such as C, Cobol or Fortran.

Generally refers to a group of high level languages used primarily for the manipulation of databases. 4GL languages have a syntax mimicking the English language and operate on sets or subsets of data rather than on single elements as do most conventional languages (such as FORTRAN or PASCAL).

(e) Fifth Generation Language

This is commonly abbreviated as 5GL. This language is based on solving problems using the constraints given to a program rather than using an algorithm. This generation of programming languages is designed to let the computer system solve the problem on its own i.e. without a programmer. These languages are mainly used in the field of artificial intelligence and expert systems which heavily use the concept of natural language. Examples include Prolog, OPS5, and Mercury.

Translators

Translation languages convert program commands into machine code. There are two main types of translation languages. These are:

o   Interpreters
o   Compilers

Interpreters convert each instruction into machine code, and then carry them out while **compilers** convert the whole program into machine code before carrying the instructions out. The following diagram shows the relationship among the translators.

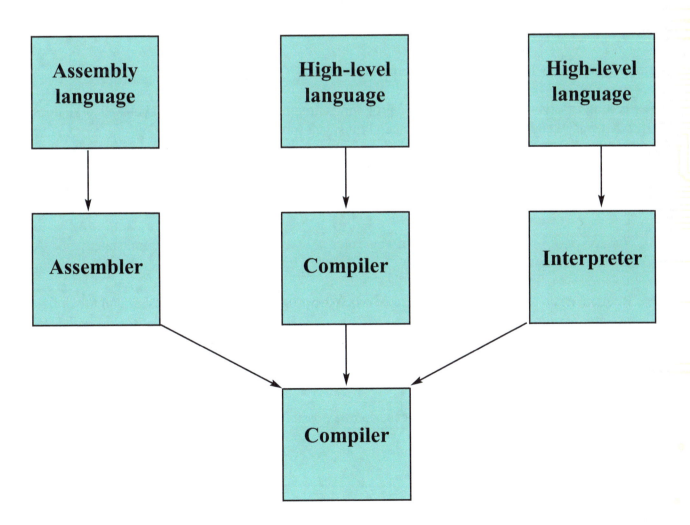

Steps in Implementing a Program

Implementing a program involves certain steps.

1. Creating the source code: Source code is the program in question. This is written in a computer language understood by the programmer.

2. Compiling the source code: Once the source code is written completely, we need to compile it. Compilation results in an executable code.

3. Linking: This function is carried out by a system software known as linker. The linker takes the object files which are generated by the compiler and combine them into a single executable file.

4. Executing: The execution of the program takes place after the linker creates the necessary executable file.

5. Maintaining: Errors, both compile time and runtime, need to be corrected and debugged. The code needs to be continuously monitored in order to ensure that the correct output is displayed to the user.

Some programming terminologies

Important Terms for Programming Implementation

- Testing Efforts - made to examine if a program is grammatically correct (no syntax errors), does what was intended (no logical errors), and runs well (no runtime errors).

- Debugging - The detection, location and correction of program errors (bugs). logical error An error in the design of the program. The program may be grammatically correct, but it is not doing what you intended it to do.

- Syntax error - An incorrect use of the rules that construct legal program statements. A grammatical mistake.

- Runtime error - Error that is first detected when the program is run. Examples: attempt to divide by zero, overflow.

- Test data - Data used to test a program. It may be wise to use normal, extreme and illegal data for testing.

- Dry Run - Testing process where a scenario of a possible failure is intentionally created

Programming in Pascal

PASCAL is a procedural programming language which was designed in 1969 and published in 1970 by Niklaus Wirth. This language intends to encourage good programming practices using structured programming and data structuring.

An object oriented version of this language has also been developed, which we know as Object Pascal. This was developed in the year 1985.

The Pascal compiler is open source and is free for download.

The software 'Lazarus' which we will be using for executing our Pascal programs run on the Free Pascal compiler. Here is what the default Free Pascal IDE looks like.

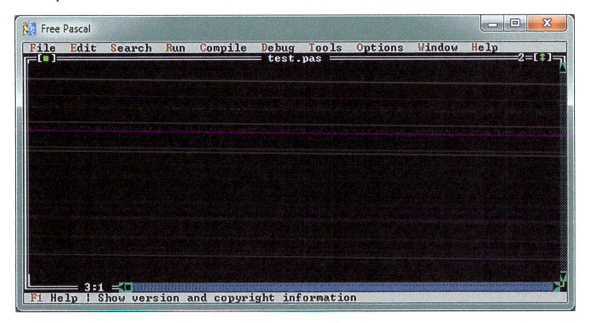

This is the basic software to execute Pascal programs. You can use this for executing the Pascal programs we will be learning soon.

Lazarus is a development software which allows both command line programming and graphics driven programming. If we click the Lazarus icon from our installation directory, we get the following screen.

We will not be using form based programming in this chapter. So we will keep ourselves to the text mode.

- Click on the File menu and then click on new.

- Click on the Program under the Project heading.

This is the source editor where we will write our code.
Now let us write some code to see whether the program works.

Sample snippet:

Writeln ('This is Free Pascal and Lazarus');
Writeln ('Press Enter key to close');
Readln;

Now, we insert this snippet into our main program between the begin and end statements.

Save this as project1.lpr.

To compile this file

* Click on **Run**
* Click on **Compile** or press CTRL + F9.

We get the following message if the program does not give compilation errors.

Project 'project1' successfully built

Once **compiled**

1. Click on Run again and then again, click on the Run menu item. Alternatively, press the F9 key.

Pressing the Enter key will result in termination of the program. The following screen will be shown.

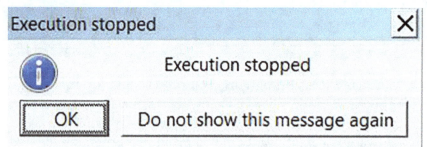

We can choose either option. If we click the button to the right, this message will not be shown again.

Go back to the program line
Writeln ('This is Free Pascal and Lazarus');

Change it to
Writeln ('This is a number:', 15);

Now run the program as before and note the output.

Now again, we will change the previous program line to
Writeln ('This is a number:', 7 + 5);
The output will be:

This is a number: 12

As we see, '+' is the addition operator when writing the program code.
Next, we check for multiplication. '*' is the operator we use for multiplication.
*Writeln ('This is a number:', 7 * 6);*

The output will be:
This is a number: 42

Let us now see what happens if you put in this line.
Writeln ('This is a number:', 5.4);

The output will be:
This is a number: 5.4

Now we will learn how to display multiple outputs in a single line.
Replace the original line with this one:
Writeln ('One, Two, Three:', 1, 2, 3);

The output will be:
This is a number: One, Two, Three: 123

Now we will write a sentence.
*Writeln ('10 * 3 :', 10 * 3);*

The output will be:
This is a number: 30

Variables and Constants

Variables and **constants** form a **key** part of any programming language. Pascal is no exception. One of the most fundamental requirements of a programming language is the ability to assign values to variables. **Variables** are symbolic names that refer to a storage location where the **value** of the variable is stored. It is called a variable because **the value that it** *contains can be changed* while the program is executing. To help programmers write robust code, variables are assigned **types** so that the value in the variable is interpreted in the correct fashion. Variables are assigned values by the use of expressions. Both of these topics are covered next.

Variables are like **data containers**. For instance, let us say we have a variable named X. We assign a value, say 7, to it. X=7 means that the variable X contains the value 7. Variables in Pascal are declared before the 'begin' statement. They are prefixed using the **'var'** keyword. Any lines following this keyword will indicate the **declaration** of variables. (The variable is introduced to the complier).

Variable Types

The types of values that can be contained in a variable belong to a few basic groups. A value can represent either a logical, numeric or character value. The numeric value is further distinguished between an integer and a floating-point value. Each of the variable types can be grouped into what is called an array or table. An array is a collection of values, all of the same type that represent multiple instances of a variable. A special case is a constant, which is a type of variable whose value never changes. Categorizing a constant as a variable type is a misnomer but for convenience sake it is defined this way.

Logical

- **Logical** variables contain **Boolean values**.

- A **Boolean value** indicates whether something is **true** or **false**. Therefore a variable that is a logical type can only contain one of two values, either **true** or **false**. In the expression section we will see how multiple logical variables can be operated upon to produce a new true or false value.

   Examples:
   Boolean logicalvar; //declaring the variable named logicalvar to be of type
   Boolean logicalvar := 1; //a variable assignment, typically 1 means true
   logicalvar := 0; //a variable assignment, typically 0 means false

   More variable assignment, some language have a keyword for true and false and the actual value that codes the true and false are hidden from the programmer.

   logicalvar := true;
   logicalvar := false;

NB: // is used to add comments to a program fro documentation so that whoever reads the code will, clearly understand what is taking place.

Numeric

- Numeric variables contain values that represent numbers. These numbers can either be **integer** or **floating-point** values.
- **Integer values** are whole numbers; they do not have a decimal point.
- **Floating-point** values have a decimal point and thus can represent fractional parts of a number like 23.341.
- Each of these types of numbers can use different amounts of memory to contain their values.
- The amount of memory reserved for the numbers will affect the range of values the number can accurately represent. Recall from the Unit on *Data Representation* that the number of bits determines all the possible values that are contained within that size bits.

Integer

Integer values are typically defined to use different amounts of memory. The motivation for this is conserve memory. If the range of possible values that the numeric integer variable is to contain can be stored in that amount of memory, then use that type so that memory is not wasted.

Let us see a sample code declaring an integer.

```
Program: firstvar;
...{code omitted}
...{until further concepts
...{are learnt}
Var
        X: Integer;
Begin
        X:      = 12; Writeln (X * 2);
        Writeln ('Press enter key to close.');
        Readln;
End.
```

Output:

We will get 24 as the output.

You can declare two variables in the same line provided they are of the same data type.

```
Var
        X, Y: Integer;
Begin
        X:=10;
        Y:=15;
        Writeln (x * y);
        Writeln ('Press enter key to close');
        Readln;
End.
```

Output:

The output of this code will be 150.

Real

- Real values are typically defined to use different amounts of memory. The motivation for this is to conserve memory.

- If the range of possible values that the numeric floating-point variable is to contain can be stored in that amount of memory, then use that type so that memory is not wasted.

- Because floating-point numbers record the value to the left and the right of the decimal point, providing greater precision for very small numbers (close to zero)

- Typical floating-point types are Float (single) or Double.

Float (single)

- Float or single, so named because the single precision of the floating-point numbers is typically defined to be 32 bits.

- Depending on the scheme used to encode the floating-point number the range of values is determined.

- Floating-point numbers are inherently signed so the range is always a plus/minus (+/-) range.

  Here is the code snippet which shows how to use this data type.

  Var:
  X: Single; Begin
  X:=2.8;
  Writeln ('John Doe stays ',x,' kms from here.');
  Writeln('Press enter key to close.');
  Readln
  End.

Output:

John Does stays 2.799999952 kms from here

Double

- Double, more aptly named because it provides double the precision of float (single), is typically defined to be 64 bits

- Again, depending on the scheme used to encode the floating-point number the range of values is determined.

Character

Character variables contain values that represent characters. This class of variable type can either be a single character or a series ("string") of characters. The typical names for these two character types are **char** and **string**.

Char

A char is defined to contain a single character. The amount of memory (number of bits, bytes) that a character uses is dependent on the encoding scheme used. The ASCII character take 8 bits, 1 byte whereas, Unicode characters take 16 bits, 2 bytes. Here is a code snippet which shows how to declare and use character variables Code:

```
Var
        C: Char;
Begin
        C:= 'B';
        Writeln ('My first letter is:', C);
        Writeln ('Press enter key to close:');
        Readln;
End.
```

Output:

My first letter is: C

String

- A **string** is defined to contain a sequence of individual characters.

- Strings are not fixed lengths like all the other type discussed so far and therefore the computer cannot directly process strings. A language must have some system of storing and managing strings.

```
Var
        X: Integer;
Begin
        Write ('Please input any number:');
        Readln (x);
        Writeln ('You have entered:', x);
        Writeln ('Press Enter key to close');
        Readln;
End.
```

Here, the value is input by the user. Let us see what output this code generates. First, it prompts the user to input a number as shown below.

Using Interaction in Coding

After the user inputs data and presses 'Enter', we get the output.

Until now, we have seen very simple programs. Let us notch the complexity up a bit. Let us now display a multiplication table of a number we will input through the command line prompt.

Variables and constants enclosed within single quotation marks will be displayed as they are written within the " " during the execution of the program. However, when they are written without, they are evaluated first and then the values are displayed.

For example:

Writeln ('5 * 3');
The output of this line of code is: 5 * 3.
Writeln (5 * 3);
The output of this line of code is: 15.
Let us perform some arithmetic operations on variables. Look at the code snippet which inputs two numbers, performs addition, subtraction, multiplication, and division on them, and then prints the results.

The output is shown.

```
Var
X, Y: Integer;
Resadd: Integer;
Ressub: Integer;
Resmul: Integer;
Resdiv: Single;
Begin
        Write ('Input a number:');
        Readln (X);
        Write ('Input another number:');
        Readln (Y);
        Resadd:= X + Y;
        Writeln (x, '+ ', y, ' = ', Resadd);
        Ressub:= X-Y;
        Resmul:= X * Y;
        Resdiv:= X / Y;
        Writeln (x, ' − ', y, ' = ', Ressub);
        Writeln (x, ' * ', y, ' = ', Resmul);
        Writeln (x, ' / ', y, ' = ', Resdiv);
        Writeln ('Press enter key to close:');
        Readln;
End.
```

Conditional Branching

Whatever programs we have dealt with so far, they follow the tenets of the **sequence control** structure. This means **every statement is executed line after line**. However, this will not work for every practical situation. There may come a time where we would want the software **to make some decisions for us**. This is where we come to the **conditional control structure**.

- The conditional control structure allows the program execution to **branch** depending on how the conditional statements evaluate.
- PASCAL provides us with the 'IF' condition statement.
- The 'IF' condition statement is usually followed by an 'else' statement should there be some message for the user if the condition evaluates to false.

Let us look at a sample program to show how the 'IF..Else' construct works.

```
Var
        Somevar: Integer;
Begin
        Write ('Please enter a value:');
        Readln (Somevar);
        If Somevar * 2 = 30 then
                Writeln ('The number you have entered is 15.')
        Else
                Writeln ('The number you have entered is not 15.');
        Writeln ('Press enter key to close.');
        Readln;
End.
```

Let us now see what the output of this code looks like.

First, let us try the input with the correct number, meaning let us now see how it branches to the statement following the evaluation of the condition to true then let us see what happens if the condition evaluates to false.

We will have multiple conditions in the program which is shown in the following code:

```
Var
X:      Integer; Begin
Write ('Input a number:'); Readln (x);
If x * 2 = 30 then
Writeln ('number you have entered is 15.')
Else
If x * 3 = 30 then
Writeln ('number you have entered is 10.')
Else
Writeln ('number you have entered is neither 15 nor 10.');
Writeln ('press enter key to close.');
Readln;
End.
```

Let us now analyse further.

Scenario 1: First condition evaluates to true.

The message corresponding to this conditional statement is displayed to the user and then control skips to the end of the construct (set of instructions).

- If this condition evaluates to false, it goes to the **else** part. Now here, the compiler sees that there is another "if" condition. This condition checks whether the input number when multiplied by 3 gives the result 30. This means the input number must be 10.

Scenario 2: Second condition evaluates to true.

The message corresponding to this "If" condition is displayed to the user and then the control skips to the end of the program.

If this condition evaluates to false, it goes to the else part. Here the compiler now knows that the number x is neither 15 nor 10. This means both the conditions have now evaluated to false. So, it displays the message corresponding to the else part and skips to the end of the program.

There may be situations where we would need to combine two conditions within a single "if" condition. Here we may come to appreciate the use of logical operators. Logical operators which we commonly use are "AND" and "OR". The condition using "AND" as logical operator evaluates to true if and only both the conditions evaluate to true. Let us now see the truth table for this. Truth Table for "AND":

Condition 1	Condition 2	Conditions 1 And 2
True	True	True
True	False	Flase
False	True	False
False	False	False

This truth table is for only two conditions. However, there may be multiple conditions in the 'If' condition. The theorem is that if there are 'n' conditions, there are 2 entries in the truth table.

In case of 'AND', it may suffice to know that the condition using this operator evaluates to true if and only if all the conditions evaluate to true. Let us now see a program incorporating this logical operator.

```
X:      Integer;
Begin
        Writeln ('Input a number:'); Readln(X);
        If (X = 5) and (X + 2 = 7) then
            Writeln ('You have input correct number.') Else
            Writeln ('You are forbidden to cross the door.'); Writeln („Press enter key to close.');
            Readln;
End;
```

Here are the outputs.

Scenario 1: Both conditions are evaluated to true
Scenario 2: Both conditions or either one evaluates to false

Notice that in the above program, both the conditions have to evaluate to false. There is no scenario where both conditions evaluate to true.

Var
X, Y: Integer;
Begin
    Readln(x);
    Readln(y);
    If (x=8) and (y=9) then
      Writeln ('You may pass.');
    Else
      Writeln ('You cannot pass.');
      Writeln ('press enter key to pass.');
End.

The output of this program is:
Both conditions evaluate to false or at least one condition evaluates to false:

An important thing to note is that there can be multiple 'if...then...else' in a program. However, as we incorporate more of this construct, the complexity becomes higher and the program is not so easily readable. To rectify this issue, PASCAL provides us with the Case...Of construct. This is another method for conditional branching.

For instance, we will now consider the following program.

Var
Meal: byte;
Begin
    Writeln ('Welcome to the shoe shop. Please select your brand.');
    Writeln ('1. Liberty');
    Writeln ('2. Nike');
    Writeln ('3. Reebok');
    Writeln ('4. Adidas');
    Writeln ;
    Write ('Please enter your selection:');
Readln (Meal);

Case Meal of
1:   *Writeln ('You have ordered Liberty shoes.');*
2:   *Writeln ('You have ordered Nike shoes.');*
3:   *Writeln ('You have ordered Reebok shoes.');*
4:   *Writeln ('You have ordered Adidas shoes.");*

Else

        Writeln ('Wrong entry.');
        End;
        Write ('Press enter key to close.');
        Readln;

End.

Output:

Welcome to the shoe shop. Please select your brand.
1. Liberty
2. Nike
3. Reebok
4. Adidas
Please enter your selection.

Depending on the number we input, we get a suitable output.

If we input 2, then we get a message that we have ordered Nike shoes.

If we enter 3, then we get a message that we have ordered Reebok shoes.

If we enter 4 then we get a message that we have ordered Adidas shoes. If we enter some other number then we get a message saying 'Wrong Entry'. This is when the control shifts to the 'else' part.

The Case…of construct is closed with an end statement.

Loops

Like conditional branching, practical situations demand the usage of iterative control structures as in loops. Using loops, we make a block of statements execute repeatedly until a condition evaluates to loop. Although the concept of an infinite loop is possible, it finds little use in actual programming. There are three looping statements provided by PASCAL. They are:

1. For loop
2. While loop
3. repeat…until loop

First, we will go through the 'for' loop.

The FOR Loop

This loop is used to execute statements for a finite number of times and when we want to use counters. Consider this example:

```
Var
I: Integer;
Count: Integer;
Begin
  Write ('Enter limit:');
  Readln (Count);
  For i:=1 to Count DO
        Writeln ('Hello world!');
        Write ('Press enter key to close');
        Readln;
End.
```

The 'i' in the loop is known as a loop variable. Always use Integer, Byte, and Char for loop variables. Loop variables arc also known as counters.

As we see, we input the limit as 5 and 'Hello World!' has been displayed 5 times. We can also display the loop counter value in every iteration. For example, consider the following code segment.

```
Var
i:      Integer; Count: Integer;
Begin
  Writeln('Enter limit:');
  Readln(Count);
  For i:=1 to Count do Begin
        Writeln('Hello World!'); Writeln('Iteration Number :', i); End;
        Writeln('Press enter key to close.');
        Readln;
End.
```

The 'begin' and 'end' statements inside the list are used to indicate that there are going to be multiple statements to be repeated using the loop.

Factorial of a number:

In mathematics, we have come across a term known as factorial of a number. It is actually the multiplication of a number by its predecessor down to the number

For example: 5! = 5 * 4 * 3 * 2 * 1 = 120. Let us see how we do this using loops.

```
Var
Fac, Num, i:
Integer;
Begin
  Writeln('Input a number:');
  Readln(Num);
  Fac:=1;
  For i:=num downto 1 do
        Fac:=Fac * i;
        Writeln('Factorial of', Num, 'is', Fac);
        Writeln('Press enter key to close.');
        Readln;
End.
```

The While Loop

- In this loop, the condition is checked first.

- If the condition evaluates to true then the statements are executed.

- This loop is also called as top testing loop.

- If the condition in the loop evaluates to false then the control skips the entire block to the statement next to the loop.

- If there are multiple statements which need to be executed repeatedly then we must enclose it within the 'begin…end' construct.

Let us now do the factorial program using while loop.

```
Var
Fac, Num, i: Integer;
Begin
  Write('Please input any number:');
  Readln(Num);
  Fac:=1;
  i:=Num;
  While i>1 DO
  begin
```

```
       Fac:=Fac * i;
       i:i-1;
       end;
           Writeln('Factorial of', Num, 'is', Fac);
           Writeln('Press enter key to close.');
           Readln;
End.
```

Repeat...Until loop:

- Unlike the For loop, this loop **does not make use of a counter**.

- This loop executes the block at least once.

- The condition is **checked at the bottom** of the loop. This is why it is known as the *bottom testing loop*.

- If the condition evaluates to true, the block is executed again otherwise the control skips to outside of the loop. Let us do the shoe program using this loop.

```
Var
Shoeschoice: Char;
Price:=Integer;
Total:=Integer;
Begin
Total:=0;
Repeat
        Writeln ('Welcome to the shoe shop. Please select your brand.');
        Writeln ('1. Liberty (200 dollar)');
        Writeln ('2. Nike (250 dollar');
        Writeln ('3. Reebok (235 dollar)');
        Writeln ('4. Adidas (240 dollar)');
        Writeln ;
        Write ('Please enter your selection:');
        Readln ( Shoeschoice);
        Case Shoeschoice of
           '1': begin
           Writeln ('You have ordered Liberty shoes.');
           price:=200;
        end;
           '2': begin
           Writeln ('You have ordered Nike shoes.');
            price:=250;
        end;
           '3': begin
           Writeln ('You have ordered Reebok shoes.');
            price:=235;
```

```
        end;
         '4':begin
          Writeln ('You have ordered Adidas shoes.');
          Price:=240;
End;
Else
         begin
         Writeln ('Wrong entry.');
         Price:=0;
         End;
End;
         Total:=total + price;
         Until(Meal= "x") or (Meal= "X");
         Writeln('Total Price = ', total);
         Write ('Press enter key to close.');
         Readln;
End
```

Arrays

Sometimes we want to store a "bunch" of values of the same type together. For this purpose we use **arrays**. An **array** is a container in which numerous variables are stored

Arrays can contain variables of the same data type only.

Arrays store the variables in contiguous memory locations.

The first step is **declaring an array**. In Pascal, we do it in the following way:

Numbers: array [1..10] of Integer;
To access the elements of an array, we just refer to the index of the array. For example, if we want to put a value in the first variable in the array, then we write it as:
Numbers [1]:=30;

The indices of an array in Pascal start with 1 unlike most other programming languages.
In the next example, we will ask user to enter ten student marks and put them in an array.
Then we will see who has passed or failed.

```
Var
Marks: array[1...10] of Integer;
i:Integer;
begin
        for i:=1 to 10 do
begin
        write('Input student number', i , 'mark:');
        readln(Marks[i]);
```

```
Eend;
for i:= 1 to 10 do
begin
        write(„Student number', i, 'mark is :', Marks[i]);
if Marks[i]>=40 then
        writeln('Pass');
else
writeln('Fail');
End;
writeln('Press enter key to close.')
readln;
End.
```

Press Enter after you include all the marks.

Trace Tables

A **trace table** is a table with one column for each variable used and one column for the output. A cell shows a change in a variable or the output as the program is executed. There are three ways to fill out a trace table.

1. Use one row for each change.
   Advantage: shows the order of events.
   Disadvantage: takes up a lot of space.

A	output
2	
4	
	4
6	
	6

```
A=2
While A < 5
    A = A + 2
    msgbox str(A)
Wend
```

2. Use one row for each time the loop runs.
   Advantage: takes up less space.
   Disadvantage: cannot be used if a variable changes more than once in the loop.

A	output
2	
4	4
6	6

3. Use next cell when there is a change.
   Advantage: takes up little space.
   Disadvantage: Does not show the order of events.

A	output
2	4
4	6
6	4

TERMS YOU NEED TO KNOW

Dry-run
A manual traversal/run of a program using a trace table.

Stepping through a program
A good debugging tool is to run a program one instruction at a time. Press F8 to get started and then click Locals Window on the View menu to see how the variables change every time you press F8 to execute the next instruction.

Source code
Program written in a computer language.

Object code
Machine language program produced by a compiler.

Compiler
A computer program, which translates a high-level language program (the source) into machine code (the object code, an executable file).

Interpreter
A computer program which analyses and executes a source program one statement at a time; without converting it to object code.

Loader
A computer program, which copies an object program held on backing store into main store.

Executing
A program is executed or run when the computer carries out the program's instructions.

Watches

One can trace the execution of a program in Lazarus. There are Step Into and Step Over functions available to us if we ever want to know the details of programming. Often it is helpful to a programmer as it helps in debugging procedure.

The Step Into function is a menu item in the Run Menu. To access, click Run -> Step Into. Alternatively press F7. Step Into executes every line of the program.

The Step Over function is a menu item in the Run Menu. To access, click Run-> Step Over. Alternatively, press F8.

PROGRAM DOCUMENTATION

The program documentation is like a comprehensive procedural description of a program. It shows how a program is written. The program documentation describes exactly what a program intends to achieve. There are two kinds of program documentation:

1. Internal Documentation
2. External Documentation Internal Documentation

Internal Documentation involves meaningful variable names, comments, indentation etc... Variable Names:

All variable names must follow the rules outlined below:

1. They must begin with a letter or an underscore.
2. They can contain only letters, numbers, or underscores.
3. They cannot have blank spaces.

Examples of illegal variable names: 5 BREADTH, AB 3, Vee.Hive, etc..

Comments

Comments are piece of code which are completely discarded by the compiler. They exist only to help the programmer and to provide him with an easy reference.

In the early days, (* and *) were used to indicate comments. However, they have been replaced by { and }. These are mostly used for multi-line comments. // is used for a single line comment.

Examples:

// This is a Hello World function
{

      This is a hello world function.
      You see hello world as output.

}

Indentation

- You should always indent two spaces for all indentation levels. In other words, the first level of indentation is two spaces, the second level four spaces, the third level 6 spaces, etc.

- Never use tab characters. There are few exceptions.

- The reserved words unit, users, type, interface, implementation, initialization and finalization should always be flush with the margin.

- The final end statement at the end of a unit should be flush with the margin.

External Documentation

External documentation is to help the user of the system to understand how the software works. It is a user manual which is a book-like document having the following contents:

1. Cover page.

2. Title and copyright page.

3. A preface covering the details of relevant documents and information on how to navigate through the guide.

4. Contents in tabular form.

5. A guide section on how to use the main functions.

6. Troubleshooting section detailing the errors which might occur and how to solve them.

7. A FAQ document.

8. Where to find further help and contact details.

9. A glossary.

PASCAL ERROR CODES

The following error codes are predefined:

Code	Meaning
1	Invalid function number
2	File not found
3	Path not found
4	Too many open files
5	File access denied
6	Invalid file handle
12	Invalid file access code
15	Invalid drive number
16	Cannot remove current directory
17	Cannot rename across drives
18	No more files
100	Disk read error
101	Disk write error
102	File not assigned
103	File not open
104	File not open for input
105	File not open for output
106	Invalid numeric format
150	Disk is write protected
151	Bad drive request structure length
152	Drive not ready
154	CRC error in data
156	Disk seek error
157	Unknown media type
158	Sector not found
159	Printer out of paper
160	Device write fault
161	Device read fault
162	Hardware failure
200	Division by zero
201	Range check error
202	Stack overflow error
203	Heap overflow error
204	Invalid pointer operation

Code	Meaning
205	Floating point overflow
206	Floating point underflow
207	Invalid floating point operation
208	Overlay manager not installed
209	Overlay file read error
210	Object not initialized
211	Call to abstract method
212	Stream registration error
213	Collection index out of range
214	Collection overflow error
215	Arithmetic overflow error
216	General protection fault
217	Invalid operation code
227	Assertion failed
300	File IO error
301	Non matched array bounds
302	Non local procedure pointer
303	Procedure pointer out of scope
304	Function not implemented
305	Breakpoint error
306	Break by Ctrl/C
307	Break by Ctrl/Break
308	Break by other process
309	No floating point coprocessor
310	Invalid Variant type operation

Task 1

Review Questions:

1. What is a programming language?

2. What is a program and why is a program so important?

3 **a)** List 4 programming languages.
   b) Explain 2 of the programming languages.

4. What are the characteristics of a good programmer?

5. List the characteristics of a good program.

6. Rewrite the following algorithm using Pascal code. (You should assume that the variables have been declared.)

   Input message
   Initialize Speed to 0
   Repeat 7 times
          If message is equal to 40 then
               Speed = Speed + 1
          Input message
   Print Speed   **(5 marks)**

7. Answer the following questions based on the code below:

   If paths = 20
   Then Speed := speed + 1
   Else writeln('Challenge a Speed');
   State

       (i) the type of control structure.   **(1 mark)**

       (ii) the relational operator used.   **(1 mark)**

       (iii) the data type of Speed.   **(1 mark)**

(iv) the location of the cursor if the statement is written.   **(1 mark)**

(v) the result when Speed has a value of 12.   **(1 mark)**

8. A one-dimensional array named ROAD is used to store the number of points for three levels in a game. Write PASCAL code to:

   (i) Declare the array ROAD   **(4 marks)**

   (ii) initialize the array to 0.   **(4 marks)**

9. Algorithms are means of recording the steps needed to solve a problem.

   Write an algorithm using simple pseudocode to: **(5 marks)**
   - Prompt a user by displaying the statement:
     Enter positive integers one by one and "−1" to designate no more input.

   - Accept the values entered until −1 is entered   **(3 marks)**

   - Determine and display
     (i) the sum of the numbers   **(2 marks)**
     (ii) the average of the numbers.   **(2 marks)**

10. Give ONE difference between EACH of the following pairs of terms :
    a) Object code and Source code   **(2 marks)**

    b) Constant and a Variable   **(2 marks)**

    c) Syntax and logic errors   **(2 marks)**

    d) Looping control structures and Conditional branching   **(2 marks)**

    e) Debugging and Testing   **(2 marks)**

11. Consider the following segment code:
    Read A,B
    While (A <>B) Do
          Print B
          B = B- + 1
    Print B

Use trace table to determine the output of the code if A = 5 and B =3. The headings should have A, B, Print.   **(5 marks)**

(Total: 45 marks)

APPENDIX A: GLOSSARY OF ICT TERMS

Term	Definition
Abacus	An early calculating device using beads moving on strings.
Address	The identification of a particular location in memory where a data item or instruction is stored.
Algorithm	A set of well-defined rules for solving a problem in a finite number of operations.
Aligning	A data can usually be aligned in one of three positions namely left-align, right-align or centered.
Antiglare screen	A polarized screen attached to the front of the monitor, which reduces eye strain
ALU	Arithmetic and Logic Unit. The part of the Central Processing Unit thathandles all mathematical calculations, addition, subtraction and multiplication; and logic operations, such as comparisons for greater than, less than, and equal to an identified number.
Backing store	A relatively permanent storage location for large quantities of data outside the processor of the computer system.
Backup copy	A copy of a disk onto a second disk that is for everyday use, protecting the original disk in case of damage.
Bandwidth	A characteristic of a communication channel that determines the speed atwhich data can be transmitted over the channel
Bar code	A series of thick and thin black bars separated by spaces of varying widths representing data.
Baud	A unit of speed in data transmission system which now represents one data signal per second.
BCD	BCD is an abbreviation for Binary-Coded-Decimal. In this number system, each digit of a number is written as a BINARY number, rather than converting the whole number. For example, 47 would be coded as 01000111, the binary codes for 4 and 7. Contrast this with 101111, which is the true binary code of 47.
Binary	Base two numbering system. A binary digit can be a 0 or a 1 [bit].
Bit	The smallest unit of memory or information. A bit is represented by a 0 or 1.
Boot	To get the computer started. [Switched on] warm boot and cold boot.
Border	In printing a spreadsheet certain groups of column or rows may be designated as left or top borders to ensure that the information they contain will appear on all pages of the print out.

Term	Definition
Bulletin	An electronic equivalent of a conventional bulletin board. It is used as part of a communication network where users can post messages, read messages posted by others users, communicate with the system operator and upload or download programs.
Byte	Represents 8 bits or a character e.g.?, . , /, 1-9, a-z, *, &, %, #, @ and so on.
CD	Compact Disk. There are two types of CDs: [I] CD writer - a peripheral device that can write once to a CD-R disk to create an audio or a CD-ROM. [ii] CD-R – [Compact Disk Recordable] The medium on which CD writers create CDs and CD-ROMs.
CD-ROM disk	Compact-Disk-Read-Only-Memory disk. A type of optical laser storage medium.
Central Processing Unit	The logical component of a computer system that interprets and executes program instructions. [CPU/Processor]
Character	Any keyboard character: letter number or symbol which can be input, stored, processed, and/or output by a computer system. [Eight bits of memory]
Chip	An integrated circuit made of a semiconductor [silicon] and containing electronic components. It can be as little as ¼ inch square.
Communication	Acts of transmitting or exchanging information, ideas or opinions over a communication channel.
Compiler	A program that translates the sources program into executable machine code, and saves the code to a file [the object program] for later execution.
Computer	An electronic device that is controlled by a stored program which accepts data, processes it and stores the results of processing, to provide an output in the form of information.
Computer system	A collective reference to all interconnected computing hardware, including processors, storage devices, input/output devices, and communications equipment. In short it's the computer and its peripheral devices.
Control Unit [CU]	Responsible for coordinating all devices connected to the system, determines which activity to perform, as well as how and when to perform it.
Cursor	A flashing symbol on the monitor's screen, which indicates the position of user activity.
CPU	Central Processing Unit.
Data	Unorganized facts or material including numbers and words that are processed by the computer.

Term	Definition
Database	A collection of data files that may be used by number of applications with storage and access to the data controlled by a set of programs known as Database Management System. [DBMS]
Database Management System	Programs and database files that allow timely and easy controlled access to data by a number of users.
Decode	To reverse the encoding process.
Desktop	The screen in windows upon which icons, windows, a background are displayed.
Device	A machine with a specific function.
DTP	Desk Top Publishing.
Download	Process whereby programs or data are transferred via communications channels, from a computer and stored on media located at the user's computer.
DVD	Digital Video Disk or Digital Versatile Disk. A high-density compact disk for storing large amounts of data, especially high-resolution audio-visual material.
E-mail/ Electronic Mail	A computer application whereby messages are transmitted via data communications to "electronic mailboxes" also called e-mail.
EPROM	Erasable programmable read-only memory. A type of memory chip that can be erased by moving it from the circuit and exposing it to ultraviolet light. The chip can then be programmed.
Field	[1] A section of a record containing data relating to one attribute of an entry. [2] Part of a machine instruction containing an operation or address.
File	A collection of related records. Transforms secondary storage into an electronic filing cabinet. Any data or set of instructions that have been given a name and stored on disk.
Floppy disk	A flexible magnetic coated disk, commonly used with microcomputers, on which data can be stored magnetically.
Flowchart	A diagram that illustrates data, information, and workflow by means of specialized symbols which, when connected by flow lines, portray the logic of asystem or program.
Folder	Similar to the file jackets you use for your research assignments or those used in a filing cabinet to store documents [files]. A holding or storage area for data files on a disk.
Font	A family or collection of characters [letters, punctuation marks, numbers and special characters] of a particular size and style.

Term	Definition
Formatting	Initialize the disk i.e. we prepare the disk for use.
Fourth generation	A computer programming language which allows the program to Language [4GL] specifics "what" is to be achieved rather than "how" it is to be achieved.
Gigabyte	The equivalent of one billion bytes.
Hard disk	A permanently installed, continuously spinning magnetic storage medium madeup of one or more rigid disk platters. [Same as fixed disk or Winchester disk]
Hardware	The physical tangible parts that make up a computer system.
Home page	The file available for access at a World Wide Web site intended chiefly to greet visitors, provide information about the site, and direct them to other sites with more related information.
HTML	Hyper Text Markup Language. A mark-up language used to structure text and multimedia documents used extensively on the World Wide Web.
HTTP	Hyper Text Transfer Protocol. A protocol used to request and transmit files, especially Web pages and Web page components, over the Internet or other computer network.
Icon	Pictures used in place of words on a screen display.
Immediate access	The memory within the central processor. Also referred to as Storage internal use or main store.
Indexing	Creating a secondary file which contains pointers items in an associated database file and allows rapid location of records in the file.
Information	Data that have been collected and processed into meaningful form.
Input	Data entered into a computer system for processing.
Integrated package	This package combines several applications in a suite of programs. Most of these packages combine a word processor; spreadsheet and database program. Data are shared easily between these integrated programs.
Interactive Processing	A processing system that allows "dialogue" between computer and user.
Internet	A global network that connects thousands of networks, multi-user computers and users in many countries.
Invoke	Process of starting up a program by using its name [or selecting its icon.
Joystick	An input device that uses a lever to control movement of the cursor or graphic images.

Term	Definition
Justification	The term justification often is used to refer to full justification of the alignment of text along both the left and right margins.
Keyboard	A device used for keying [typing] in data entry.
Key-to-disk	Keyboard of rapidly and accurately entering data into a computer via the keyboard as an input device.
Kilobyte	Approximately one thousand bytes but precisely 1026 bytes.
LAN	Acronym for Local Area Network. A type of computer network where two or more computers are directly linked within a small area such as a room or building site. A common characteristic of this system is that computers are linked by direct cables rather than by telecommunication lines.
Light pen	A light-sensitive input device which when it touches the screen detects the presence or absence of light. It is used to select an entry or indicate a position.
Load	To transfer data or programs from secondary to primary storage.
Magnetic disk	A mylar [floppy disk] or metallic [hard disk] circular plate on which electronic data can be stored magnetically. Suitable for direct or random access data storage and retrieval.
Magnetic tape	A storage medium consisting of a flexible plastic strip of tape covered with magnetic material on one side, used to store date. It is available in spools or cassettes.
Mainframe	A large computer that can service many users simultaneously.
Mail-merge	A facility found in full-fledged word processing programs that draws information from a database, usually a mailing list, to print multiple copies of a document. Each copy contains some common text but each bearing different address.
Media	Materials on which data and instructions are stored as electromagnetic signals e.g. magnetic tapes, diskettes, CDs.
Menu	A display with a list of processing choices from which a user may select.
Menu driven	The characteristics of a software program that provides the user with a menu.
Merge	The combination of two or more files on the basis of common field [key field]
Microsoft Disk Operating System	MS-DOS. A microcomputer operating system. An operating system is the software that controls the execution of all applications and system software.

Term	Definition
Microcomputer	A small computer designed for use by an individual. [Also called a Micro or PC-Personal Computer].
Microprocessor	The processing component of a microcomputer.
Minicomputer	A mid-sized computer also called a Mini.
Modem	Acronym for modulator-demodulator. A device that converts signals from analogue to digital and vice versa. A model allows computers to exchange information through telephone lines.
Monitor	A television-like display for soft copy output in a computer system.
Mouse	A point-and-draw device, that when moved across a desktop pad a particular distance and direction, causes the same movement of the cursor on a screen.
Natural Language Processing	The use of the computer to understand and translate a natural language, like English, into commands to perform a given operation.
Network	Two or more communicating devices that are connected electronically to form a system which shares information and resources.
On-line	A processing technique whereby terminals and other peripherals are connected to and controlled by the central processor. It provides the means for using computers on the basis of time interactive sharing and data input.
Operating system	A set of programs that controls and supervise the resources of a computer system. It also acts as an interface between the user and the computer.
Output	Data transferred from RAM to an output device for processing.
Peripheral device	Any hardware other than the processor.
Plotter	An output device specially designed to produce a hard copy of graphical data.
Printer	A device specially designed to produce a hard copy of computer output.
Processing	Manipulating or handling data to produce information.
Processor	A logical component of the computer system that interprets and executes program instructions
Protocol	A set of rules and procedures controlling the transmitting and receiving of data so that different devices can communicate with each other.
Pseudo code	A language consisting of English-like statements used to define algorithm.

Term	Definition
Program	Computer instructions structured and ordered in a manner that, when executed, causes a computer to perform a particular function.
RAM	Random Access Memory. The memory area in which all programs and data must reside before programs can be executed or data manipulated. [Provides temporary storage for programs and data]. Also called primary memory/storage.
Record	A collection of fields on data related to one entity.
Register	A permanent location in the internal memory of a processor used for the temporary storage of data during processing operations.
Resolution	A characteristic of a monitor's screen, determined by the number of pixels that can be displayed by it.
Retrieve	The process of recalling stored information for use.
ROM	Read Only Memory. Memory or storage area that can be read only, not written to. [Used to hold permanent instructions that your computer needs to get started].
Save/Store	The process of storing information for future uses.
Software	The programs/instructions used to direct the functions of a computer system.
Scrolling	The act of shifting the contents of the screen up, down, left or right. The lines formerly appearing at the top of the screen are "scrolled away", those upward scrolling below are moved up and new lines of data which exist below those formerly on screen now come into view. In downward scrolling the reverse takes place. Scrolling usually proceeds a line at a time, [may be facilitated on some computers by use of a scroll-on/off key] in combination with up and down cursor movements.
Search	Process of locating data in a database file by reference to a key field[s] in the records.
Sort	Redistribution of data into an order on the basis of the contents of a key item [sort-key]
Spell-check	A directory feature associated with a word processor which allows the user to easily detect and correct errors in spelling. One can add new words to the directory so of the Word processor.
Super computer	The category that includes the largest and most powerful computers.
System	A set of arranged parts acting together to perform a function.
Syntax	A set of rules defining the structures of a computer program or of functions in a spreadsheet.
Template	A specification of the number of fields and the kinds of data which fields in a database are allowed to hold.

Term	Definition
Terminal	The combination of a monitor and keyboard to input and check data and to view output. A terminal does not necessarily include a processor.
Title	In a spreadsheet a group of rows or columns may be designated as a horizontal or vertical title respectively, which ensure that they always appear on the screen irrespective of where the cursor has moved in the spreadsheet.
Touch terminal	Also called a touch screen. A device that allows data to be input touching a screen with the finger or other object. The surface of the screen consists of a number of programmed touch points each of which may trigger a different action when selected by the user.
Two's complement	A method of representing numbers in which the computer does not perform subtraction in the normal way but inverts digits to be subtracted and adds to them.
Up-load document	Process of reading data from a user's computer storage and sending it to another computer via communication channel.
URL	Each page on the Web has a unique address called the Uniform Resource Locator [URL].
Volatile memory	Solid-state semiconductor RAM in which the data are lost when the electrical current is turned off or interrupted.
Web page	A document on the World Wide Web, consisting of HTML file and any related files for scripts and graphics and often hyperlinked to other Web pages.
Web site	Set of interconnected Web pages, usually including a home page, generally located on the same server, and prepared and maintained as a collection of information by a person, group, or organization.
Web browser	A web browser is a programme that allows users to view and explore information on the World Wide Web. Examples of popular browsers are: Microsoft Internet Explorer , Google Chrome, Mozilla Firefox and Netscape Navigator.
World Wide Web[WWW]	The World Wide Web commonly referred to as the 'Web', is a graphical easy-to- use system of inter-linked files on the Internet. Vast amounts of information can be obtained through the use of the 'Web'.
Window	A rectangular section of a display screen that is dedicated to a specific document, activity or application.

INDEX